Paul Ricoeur's Hermeneutics of the Imagination

American University Studies

Series VII
Theology and Religion

Vol. 143

PETER LANG
New York • Washington, D.C./Baltimore • San Francisco
Bern • Frankfurt am Main • Berlin • Vienna • Paris

Jeanne Evans

Paul Ricoeur's Hermeneutics of the Imagination

PETER LANG
New York • Washington, D.C./Baltimore • San Francisco
Bern • Frankfurt am Main • Berlin • Vienna • Paris

BL
43
.R53
E83
1995

Library of Congress Cataloging-in-Publication Data

Evans, Jeanne.
Paul Ricoeur's hermeneutics of the imagination/
Jeanne Evans.
p.   cm. — (American university studies.
Series VII, Theology and religion ; vol. 143)
Includes bibliographical references.
1. Ricoeur, Paul—Contributions in hermeneutics. 2. Hermeneutics—Religious
aspects—History of doctrines—20th century. 3. Imagination—Religious
aspects—History of doctrines—20th century. I. Title. II. Series.
BL43.R53E83   121'.68—dc20   93-42528
ISBN 0-8204-2060-3
ISSN 0740-0446

Die Deutsche Bibliothek-CIP-Einheitsaufnahme

Evans, Jeanne:
Paul Ricoeur's hermeneutics of the imagination/ Jeanne Evans. - New York;
Washington, D.C./Baltimore; San Francisco; Bern;
Frankfurt am Main; Berlin; Vienna; Paris: Lang.
(American university studies : Ser. 7, Theology and religion ; Vol. 143)
ISBN 0-8204-2060-3
NE: American university studies / 07

The paper in this book meets the guidelines for permanence and durability
of the Committee on Production Guidelines for Book Longevity
of the Council of Library Resources.

© 1995 Peter Lang Publishing, Inc., New York

Printed in the United States of America.

In Memory

Richard D. Evans
Mary Thornhill

"So we make up and supplement each other .
We give and others give to us."
—Fredrich von Hügel

TABLE OF CONTENTS

PREFACE xi

Chapter I   THE PROBLEM OF METAPHOR, NARRATIVE
                  AND IMAGINATION FOR THEOLOGY.......................1

Chapter II   RICOEUR'S PHILOSOPHICAL
                  AND HISTORICAL CONTEXT....................................27

Chapter III.   RICOEUR'S TURN TO HERMENEUTICS..................47

Chapter IV   RICOEUR'S RULE OF METAPHOR AND THE
                  PHILOSOPHY OF THE IMAGINATION 87

Chapter V   RICOEUR'S BIBLICAL HERMENEUTICS:
                  IMAGINATION AND RELIGIOUS LITERACY 151

CONCLUSION..183

BIBLIOGRAPHY...189

INDEX 211

PREFACE

This study of Ricoeur's hermeneutics in terms of his correlation of the theory of metaphor to the philosophy of the imagination is inspired in part by my first reading many years ago of the "Conclusion" to *The Symbolism of Evil*. His meditation on the aphorism: "the symbol gives rise to thought" to which "no concept is equal" made a deep impression, and raised the question of the significance of the role of the imagination and symbolic forms of discourse for theological reflection. My participation, while a student, in a seminar Ricoeur held at the University of Toronto fueled my decision to pursue the question of the philosophy of the imagination and its relation to metaphor in his work. I will always treasure the memory of the energy and enthusiasm with which Ricoeur shared his work in progress on "Time and Narrative" as well as his gift of encouragement and openness.

I have tried throughout this work to adopt inclusive language. Citations from Ricoeur's work reflect that over the years, as he has become more conscious of the feminist critique, he has shifted to the use of inclusive language.

There are many people to whom to express my thanks for their support and encouragement toward the completion of this work. I am particularly grateful to my colleagues and friends Leo Bostar, James S. Farris, Margaret Hutaff, Lou McNeil, Janet Minor, and John Van Den Hengel, who either read and encouraged me through this process. I also wish to thank my mother, Annette Evans, who has understood and supported me throughout the years.

CHAPTER ONE

THE PROBLEM OF METAPHOR, NARRATIVE AND IMAGINATION FOR THEOLOGY

It is the purpose of this study to focus on Paul Ricoeur's theory of metaphor and narrative in relation to the philosophy of the imagination for its contribution to the development of a theological hermeneutics. Ricoeur's starting point is on the level of the functioning of language, particularly metaphor and narrative, rather than on conceptual, doctrinal interpretation.

A study of the inherently reflective and creative dynamic of narrative in relation to a theory of metaphor is especially relevant to an interpretation of the Judeo-Christian tradition, since the primary genre of its first order texts is narrative. Although these primary texts have traditionally been considered the touchstone of any interpretation of the Judeo-Christian faith, their equivocal language has generally been reduced by the second order doctrinal interpretations of their meaning, and overlooked by the historical critical methods of biblical scholarship.[2] As the literary critic Northrop Frye comments in the closing chapter of his book *The Great Code: The Bible and Literature:*

> We said earlier that the great doctrinal structures of the past that we identify as Catholic and Protestant or the like have always tended to make themselves the anti-types of the Biblical narrative and imagery. They are designed to establish the claim: this is what our central revelation really means, and this is how you have to understand it. Such systems of faith, however impressive and useful still, can hardly be definitive for us now, because they are so easily conditioned by the phases of language ascendant in their time, whether metonymic or descriptive. A reconsideration of the Bible can take place only with, and as part of, a reconsideration of language and of all the structures, including the literary ones that language produces.[3]

It is only recently that greater attention has been given to the functioning of the metaphoric[4] and narrative dimensions of the primary texts of the Judeo-Christian tradition, as these unfold a model of interpretation which is in fact shaped by the rules governing this type of language.

I

In order to give an overview of the problem, I will first sketch schematically the historical development of the prejudices that blocked a method of interpretation open to the symbolic/metaphorical/narrative language of the Judeo-Christian scriptures.

Typically, the historico-critical method of biblical scholarship has focussed upon what the text meant, while systematic theology addressed what it means.[5] Both approaches imply the ideal of a static and finished interpretation. In its extremes this has led to literalist pietism and rightist dogmatism, which has split roughly along the lines of Protestant versus Catholic interpretation.

On the whole, the poetic dimensions of the primary texts of the Judeo-Christian tradition have at best usually been considered allegorically[6] or treated as peripheral to the essential meaning of the text. On the secondary level of interpretation, conceptual and univocal expression has for the most part dominated theology in the west, stemming from the impact of Platonic and Aristotelian metaphysics upon the evolution of theology as a science.[7] According to Hans-Georg Gadamer:

> since late antiquity there has been a kind of art of interpretation, and there was even a rather differentiated doctrine of the diverse modes of interpreting the Holy Scriptures. But the variously distinguished forms of scriptural interpretation from the time of Cassiodorus served more as guidelines for making the Holy Scriptures useful to the dogmatic tradition of the Church. They were not at all intended by themselves to supply a way of interpreting Holy Scriptures for the sake of mediating correct doctrine.[8]

A belief in the possibility of a final and authoritative interpretation of the faith by the higher science of theology certainly was one of the presuppositions of medieval scholastic theology. As Matthew Lamb states in his book *Solidarity with Victims*:

> The internal relation between Christianity and theory was assured by the medieval shift toward theory through the assimilation of an Aristotelian *Begrifflichkeit*. Theology, the object of which was God himself and all things related to him, was both speculative and practical since it dealt more with God than with human acts, and only with the latter as oriented to *perfect knowledge* of God in eternal beatitude. *Theoria* was supreme as the knowledge of necessary and eternal truths or first principles. This transposition of Aristotle did not include his distinctions between *praxis*, as the acts of citizens and statesmen who identified the good with honor, and *poiesis* concerned with the production of material objects. Thus praxis was rendered *actio* and *factio*; and the doctrine of creation represented God, as infinite intelligence, as the *Artifex Mundi*.[9]

Thus *theoria* dominated theological reflection, aligned with the desire for necessary and unchanging truth. This deductive model of interpretation prescinded from the sphere of human action and praxis in its interpretation of the Christian faith. God served as the gravitational center of this onto-theology, removed from the events of history and human subjectivity.[10]

The Reformation's break with this type of authoritative interpretation of the faith by the Roman Catholic magisterium led to a renewed focus upon the language of the Judeo-Christian scriptures, and a reorientation to a more practical and pastoral level of interpretation. Unfortunately the Reformation's reaction to the conceptualism of neo-scholasticism created a distrust of philosophical theology. The new science of biblical criticism modeled itself instead upon the more traditional discipline of rhetoric as well as such emerging human sciences as philology and historical criticism. Hans-Georg Gadamer emphasizes though that:

> The decisive point...is not that one was dealing with the Holy Scriptures in texts in foreign tongues, whose adequate translation into the vernacular languages and whose exact understanding brought into play an entire armature of linguistic, literary, and historical information; the decisive factor was rather that by reason of the radicality of the Reformation return to the New Testament and in virtue of the demotion of the Church's dogmatic tradition, the Christian message itself confronted readers with a new, uncanny radicality.[11]

Despite the innovation of this renewed interpretation, which seemed energized, at least in part, through the attention given to the language of the scriptures, the Protestant tradition eventually arrived at its own authoritative reading of their meaning.[12] The historian B.M.G.Reardon comments:

> The Protestant Reformation, as well as its Catholic counterpart, was as a religious movement not so much the beginning of a new era as a temporary infusion of fresh life into the old. Medieval and even ancient modes of thought persisted. The watchword was Back! rather than Forward! The distant past, it was believed, possessed a truth which later generations had corrupted or obscured.... It is no exaggeration to say, therefore, that despite the great doctrinal cleavage of the sixteenth century and the bitter theological controversies to which it gave rise, the fundamental unity of Christian thought in the West continued unimpaired until the latter part of the eighteenth century. But by that time it was becoming increasingly evident that the dogmatic tradition in both its Catholic and Protestant forms would have to meet the incursion of intellectual forces tending increasingly to isolate it from the prevailing outlook.[13]

Therefore the new discipline of biblical criticism, as noted above, focussed more on the problems of translation and a determination of the original situation of the text than an analysis of its final literary form and its relation to the contemporary situation. A consideration of the metaphorical and narrative dimensions of the scriptures by biblical criticism was discouraged more fundamentally by the combined influence upon it of the rhetorical and scientific ideal of univocal expression,[14] along with the Cartesian prejudice for clear and distinct ideas. Biblical exegesis, in its extremes, veered in the direction of positivism and literalism, in contrast to the earlier, conceptual and speculative excesses of neo-scholasticism. Thus a set of presuppositions affected the methodology of biblical criticism similar to those of scholastic theology, since the belief in univocal and final truth remained a constant of the scientific ideal of knowledge from Aristotle through Descartes to Kant. Such sacred texts embodied the notion of absolute truth, untouched by the historical process,[15] despite the historical character of the Judeo-Christian tradition.

Romanticism, in defiance of neo-classicism, contributed to the emergence of a new way of thinking by advocating the case of symbolic and poetic expression.[16] Romanticism treated the latter as work of the creative imagination of the genius,[17] and considered it to be profoundly revelatory of the human condition. This movement began to shatter the notion of reality as seeing, and to erode the dominance of literal, univocal expression as the ideal language for expressing the order of things. Romanticism opened the way for a recognition of the creative and historical character of human beings objectified through the works of culture, art, language and religion.[18]

Kant was the preeminent philosophical influence of this period, heralding the end of metaphysics by questioning the limits of knowledge. He was unappreciative of human experience in its historical dimension, and depicted reason in terms of the isolated individual thinker, but he is to be credited with recognizing that time and experience are fundamental to human understanding, linking them through the schematization of the transcendental imagination.[19] The turn to experience, the recognition of time, and the expanded foundational role of the imagination in relation to the act of understanding are presented by Kant in his *First* and *Third Critiques*. In the latter work Kant captures Romanticism's new and radical respect for the symbolic with his aphorism: "the symbol gives rise to thought", to which he added: "no concept is equal".[20] The work of the preeminent Liberal Protestant theologian Friedrich Schleiermacher developed these notions further, influenced both by Kant and the Romantic movement. For example he reoriented theology from a focus on the propositions of faith to religious experience as a feeling of absolute dependence on God, transcending Kant's narrow notion of empirical experience.[21] Inspired by Kant's critique of knowledge, he redirected the various hermeneutical disciplines, such as philology, law and theology, by his conception of a general hermeneutics as the art of understanding the expressions of life. General hermeneutics serves as the basis and core of all "special" hermeneutics, and is founded on his recognition of the common reference to language by these different disciplines.[22] This general hermeneutics may be considered as an emerging alternative philosophical framework for theology,[23] in place of neo-scholastic metaphysics on the one hand and neo-classical rhetoric and the natural sciences on the other.

In 1799 Schleiermacher had already, in his famous tract addressed to the cultured despisers of religion, decisively rejected metaphysics and morals as a basis for the phenomenon of religion. Religion had to do not with man living according to some rational ideal but rather living, acting and feeling in relation to his creaturely dependence on God. Similarly, hermeneutics was held by Schleiermacher to be related to the concrete, existing, acting human being in the process of understanding dialogue. When we start with the conditions that pertain to all dialogue, when we turn away from rationalism, metaphysics and morality and examine the concrete, actual situation involved in understanding, then we have the starting point for a viable hermeneutics that can serve as a core for special hermeneutics, such as the biblical.[24]

But he also conceived of this art of understanding as a science, which uncovers the laws of understanding common to the act of interpreting texts in terms of the principles of language.[25] However he later focussed the task of hermeneutics more upon a psychological recovery of the creative imagination of the author, rather than upon the intentionalty of the text projected through its literary structure and language. This reflected the influence upon his work by the Romantic Movement's psychological definition of the creative imagination, a definition which he related to his concept of hermeneutics as an empathetic dialogue[26] between the author and the reader of the text.

The advent of a new consciouness of history as dialectical was prepared by Schleiermacher's development of general hermeneutics as the art of understanding the expressions of life in terms of the hermeneutic circle[27] between the author and reader. Wilhelm Dilthey, his successor, considered the father of modern conceptions of history,[28] broadened this hermeneutical circle to the historical dialectic of past, present and future[29] which further conditions the exchange between author and reader. General hermeneutics as history, according to Dilthey, is the hermeneutical science grounding the human sciences.[30] As Palmer states, quoting Dilthey:

'Not through introspection but only through history do we come to know ourselves.'The problem of understanding man was for Dilthey one of recovering a consciousness of the 'historicality' (*Geschichtlichkeit*) of our own existence which is lost in the static categories of science. We experience life not in the mechanical categories of 'power' but in complex individual moments of 'meaning,' of direct experience of life as a totality and in loving grasp of the particular. These units of meaning require the context of the past and the horizon of future expectations; they are intrinsically temporal and finite, and they are to be understood in terms of these dimensions—that is historically.[31]

Thus Dilthey extended Schleiermacher's definition of hermeneutics to a recognition of the fundamental historicality of human understanding. As he says:

> The totality of man's nature is only history.... It is in no way possible to go back behind the relativity of historical consciousness.... The 'type' man dissolves and changes in the process of history.... What man is and what he wills, he experiences only in the development of his nature through the millennia and never completely to the last syllable, never in objective concepts but always only in living experience which springs up out of the depths of his own being.[32]

For Dilthey the process of understanding through history is creative and always unfinished. His development of hermeneutics as the foundation of the human sciences exemplifies the struggle to give such claims a critical foundation in the face of the dominance of natural science[33] and its objectivist criteria of truth. But Dilthey was hindered by his acceptance of the subject-object dichotomization, which was characteristic of the neo-Kantian epistemology of his day.[34] He designated understanding as the proper mode of knowledge for the human sciences, while explanation was assigned to the realm of natural science, and he assumed the latter's method to be superior in its validation of objective truth.[35] Although he advanced beyond Schleiermacher's psychologism, he remained caught by his subjective focus.[36] As Palmer states:

> We note....that he did not fully succeed in extricating himself from the scientism and objectivity of the historical school which he had undertaken to transcend. We see more clearly today that the quest of "objectively valid knowledge" was itself a reflection of scientific ideals wholly contrary to the historicality of our self-understanding.... We may criticize the fact that Dilthey saw understanding—as did Schleiermacher—as reexperiencing (*Nacherleben*) and reconstruction of the author's experience and therefore analogous to the act of creation.[37]

Liberal Protestant theology was more directly affected by the work of Schleiermacher,[38] particularly by his emphasis on religious experience and his dissatisfaction with all philosophical systems that deal with religious faith as a set of conceptual theological propositions. On the other hand the success of the natural sciences competed as an alternative model of knowledge which fueled, for example the quest for the historical Jesus,[39] as a theology in search of a sound empirical basis for faith.

The response of Roman Catholicism through the nineteenth century to these different currents of thought remained almost consistently closed until the advent of the Second Vatican Council in the twentieth century. Reardon comments: "[Catholicism fell] back on the stronghold of an absolute authority...and matched it with an appropriate ecclesiastical policy."[40] It was unwilling to accept the dawning Liberal Protestant view that in Palmer's words:

> If man is not a disincarnate intelligence but a creature of time and place, if, that is, his life is historically determined, then his apprehension even of ultimate truth must be subject to historical conditions.[41]

These currents of thought were forcefully suppressed by the Vatican at the turn of the century.[42] In an anthology entitled *Consenus in Theology?*, Hans Küng, reviewing the situation prior to the Vatican II, points out that the reigning theological method in Roman Catholicism mandated by the First Vatican Council, reflected the categories and methods of neo-scholastic theology.[43] This deductive "Denzinger theology" was ahistorical and ruled by the apologetic dictates of the magisterium and was opposed to any consideration of modern biblical scholarship and the questions of the society of the day.

In contrast Vatican II yielded an extraordinary period of renewal with far reaching consequences, particularly due to its encouragement of biblical and historical scholarship and its openness to the modern world.[44] This in turn has led to a growing recognition of the inadequacies of neo-scholastic theology or any hierarchical model of interpretation that disregards the primacy of experience and the refractoriness of reality.[45] For contemporary Catholic theologians the legacy of Vatican II is the demand for greater knowledge of the contemporary world and its problems, as well as a utilization of the methods of modern scholarship.

The tragic events of the twentieth century have forced a consciousness of the complex character of modern society and the fallibility of the human condition. New disciplines have arisen since the nineteenth century to analyze the diverse factors at work in human society, for example, political science, economics, psychology, sociology, linguistics, as well as the impact of various new technologies affecting the limits and possibilites of human existence.

Vatican II, through its openness to the modern world, shifted the emphasis of the task of interpreting the Christian faith from contemplation of the truths of faith, apart from the world, to the meaning and praxis of faith, in response to the world. The spectrum of the audience for this translation of the Christian faith to the contemporary world now runs the gamut from the secular scientific consciousness of the first world to the beleaguered consciousness of the oppressed and impoverished of the third world.[46]

II

The general problem bequeathed by Vatican II is to construct a theological model of interpretation that can integrate the various methods of modern scholarship and respond to the contrast of the situations of the first and third world, particularly the questions raised by those outside the magisterium of the Church and the academy.[47] A partial answer seems to lie in the development of a theological hermeneutics which can overcome the shortcomings of nineteenth century hermeneutics[48] and encompass not only an hermeneutics of appropriation,[49] but also a hermeneutics of suspicion.[50]

In the anthology mentioned above, Hans Küng, Edward Schillebeeckx, David Tracy, George Lindbeck and Rosemary Ruether, among others, agree that the post-Vatican II situation requires a method of interrelating current scholarship on the biblical and post-biblical texts of Christianity with the questions and concerns of the present horizon of the contemporary world.

Küng makes the point that "if an unhistorical exegesis is definitely out of date in this era, so also is an unhistorical dogmatic theology".[51] In other words biblical scholarship and systematic theology are vitally connected disciplines. Systematic theology can no longer ignore or dominate the former. It must find a way to interrelate more dynamically the experiential testimony of the past with the present. Time, and its great importance for understanding the process of the mediation and interpretation of the meaning and truth of experience through language and the imagination, has come more to the forefront in this era.

Both Küng and Schillebeeckx, along with Tracy, are examples of post-Vatican II Catholic theologians who have attempted to wrestle with this problem by developing a correlative theological model.[52] As Küng states:

> In our current decade it has become increasingly evident that the only theology (primarily systematic and especially dogmatic theology) that could survive the future would be one that was daringly able to blend two vital elements in a non-traditional and highly convincing manner. These two elements are a "return to the sources" and a "venturing forth on to uncharted waters," or to put the matter less poetically, a theology of Christian origins and center enunciated within the horizon of the contemporary world.[53]

The development of this correlative model, as opposed to the deductive method of neo-scholastic theology, has much to gain by attending to the contributions of contemporary hermeneutics, literary criticism and the philosophy of language. They address the functioning of language in the mediation of experience and its relevance to the act of interpretation, particularly in terms of the philosophy of the imagination. For Schillebeeckx such a critical correlation is defined by a broad hermeneutic circle of three moments:

> 1) An analysis of our contemporary world of experience, 2) an investigation of the constant structures of the basic Christian experience spoken of by the New Testament and subsequent Christian tradition and 3) a critical relating of these two 'sources'.[54]

For Küng the essential method that enlivens the dialectic of this hermeneutic circle is the application of the historical critical method to the investigation of the "basic Christian experience of the New Testament". He argues that this is fundamental to a critical correlation of Christianity's understanding of its past in relation to its present. He notes that one of the most important developments for Roman Catholic scholarship since Vatican II is the recognition and acceptance of modern biblical scholarship, which challenges the responsible theologian to struggle with its implications for an interpretation of Christian dogma in the present situation.[55] For Küng the historical critical method provides a basis for a hermeneutics of suspicion with regard to established belief and practice.[56]

Although Schillebeeckx, Tracy and Küng have all made the turn to hermeneutics, the first two more than Küng recognize the relevance of the developments of literary criticism and its analysis of the narrativity of experience to the hermeneutic circle. In theological terms this calls for the critical correlation of experience of the New Testament with contemporary Christian experience. In terms of the presuppositions of philosophical hermeneutics, literary critical method examines the temporal mediation of experience through language and the transcendental imagination. At this level the prior conceptuality that has dominated biblical and theological interpretation needs to be questioned and reconstituted by a hermeneutical model of interpretation, in which the historical critical method has its place.[57] But as Schillebeeckx states in the Introduction to his book *Christ*:

> even if our concern is historical—and this can be pursued only by means of particular text—we must first use the method of literary criticism and only then use other methods to get through to the historical 'substratum'. If that happens, I believe that we shall arrive at a more varied and even richer historical picture of Jesus than we discover (as at present) when we follow the reverse sequence. Furthermore, this points to what I have called the never finished study of the Jesus event. The use of particular methods also occurs as an event in history.[58]

Contemporary hermeneutics questions the notion of univocal and final interpretation at the level of the mediation of experience and expression. A chief hermeneutical principle is that experience is always *interpreted* experience,[59] and narrative is one of the fundamental ways in which experience is mediated.[60] It is a form of mediation that is a constant of both the Judeo-Christian testimony of the Old and New Testaments as well as a key form of expression of contemporary experience. Literary critical method brings to the forefront the capacity of certain narratives to challenge and disrupt established assumptions and to stimulate a rethinking of the *status quo* interpretation of tradition.[61]

For Schillebeeckx and Tracy it is on this fundamental level that a clue to the dynamic of a correlative hermeneutical model for systematic theology can be constructed, one which circumvents the conceptuality of the previously dominant deductive model of interpretation and its univocal ideal of truth and meaning. The latter model simply reduced equivocal language, ignoring its capacity to mediate the refractoriness of reality. As Schillebeeckx states:

> The hermeneutical principle for the disclosure of reality is not the self-evident, but the scandal, the stumbling block of the refractoriness of reality. Reality is always a surprising revelation for thought, for which thought can only be a witness.[62]

What is uncovered in the analysis of the relation between experience and narrative is a more dynamic and open-ended character to the process of interpretation. Schillebeeckx recognizes that a living interpretation of tradition is defined by its ability to mediate and respond to the refractoriness of reality.

> Anyone who has had an experience *ipso facto* becomes himself a witness: he has a message. He describes what has happened to him. This narration opens up a new possibility of life for others, it sets something in motion. Thus the authority of experience becomes operative in the telling. The authority of experience has a narrative structure.[63]

He observes that tradition and experience are not opposites, rather they make one another possible, since we never experience without presuppositions. On the other hand the act of interpretation is stimulated by new experiences which offer fresh perspectives on the narratives of the tradition, enabling the tradition thereby to be renewed and critiqued.

> Our thought and experience are subject to historical and social influence. Reflection means thinking with presuppositions. This bond to a particular cultural tradition of experience is on the one hand positive: it makes understanding possible. On the other hand it is negative: it limits our understanding, is selective, and already guides new experiences in a particular direction.... That is why even a very old tradition of experience is always subject to the challenge of new experiences.[64]

And earlier he comments:

> The permanent resistance of reality to our rational intentions forces us to constantly new and untried models of thought. Truth comes near to us by the alienation and

disorientation of what we have already achieved and planned. This shatters the so-called normativeness or the dogmatism of the factual, of what is 'simply given'...................

....

Reality is always a surprising revelation for thought, for which thought can only be a witness.[65]

David Tracy, who also seeks to develop a correlative theological method bringing together biblical scholarship and theological reflection, adds:

on methodological grounds, historico-critical exegesis is a major but not sole method of analysis for these texts. A hermeneutical method with a more literary-critical than historico-critical bent has, in my judgment, also proved itself for theological usage. Minimally hermeneutical-literary critical methods provide another and distinct route to the Christian mode of being-in-the-world disclosed in front of (not behind)...these texts.... Greater sensitivity to these literary-critical and hermeneutical concerns promises at least as secure and, in general, a more relatively adequate methodological approach to the New Testament.[66]

In his book *The Analogical Imagination*, he affirms:

The heart of any hermeneutical position is the recognition that all interpretation is a mediation of past and present, a translation carried on within the effective history of a tradition to retrieve its sometimes strange, sometimes familiar meanings. But the traditionalist's use of tradition betrays the enriching, even liberating notion of tradition.[67]

Both Schillebeeckx and Tracy in their quest for a living interpretation point out the need to explicate the innovative and critical capacities of the texts of the Judeo-Christian tradition. Both make the turn to hermeneutics and literary criticism to construct such a model by attending to the primary level of experience and language. Paul Ricoeur, a philosopher of religion and a major contributor to the explication of contemporary hermeneutics, has influenced the work of these theologians[68] in a major way.

This study will concentrate on Ricoeur's argument for a model of creative interpretation[69] through his development of a theory of metaphor and narrative which stands in relation to the philosophy of the imagination. I will argue that this model, through Ricoeur's analysis of metaphor and imagination, offers a central key to account for a creative and critical interpretation of tradition oriented to authentic praxis. As Ricoeur puts it:

> Now whatever may be the epistemological status of "concepts" appropriate to our
> present cultural and philosophical situation, the problem is to look at religious language
> itself and explicate its conceptual potentialities, or, if you prefer, its capacity to be
> conceptually articulated in the space of confrontation with our culture. Our regressive
> method leads us from a mere extrinsic encounter between religious language and
> philosophical concepts, through the notion of *correlation*, toward a direct inquiry into
> religious language from the standpoint of its conceptual potentialities.[70]

III

In the past the dominant conceptual presuppositions that affected the development of theology as a science, and later biblical criticism, prevented a recognition of the contribution of metaphor and narrative to a creative interpretation of the Judeo-Christian tradition. The nineteenth century inaugurated the development of general hermeneutics and historical consciousness. However the emerging human sciences were ensnared by their struggle against the dominance of natural science's criteria of truth. Dilthey failed in his attempts to give a critical foundation to the human sciences equal to that of the natural sciences. The Romantic claims for the power of poetic expression foundered on the narrow psychological and subjective definition of the creative imagination, which influenced both Schleiermacher and Dilthey.

Heidegger's development of hermeneutics overcame the impasse of Dilthey's struggles to develop hermeneutics in terms of neo-Kantian epistemology and a psychological interpretation of the imagination. He overturned the subject-object dualism of neo-Kantian epistmology and radically defined hermeneutics as ontology, in which case understanding (as the transcendental imagination) is redefined as a mode of being.[71] On the other hand Heidegger's ontology does not address Dilthey's concern for method and critical reflection on the level of the interpretation of texts.

Both Gadamer[72] and Ricoeur have continued to develop this ontological hermeneutics, particularly in relation to language and aesthetics. But it is Ricoeur who focusses most directly on the study of symbolic/metaphoric[73] expression and the question of the creative interpretation of such texts. In contrast to Heidegger and Gadamer, Ricoeur explicitly addresses the earlier concerns of Dilthey for method and critical reflection[74] and seeks to overcome the weakness of Romanticism's earlier claims for symbolic and poetic expression and the inadequacies of its psychological definition of the imagination.

Contemporary hermeneutics in general, especially as advanced by its principal twentieth century authors (Heidegger, Gadamer and Ricoeur), offers the possibility of a more adequate philosophical model of interpretation. It overcomes the epistemological dilemmas of nineteenth century dualism through the development of the ontological hermeneutics of Heidegger's foundational work. It is particularly this conceptual framework that carries within it the possibility of a critical interpretation of symbolic/poetic/narrative[75] expression, treating it as non-reducible and capable of demonstrating the innovative relation of such language to thought and praxis.

The hermeneutics of Ricoeur specifically explicates an interrelationship between poetics, theory and praxis from the vantage point of practical philosophy.[76] It does this by being attentive to language and its mediation of time and human action. This ontological hermeneutics represents an alternative both to traditional metaphysics and to such modern philosophical positions as positivism, empiricism and lingusitic analysis.

In general it recognizes the ontological character of language as a fundamental vehicle of human expression and self-understanding which transcends and grounds the self by its capacity to mediate the meaning of human events. We are beings in the world, thrown and situated within it, prior to any of our attempts to control and objectify it. Primarily through language we receive access to the cultural and historical well-springs; to the stories and myths that form the repertoire of our heritage, the sources of its identity and sustenance. Hermeneutics as pursued by Ricoeur and Gadamer insists that self-understanding is never immediate, but emerges through the more indirect routes of interpretation and reappropriation of these works of culture, art and tradition.[77]

To be human is to be involved in the process of the making and remaking of ourselves and our world. Although generally unrecognized, narrative is one of the central forms we use to comprehend human experience and to project the limits and possibilities of this world we both inherit and continue to create. It is particularly the narrative mediation of the dialectic of past, present and future, through the literary works of the imagination, which has a covert ability to interpret our situation and to project new ways of being in the world. Both fictional and historical narratives have a capacity to intersect with the ordinary narrative of our lives and to effect a confirmation of the norm or to awaken us to the innovative possibilities of existence.

Unlike the traditional philosophy of nature that concerns itself with the conditions of objectivity, truth and the absolute order of things, contemporary hermeneutics attends to the conditions of possibility for finite human existence through the dialectic of past, present and future. Thus it is able to take more seriously the reflective power of metaphor and narrative, particularly the ability of narrative to redescribe human existence and to play with the possibilities of existence.

Traditional philosophy has been imbued with the representative illusion,[78] in which case space and the order of things, rather than time and history as future directed, describe the traditional sphere of investigation. This position is largely unaware of the significance of the process of time to the production and definition of human subjectivity and the works of culture. Art is simply the imitation[79] of nature and the order of things. In contrast hermeneutics contends that the world is a mediated and interpreted reality in which time is constitutive of understanding and being. Thus it is integral to the way in which we construe, express and understand meaning.[80] Such understanding, objectified through art and literature, is not simply an imitation of what is, but is potentially critical of the praxis of the human situation and a means of projecting new possibilities for existence in terms of its *mimetic*[81] mediation of experience.

In contrast to later developments of traditional philosophy which were in search of an original starting point (for example, Descartes) or final vision of the whole (for example, Hegel), a key hypothesis of contemporary hermeneutics is that interpretation is a continuous spiral of understanding, an open-ended process, in which case there is no presuppositionless starting point[82] nor the possibility of absolute knowledge. Instead through the process of interpretation of finite human history, being manifests itself in many ways, as a dialectic of the determined and undetermined. The latter view differs from classical metaphysics' definition of pure being as univocal, determined, and one in its essential nature, above the accidents of history and the human condition.

Ricoeur is distinguished from Heidegger and Gadamer by his more specific focus upon symbolic /metaphoric/narrative expression and by his greater concern for critical reflection[83] and method. This has required of him an openness to the various methods of the human sciences and has led him to a more precise study of language. This analysis of language has brought him into dialogue with structuralism, semiotics and literary criticism. In addition he is more explicitly attuned to the sacred, particularly the symbols, myths and narratives of the Judeo-Christian tradition.[84]

The philosophy of Ricoeur addresses the relation between symbol and thought as a dialectic. This dialectic is weighted in the direction of the symbolic. That is, according to his earliest formulation of the problem, there is always more meaning in reserve in the symbol which precedes thought. True symbols have an inexhaustible reservoir of meaning that constantly calls forth the engagement of thought; of interpretation in the search for greater understanding in relation to the contemporary situation of the reader. As he states in his early article, "The Hermeneutics of Symbols and Philosophical Reflection: I":

> the task is now to think starting from the symbolic and according to the genius of the symbolic. And it *is* a matter of thinking. For my part, I do not in the least abandon the tradition of rationality that has animated philosophy since the Greeks. It is not at all a question of giving in to some kind of imaginative intuition, but rather of thinking, that is to say, of elaborating concepts that comprehend, and make one comprehend, concepts woven together, if not in a closed system, at least in a *systematic* order. But at the same time it is a question of transmitting by means of this rational elaboration, a richness of meaning or signification that was already there, that has already preceded rational elaboration. For such is the situation; on the one hand, all has been said *before* philosophy, by sign and by enigma...on the other hand, we have the task of speaking clearly, by taking the risk of dissimulating.[85]

Ricoeur projects the possibility of a creative interpretation in which thought is both bound to the symbol and free to interpret the symbol creatively.

> I would like to try another way, the way of creative interpretation, an interpretation that
> would respect the original enigma of symbols, let itself be taught by this enigma, but,
> with that as a start, bring out the meaning, give it form, in the full responsibility of an
> autonomous sytematized thought. But how can thought be at once *bound* and *free*?
> How can one maintain the immediacy of symbol and the mediation of thought?[86]

His strategy is inductive in that his investigation of hermeneutics is centered and wagered upon an intense study of symbolic/metaphoric/narrative expression which proceeds from the level of metaphor and the sentence to narrative with a concern to uncover the conceptual potentialities of this type of language.[87] His route to an ontological[88] hermeneutics is circular, indirect and endless conducted as a continuous journey of exploration and provisional definition, which is guided by his study of language and his dialectical conversation with the history of philosophy. So, unlike Husserl, he does not bracket the question of ontology, but rather assumes a truncated and concrete ontology[89] in his effort to define a general hermeneutics in touch with the methodology of the human sciences.

Ricoeur is always careful to admit the difference between poetic discourse and philosophic discourse.[90] On the other hand he maintains that metaphoric strategy[91] is common to the innovative rule of both types of discourse, and that hermeneutics functions at the intersection of these two domains.

> It is a composite discourse therefore and as such cannot but feel the opposite pull of
> two rival demands. On the one side interpretation seeks the clarity of the concept; on
> the other it hopes to preserve the dynamism of meaning that the concept holds and pins
> down.[92]

His own philosophic method utilizes what he later refers to as metaphoric strategy, in his development of this problem. I will point out that Ricoeur's resolution is a testimony to the adequacy of metaphoric strategy at the level of philosophic discourse. It is an example of a philosophic creativity in keeping with his understanding of creativity at the level of poetic discourse. Mary Schaldenbrand comments on the application of Ricoeur's concept of metaphoric stategy to the level of philosophic discourse as follows:

a philosophic use of metaphoric strategy corresponds to a sense of expanding reality. If as Mary Hesse points out, "a world in continuous expansion" obliges practioners of scientific method to "continuous adaptation of their language," their philosophic counterparts are no less obliged. It thus appears that metaphoric strategy enables, not only scientific and poetic creativity, but philosophic creativity as well.[93]

The position I want to explicate through the work of Ricoeur is the centrality of his understanding of the strategy of metaphor to the development of a general hermeneutics, which can critically account for the plurivocity of meaning of symbolic/metaphoric/narrative language. I will attempt to show that this strategy offers innovative resources for enpowering (in particular) a living interpretation of the texts of the Judeo-Christian tradition.

According to Ricoeur, the theory of metaphor and the philosophy of the imagination[94] are key to understanding the potentially creative power of symbolic/metaphoric/narrative works and their capacity to enliven or critique our understanding of the authenticity or inauthenticity of existence. The imagination, objectified through the language and structure of literary works, acts, from the perspective of the reader, as the instructive axis of interpretation governing a creative reading of the poetic and narrative texts which give expression to our culture. Specifically I will argue that he develops his definition of the role of the imagination correlatively in terms of his theory of metaphor. As Ricoeur states in the *Rule of Metaphor*:

This is the situation Kant considers in the celebrated paragraph 49 of the *Critique of the Faculty of Judgment*. He calls 'the spirit' (*Geist*) in an aesthetic sense,'the life-giving principle of mind (*Gemut*).' The metaphor of life comes to the forefront at this point in the argument because the *game* in which imagination and understanding engage assumes a task assigned by the Ideas of reason, to which no concept is equal. But where the understanding fails, imagination still has the power of presenting' (*Darstellung*) the Idea. It is this 'presentation' of the Idea by the imagination that forces conceptual thought *to think more*. Creative imagination is nothing other than this demand put to conceptual thought. This sheds light on our own notion of living metaphor. Metaphor is living not only to the extent that it vivifies a constituted language. Metaphor is living by virtue of the fact that it introduces the spark of the imagination into a 'thinking more' at the conceptual level. This struggle to 'think more,' guided by the 'vivifying principle,' is the 'soul' of interpretation.[95]

It is my thesis that through his wedding of a theory of metaphor to the philosophy of the imagination, within the framework of a general hermeneutics, he successfully grounds and explicates the meaning of creative interpretation[96] (which he presupposes such texts demand). Thus I will argue that he is able to overcome the limitations of Romanticism's claims for symbolic/metaphoric expression, which relied too heavily upon a psychological definition of the imagination, and at the same time overcome the limits of neo-Kantian aesthetics and epistemology.

I will then illustrate and support the implications of Ricoeur's theory of creative interpretation for biblical hermeneutics[97] by applying it, at the level of metaphoric religious language, to a poem in Isaiah 14:4-20. At the center of this poem is a myth which was taken over by the poet from the surrounding culture. Typical interpretations by scholars in the past have ignored the significance of the myth to the design and intentionality of the poem as a whole.[98] Instead it has been generally considered as simply decorative and incidental to the text and its overall meaning. I will argue that Ricoeur's theory of metaphor uncovers the subversive power of the imagination at work in the narrative of this poem, particularly through the incorporation of the myth at its center.

I will limit my discussion of the problem of the interpretation of symbolic/metaphoric/narrative language to Ricoeur's address of it within the framework of a general hermeneutics and then, in conclusion at the level of biblical hermeneutics. This is in keeping with Ricoeur's path, since he develops his theory of metaphor and imagination first with reference to language and hermeneutics in general[99] and then to religious language and biblical hermeneutics in particular. Thus the scope of this study will remain in keeping with the limits Ricoeur sets to the problem.

In summary then this analysis will argue through examination of the work of Paul Ricoeur that symbolic/metaphoric/narrative expressions are key to a living interpretation of the Judeo-Christian tradition in terms of their capacity to maintain its authenticity and vision through the strategy of metaphor and imagination. This metaphoric strategy, pursued in the present, acts through the dialectic of the text and the reader to foster a hermeneutics of suspicion and a hermeneutics of creative appropriation, oriented to an understanding of the praxis of the Kingdom of God.[100] In the area of biblical hermeneutics, the adequacy of this theory will be demonstrated by applying it to a text in Isaiah. The theory will be shown to uncover the subversive and creative power of the imagination at work in this text.

ENDNOTES OF CHAPTER ONE

[1]Stephen Crites, "The Narrative Quality of Experience", *Journal of the American Academy of Religion*, 39(1971), 291-303.

[2]Hans Frei, *The Eclipse of Biblical Narrative* (New Haven and London: Yale University Press, 1974). Northrop Frye *The Great Code: The Bible and Literature* (Toronto: Academic Press Canada, 1981), xvii.

[3]Frye, pp. 226-227.

[4]Sallie McFague, *Metaphorical Theology* (Philadelphia: Fortress Press, 1982). David Tracy, *Blessed Rage for Order* (New York: Seabury Press, 1975), pp. 120-131 and *The Analogical Imagination* (New York:Crossroad, 1981).

[5]Elisabeth Schüssler Fiorenza, *Bread Not Stone* (Boston: Beacon Press, 1984), p. 121. Raymond Brown, "What the Biblical Word Meant and What It Means", in his *The Critical Meaning of the Bible* (New York: Paulist Press, 1981), pp. 23-44.

[6]Henri de Lubac, *Exégèse medievale. Les quatre sens de l'Ecriture*, 4 vols. (Paris: 1959-64). Tzvetan Todorov, *Symbolism and Interpretation*, trans. Catherine Porter (Ithaca: Cornell University, 1982), p. 140. Frei, p. 2.

[7]Karl Rahner, ed., *Encyclopedia of Theology: The Concise Sacramentum Mundi* (New York: Seabury Press, 1975), pp.55 and 44.

[8]Hans-Georg Gadamer, *Reason in the Age of Science*, trans. F. G. Lawrence (Cambridge: MIT Press, 1982), pp. 127-128.

[9]Matthew Lamb, *Solidarity with Victims* (New York: Crossroad, 1982), pp.65-66.

[10]Rahner, p. 1690.

[11]Gadamer, p. 128.

[12]B. M. G. Reardon, *Religious Thought in the Nineteenth Century* (Cambridge: Cambridge at the University Press, 1966), p. 2.

[13]Ibid., p. 3.

[14]Todorov, *Theories of the Symbol*, trans. Catherine Porter, (Ithaca: Cornell University Press, 1982), pp. 108-109.

[15]Frei, p. 7. See also Ian G. Barbour, *Issues in Science and Religion* (New York: Harper & Row, 1966), pp. 52, 60f.

[16]Lilian R. Furst, *Romanticism* (London: Methuen & Co. Ltd., 1969), pp.   15f.

[17]Ibid., p. 40. See also Kant's definition of genius in his *Critique of Judgment*, trans. J. H. Bernard (London: Hafner Press, 1951), pp. 150-164.

[18]Todorov, pp. 167f.

[19]Kant, *Critique of Pure Reason*, trans. Norman Kemp Smith (New York: St. Martin's Press, 1929), pp. 181, 185. See also Martin Heidegger, *Kant and the Problem of Metaphysics*, trans. James S. Churchill (Bloomington: Indiana Press, 1962).

[20]Kant, *The Critique of Judgment*, p. 158.

[21]Reardon, p. 42. Richard E. Palmer, *Hermeneutics:Interpretation Theory in Schleiermacher, Dilthey, Hiedegger, and Gadamer.* (Evanston: Northwestern University Press, 1969), p. 102.

[22]Palmer, pp. 85-86.

[23]Hermeneutics as the art of understanding the expressions of life serves to return theology to recognizing the basic interpretive character of the Judeo-Christian tradition, and developing an inductive model of interpretation, which attends to language and the historicity of the human condition.

[24]Palmer, p. 85.

[25]Ibid., p. 92.

[26]Ibid., p. 86.

[27]Ibid., p. 87.

[28]Ibid., p. 117.

[29]Ibid., p. 101.

[30]Ibid.

[31]Ibid.

[32]Ibid., pp. 116-117.

[33]Ibid., p. 123.

[34]Ibid., p. 122.

[35]Paul Ricoeur, "The Task of Hermeneutics", in *Hermeneutics and the Human Sciences*, ed. and trans. John B. Thompson (Cambridge: Cambridge University Press, 1981), p. 49.

[36]Ibid., p. 52.

[37]Palmer, p. 123.

[38]Reardon, p. 20.

[39]Ibid., p. 22.

[40]Ibid., p. 3.

[41]Ibid., p. 4.

[42]Ibid., pp. 30-31.

[43]Hans Küng, "Toward a New Consensus in Theology", in *Consensus in Theology?*, ed. Leonard Swidler (Philadelphia: Westminster Press, 1980), p. 1.

[44]Ibid., pp. 1-4.

[45]Edward Schillebeeckx, *Christ*, trans. John Bowden (New York: Seabury Press, 1980), pp. 31-42.

[46]Rosemary Radford Ruether, "Is a New Christian Consensus Possible?", in *Consensus in Theology?*, p. 67.

[47]Ibid., p. 65.

[48]Ricoeur, pp. 48-53.

[49]Ricoeur, "Appropriation", in *Hermeneutics and the Human Sciences*, pp.182-93.

[50]Ricoeur, "Hermeneutics and the Critique of Ideology", in *Hermeneutics and the Human Sciences*, p. 63ff.

[51]Küng, p. 8.

[52]Tracy, *Blessed Rage for Order*, pp. 45-46. See also Kung, p. 12.

[53]Ibid., pp. 2-3.

[54]Ibid., p. 13.

[55]Ibid., p. 8.

[56]Ibid.

[57]Tracy, "Particular Questions Within General Consensus", in *Consensus in Theology?*, p. 37.

[58]Schillebeeckx, p. 24.

[59]Ibid., p. 33.

[60]Ibid., pp. 37-38.

[61]Ibid., p. 43.

[62]Ibid., p. 35.

[63]Ibid., pp. 37-38.

[64]Ibid., p. 38.

[65]Ibid., p. 35.

[66]Tracy, "Particular Questions", p. 37.

[67]Tracy, *Analogical Imagination*, pp. 99-100.

[68]Tracy, *Blessed Rage for Order*, p. 120ff.

[69]Ricoeur, "The Hermeneutics of Symbols and Philosophical Reflection: I", trans. Denis Savage in *Conflict of Interpretations*, ed. Don Ihde (Evanston: Northwestern University Press, 1974), p. 300.

[70]Ricoeur, "Biblical Hermeneutics", *Semeia* 4(1975), p. 132.

[71]Ricoeur, "The Task of Hermeneutics", p. 55. See also Heidegger, *Kant and the Problem of Metaphysics.*

[72]Ricoeur, pp. 59-62.

[73]Ricoeur, "Existence and Hermeneutics", trans. Kathleen McLaughlin in *Conflict of Interpretations*, pp. 14-16, 22-24.

[74]Ricoeur, p. 11.

[75]Ricoeur, "Existence and Hermeneutics", p. 15.

[76]Ricoeur, "*Mimesis* and Representation", *Annals of Scholarship* 2 (1981), 15-31. Gadamer, "Hermeneutics as a Theorectical and Practical Task", in *Reason in the Age of Science*, pp. 113-137.

[77]Ricoeur, "Existence and Hermeneutics", p.17.

[78]Richard Rorty, *Philosophy and the Mirror of Nature* (Princeton: Princeton University Press, 1979), pp. 315ff.

[79]Todorov, *Theories of the Symbol*, pp. 111ff.

[80]Heidegger, *Being and Time*, trans. John Macquarrie and Edward Robinson (Oxford: Basil Blackwell, 1978), pp. 274ff.

[81]Ricoeur, "*Mimesis* and Representation".

[82]Ricoeur, "Existence and Hermeneutics", p.17.

[83]Ricoeur, p. 10.

[84]Ricoeur, *The Symbolism of Evil,* trans. Emerson Buchanan (Boston: Beacon Press, 1967), p. 20.

[85]Ricoeur, "The Hermeneutics of Symbols: I", p. 296.

[86]Ibid., p. 300.

[87]Ricoeur, "Existence and Hermeneutics", pp. 11-16.

[88]Ibid., p. 23.

[89]Ibid.

[90]Ricoeur, *The Rule of Metaphor,* trans. Robert Czerny, Kathleen McLaughlin and John Costello (Toronto: University of Toronto Press, 1977), pp. 258-259.

[91]Mary Schaldenbrand, "Metaphoric Imagination: Kinship Through Conflict" in *Studies in the Philosophy of Paul Ricoeur*, ed. Charles E. Reagan (Athens: Ohio University Press, 1979), p. 79.

[92]Ricoeur, *The Rule of Metaphor*, p. 303.

[93]Schaldenbrand, pp. 79-80.

[94]Ricoeur, "A Response by Paul Ricoeur", in *Hermeneutics and the Human Sciences*, pp. 38-39.

[95]Ricoeur, *The Rule of Metaphor*, p. 303.

[96]Ricoeur, "The Hermeneutics of Symbols: I", p. 300.

[97]Ricoeur, "The Bible and the Imagination", *The Bible as a Document of the University,* ed. Hans Dieter Betz (Ann Arbor: Scholars Press, 1981), pp. 66-72.

[98]Brevard Childs, *Myth and Reality in the Old Testament* (London: SCM Press, 1960), pp. 95-96.

[99]Ricoeur, "Philosophical Hermeneutics and Theological Hermeneutics"in *The Center for Hermeneutical Studies* 17 (1976), pp.1-2.

[100]Ricoeur, "Biblical Hermeneutics", p. 32.

CHAPTER TWO

RICOEUR'S PHILOSOPHICAL
AND HISTORICAL CONTEXT

This chapter gives a biographical sketch of Ricoeur emphasizing the philosophical influences and political context that condition his development of hermeneutics, in terms of his lifelong effort to connect philosophy to praxis. In particular I will note the contrast between Marcel, Jaspers and Husserl on the one hand and Heidegger on the other. It is Ricoeur's allegiance to the former that fuels his desire to explicate a critical hermeneutics despite his debt to Heidegger's monumental redefinition of hermeneutics. The controversial actions of Heidegger throw light upon Ricoeur's dissatisfaction with Heidegger's ontological hermeneutics and Ricoeur's recognition of the need for a hermeneutics of suspicion to compliment a hermeneutics of appropriation.

Political forces and the response to them affected the philosophical agendas of Heidegger and Ricoeur, men of different generations and opposing sides of war. The historical context speaks to the complexity of Ricoeur's dialectical relationship to Heidegger, which may be characterized as one of both conflict and kinship with the man and his work.

In the next chapter I explicate Ricoeur's turn to hermeneutics against the backdrop of Heidegger's ontological hermeneutics, which fundamentally transformed the horizon of the contemporary discussion, by establishing the priority of being-in-the-world to the subject/object dualism of the neo-Kantian framework. Heidegger cast aside epistemology in the wake of his deconstruction of western metaphysics and retrieval of the forgotten question of Being. But Ricoeur's quest for a critical hermeneutics leads him to make the return to epistemology, in view of the horizon of the Heideggerian achievement.

I

Paul Ricoeur was born in Valence, France on February 27, 1913 and raised in the Calvinist Protestant tradition.[8] His university and graduate years took place during the 1930's at the University of Paris. At an early age he lost his father, which perhaps deepened the influence of the mentors he encountered at the university, particularly Gabriel Marcel and Emmanuel Mounier. Both were exemplary human beings, who engaged their students in their attempts to create a more concrete philosophy, responsive to life and the mediation of its meaning.

The horizon of the nineteen thirties was shaped by the uncertainties of economic depression, which fueled political unrest and the search for a new order. Fascism, socialism and communism represented the political spectrum of opposing responses and solutions to the economic struggle of this era, foreshadowing the fuller conflict of war. As William Barrett vividly describes the France of the 1930's:

> The atmosphere of Leftist politics was over everything.... But over France also was the stale and tired atmosphere of a world already doomed to defeat: The Popular Front Government of Léon Blum drifted, nerveless and flaccid, incapable of meeting the crisis of the times; the French bourgeoisie hung on, entrenched and petty, unable to conceive the possibility of any great action.[9]

Against this malaise the leftist philosophical style of both Marcel and Mounier endeavored to define a philosophy responsive to the concrete, existential circumstances of the human condition, in contrast to the reigning philosophical approach of the University of Paris, which maintained a standard of intellectual detachment and objectivity, abstracted from the political and social context.[10] The type of philosophizing of both these men was at variance with the prevalently neo-Kantian tone of the university. As Ricoeur states:

> Up to the pre-war period, French philosophy was obviously a part of the teaching function in the broadest sense. That teaching function points up rather well the strength and weakness of university philosophy. Its weakness was in situating its problems on the fringes of life and history, which strictly speaking, were unrealistic. Its strength, however, was its ability to deal with problems of method and fundamental questions, the quest for a "point of departure" and the "first truth," and, naturally, the orderly command of discourse.[11]

Marcel, a Catholic, in revolt against the neo-Kantianism of the university resorted to Kierkegaard (the nineteenth century precursor of existentialism). He responded to Kierkegaard's call for a redirection of traditional philosophy and theology, by focussing upon depth experiences of life, in order to retrieve the sources of authentic subjectivity. He also adapted Kierkegaard's radical innovation of using poetic and literary genres for philosophical and theological expression, particularly the genre of the journal.

In Marcel's case this is exemplified by his development of the philosophical diary and revival of the socratic method of dialogue.[12] He addressed the theme of embodied existence, as well as such depth experiences as death, betrayal, despair and hope, in order to circumvent the pretensions of the Cartesian *Cogito* and to reveal the primacy of "I am" and existence over objectivity. Like Kierkegaard he did not bracket his faith from his philosophical reflection, but it served as the source of his experience of the Mystery of Being which led Marcel to refuse to equate God with a definition of Being, in relation to his explication of a concrete ontology.

Ricoeur took part in the seminars held in Marcel's apartment, with their demand to practice the socratic method, and the reference to one's own experience, prior to any citing of established authors and commentaries. As he recalls:

> Every Friday evening in his home Gabriel Marcel brought together twenty or so of his disciples and friends; we tried never to cite ready-made analyses or interpretations. Instead, we were required to think on the basis of fresh examples, whether real or imaginary, investigating the ontological implications of the situation under consideration, exploring new avenues, taking chances, using the resources of our dialogue alone. In this way we participated to a greater or lesser extent in developing and discussing the great themes (of his concrete ontology).[13]

Mounier, the other mentor of this period for Ricoeur, challenged his students to use philosophy to address the political and spiritual crises of this pre-war era. Emmanuel Mounier, like Marcel a Catholic, sought to reshape philosophy in terms of faith and activism[14] through attention to the practical and political realm. He recognized a crisis of civilization that must be addressed. His philosophy of Personalism argued that the realization of authentic subjectivity is concomitant with the effort to create a just and authentic society. He founded a journal, *Esprit*, which provided a forum for reflection upon the interrelationship between philosophy/faith and activism. In order to pursue these themes, he stepped outside the university, which he found too constricting because of its definition of the philosopher as detached from the political and practical realm. Mounier's movement reached people through adult education, attempting to serve a wider and less elite audience. The term Personalism was intended "to designate the first investigations of the review *Esprit* and of some allied groups concerned with the political and spiritual crisis which was then breaking out in Europe."[15]

This movement was for Ricoeur a pedagogy, advocating the relation of the individual to the communal. It was not a philosophy in the strict sense of the university, which defined itself through a philosophical problematic, concerning questions of starting point, methods and order. Mounier critiqued the individualism of the bourgeois as well as the pseudo-universalism of the fascists. Overall he endeavored to think the connection between theory–practice and reflection–action and to broaden ethics to encompass social justice. Moreover he fostered a strong suspicion of the hidden authoritarianism of philosophical systems.

Ricoeur combined the influences of Marcel and Mounier with his classical philosophical training at the University of Paris. Aristotle and Kant are the great architects of western philosophy that made an enduring impact upon Ricoeur's thought. The dialectical style of his reflection is founded upon both his fundamental respect for the philosophical tradition of the university, and its classics, as well as his recognition of the need for philosophical innovation. His wager is that innovation acts to regenerate the philosophical tradition by drawing upon the classics as resources and avenues to philosophical renewal and creativity.

Both Marcel and Mounier challenged Ricoeur to develop his philosophy and his Christian commitment in relation to the ethical and existential questions and crises of the day. Thus his commitment to philosophical innovation and social justice finds its inspiration in the work and example of these two early mentors. They demanded a rebuilding of philosophy by going back to experience, and in the case of Marcel, encouraged an analysis of such primary forms of expression as symbol, myth and poetic/literary works, the resources for the development of a concrete ontology, undercutting the reign of conceptual absolutes.

II

Ricoeur began reading the contemporary German philosophical work of Husserl, Heidegger and Jaspers through his contact with Marcel's circle.[16] He was fundamentally drawn to Husserl's phenomenological method, since it offered a precision of thought, which he found lacking in Marcel's method and style.

The desire for this concrete ontology has never left me. But it encountered the force of another desire, just as strong—the desire for a certain systematism, which I had first admired in my student days in the great architects of the Treatises of the Categories, Aristotle and Kant.... Now this desire for systematism in philosophical method I found in Husserl, more precisely, in the *Ideas.*[17]

This reading together of the thought of Marcel in relation to Husserl, early in Ricoeur's philosophical development, exemplifies a consistent hallmark of his philosophical style of reflection. It is a strategy central to his later definition of hermeneutics and the philosophy of the imagination; that is the dialectical interrelation and mediation of opposing viewpoints. As Ricoeur states "[there are] two requirements of philosophical thought—clarity and depth, a sense for distinctions and a sense for covert bonds—[which] must constantly confront each other."[18]

In the case of Marcel and Husserl their common endeavor was to cut beneath the preconceptions of abstract philosophical systems in order to return to the more fundamental level of primary experience and its mediation of meaning. A point of conflict is Husserl's idealist interpretation of phenomenology, which brackets being in order to return to intentional consciousness, from Marcel's perspective this bracketing of being undermines the priority of ontology to subjectivity. Ricoeur set himself the task of creatively conciliating phenomenology with ontology by overcoming Husserl's idealist interpretation of the reduction and placing it at the service of a concrete ontology.

In Husserl I admired not only the care taken in his descriptions but the way they were linked together. Some of Husserl's theses could be made, without distorting them too much, to agree with the thought of Gabriel Marcel: the central nature of the question of meaning, the subordination of the linguistic and propositional level to the fundamental level of experience itself, the privileged position of perception in apprehending reality and that of intersubjectivity in developing any sort of being in common. Other theses of Husserl ran counter to Gabriel Marcel's concrete ontology, in particular, the claim to bracket the natural attitude by means of the reduction. Of course, the Marcellian opposition between existence and objectivity did not lack a certain affinity with the Husserlian opposition between the intentional sphere of consciousness and so-called natural givens. In the eyes of a disciple of Marcel, Husserlian bracketing, however affected the ontological commitment of the concrete subject.... In short Husserlian idealism did run counter to Marcel's concrete ontology.[19]

The German philosophers, Husserl, Heidegger and Jaspers acted as rival influences[20] upon Ricoeur. They represent a generation which developed in the German situation of Post-World War I disenchantment with humanism and technology, in which an economically unstable and defeated Germany fueled a movement to recover the national pride of the German spirit.

The role of the university professor of this generation, as in France, functioned in an academic arena that mandated detachment and political neutrality. On the other hand Husserl (paralleling Marcel) quietly enacted a revolution in the abstract university atmosphere against the reign of objectivism and the grand conceptual systems advocated by such neo-Kantians as Heinrich Rickert. Husserl's phenomenological challenge was "Back to the things themselves!"[21] Heidegger came under the influence of this revolution. "[He] became Husserl's assistant, learning directly from the master about his phenomenonological method and giving seminars in which he both practiced the method and began to question it...."[22]

Heidegger transformed phenomenology through his quest to retrieve the forgotten question of the meaning of Being. By grafting Husserl's phenomenological method to an ontological definition of hermeneutics, he transcended Husserl's idealist interpretation of subjectivity. Heidegger more than any other philosopher of this century made a monumental impact upon the philosophical tradition through the publication of *Being and Time*,[23] in which he returns to the question of Being and reinterprets understanding as a mode of being, undercutting the epistemological dualism of subject and object that held sway from Descartes to Dilthey to Husserl. Heidegger makes explicit the prior belonging of *Dasein* to *Sein*, which precedes the differentiation of subject and object. The groundwork for this Copernican revolution is developed by Heidegger's radical interpretation of Kant's definition of the transcendental imagination in the *Critique of Pure Reason*.[24]

Kant's *Critique of Pure Reason* stood, for Heidegger, at the end of a long process of "forgetfulness of Being," and it provided him with the possibility for his mode of remembrance, a transcendental inquiry into the ground of Being. While he was formulating his philosophical project in the 1920's, Heidegger prepared a series of lectures on Kant which were to be the centerpiece of the second part of *Being and Time*. These were presented in his classes in 1925-26 and finally published in 1929 as *Kant and the Problem of Metaphysics*.[25]

Heidegger's pursuit of the question of Being meshed with the German nationalist desire to retrieve the foundations of the German *Geist,* its history and traditions.[26] Jaspers and Heidegger shared with Husserl the effort to chart a new beginning for philosophy, particularly to cut beneath the abstractions of neo-Kantianism and overcome the limitations of positivism. After the 1927 publication of *Being and Time* however the friendship became more strained, since Jaspers found the book alien in tone and style, because of its subordination of subjectivity to the question of Being and its abstraction from the historical context.[27] By contrast Jaspers's publication, *Man in the Modern Age* in 1930, focussed upon the struggle for authentic subjectivity in relation to the conflicting historical forces of society. As Barrett comments:

Jaspers sees the historical meaning of existential philosophy as a struggle to awaken in the individual the possibilities of an authentic and genuine life, in the face of the great modern drift toward a standardized mass society. Jaspers wrote his book in 1930, three years before Hitler came to power and precisely at the end of a postwar decade in Germany of great intellectual brilliance and greater economic bankruptcy under the Weimar Republic. The book is thus saturated from beginning to end with the dual feeling of the great threat and the great promise of modern life.[28]

Heidegger's actions during 1933 were a more major source of disillusionment. According to the German-Jewish political philosopher, Hannah Arendt, a contemporary of Ricoeur's and student of Heidegger's, in his role as philosopher, Heidegger was aloof to the political currents of the time and in Arendt's judgment naive. He joined the National Socialist Party, which she believes he viewed romantically as renewing the tradition of German nationalism and culture.[29] At the same time he accepted from the Nazi Party the rectorship at Freiburg University in 1933 and proceeded to carry out the policies it dictated to the university. One of his more infamous actions during this period, Arendt reports, was that he forbade Husserl, his former teacher and friend, whose lecture chair he had inherited, to enter the faculty, because Husserl was a Jew.[30]

Both Husserl and Jaspers, colleagues of Heidegger, became outsiders in Nazi Germany, in part due to their connection to Judaism, as well as their questioning of Nazi ideology. Husserl and Jaspers's wife, Gertrud, as Jews, both felt the effects of Heidegger's loyalty to the Nazi Party and its policy of anti-semitism. Jaspers[31] related to Arendt that on a social visit Heidegger pointedly insulted his wife Gertrud because, as a Jew, she was forthright in her criticism of the Nazi Party. Thus in the end it was the prejudicial actions of Heidegger in 1933 that finally destroyed the friendship with Jaspers. According to Arendt Jaspers was everything during this period that Heidegger was not able to be, that is "a moral example, a cosmopolitan, a model of the public philosopher."[32] Like Marcel and Mounier, Jaspers strove to transcend the detachment of the university from the life situation, and to meet the crises of his day through words and action, directed against the *status quo*. Heidegger, recognizing his mistake, retreated into the role of the university professor and a shift to greater interior reflection. Arendt interprets the "irresponsible" behavior of Heidegger as due to the delusion of genius and the dictates of desperate action in a desperate situation.[33] However Heidegger's reputation was significantly marred by these events. Thus despite his monumental contribution to European philosophy and retreat from the Nazi Party,[34] his work was read with greater ambivalence by the European community outside of Germany.

III

Early in the war in 1940, Ricoeur was captured by the Germans and as a French officer he experienced a number of Prisoner of War Camps, which deteriorated to the level of Concentration Camps toward the war's end in 1945.[35] But for the first half of that time of imprisonment, the conditions were less severe and he was able to read intensely all that was available of the works of Jaspers and Heidegger. The influence of these two German philosophers was grafted onto the earlier dialectical pairing of Marcel and Husserl and the desire to conciliate ontology and phenomenology.[36] Early during this period he met Mikel Dufrenne, a fellow philosopher and prisoner, and together they read the work of the German philosophers, co-publishing a book on Jaspers after the war.

His period of imprisonment is described by Ricoeur as a time of enforced leisure, which informed his decision after the war to develop a philosophy of freedom. In keeping with Husserlian vocabulary, this time functioned as an *epoche*[37] in his life, between the years as a student and his return to the university after the war when as a teacher and philosopher in his own right, he was concerned to respond to the post-war desire for a new beginning. It presented Ricoeur with a depth experience far beyond anything he may have imagined as a member of Marcel's circle and heightened the significance of Mounier's project to envision a just society. Thus this time of intense reading of Jaspers and Heidegger represented an ironic setting, an enforced bracketing of his life in which prison functioned as an odd university, a setting which at the time more readily acerbated identification with Heidegger, while fostering it with Jaspers. It served for Ricoeur as a time of retreat that energized his political awareness and commitment.

> My forced leisure allowed me to read all that was available of (Heidegger and Jaspers) before 1945. I must say that my preference at the time tended toward Karl Jaspers, whom I found much closer to Gabriel Marcel and whose thought possessed an architecture I found most attractive. Even more than Jaspers confrontation with Kierkegaard and Nietzsche, it was the majestic composition of the three volumes of his *Philosophy:* "Orientation in the World", "Illumination of Existence", "Metaphysics", which won me over. Upon my return from captivity, I along with Mikel Dufrenne, my friend and companion in misfortune, made a sort of synopsis—more systematic than usual!—of the thought of Jaspers.[38]

Both Jaspers and Husserl, in contrast to Heidegger, maintained a commitment to the subjective tradition, and Jaspers more closely paralleled Ricoeur's previous mentors, Marcel and Mounier, due to Jaspers's "concern for communication, for modest and systematic socratic exploration, ...and especially, for human freedom and a 'new concept of humanity'".[39]

Ricoeur's time in prison occurs between Heidegger's infamous actions in 1933 and Heidegger's post-war publication of the *Letter on Humanism* in 1946-47.[40] Thus Ricoeur's alienation from Heidegger flowed in part from his awareness of

Heidegger's affiliation with the Nazi Party that led to his betrayal of Husserl and break from Jaspers, men that Ricoeur deeply admired and emulated. After the war Ricoeur published a work on Jaspers[41] and became a prime advocate of Husserl's[42] work in France in the capacity of translator and commentator. All along Ricoeur's chosen mentors were men who connected their lives and philosophical work to ethical and political action, rejecting the detachment of the university from the political sphere, while questioning the injustice of authoritarian systems. Heidegger's *Letter On Humanism*, served to differentiate Ricoeur's position further from Heidegger. As Ricoeur comments:

> In truth, my respect for Heidegger, although it has never ceased to grow to this very day, has always been marked by certain ever increasing reservations. So, while the careful and frequent rereading of *Sein und Zeit* has always filled me with great admiration, I have remained hostile to the critique of humanism, in particular in the *Letter on Humanism*. This reservation conveyed no doubt, my former allegiance to Karl Jaspers, but it also expressed my profound attachment to Husserlian reflection on subjectivity.... I was able to see that by contributing to the collapse of the question of the subject, Heideggerian ontology, in spite of itself, played into the hands of the new scientism represented (later) by structuralism, even though the latter was world's apart from Heidegger.[43]

Ricoeur could more readily identify with Jaspers's post-war statement that "philosophy must become more concrete and practical, without forgetting for a moment its origins".[44] Heidegger's publication of the *Letter on Humanism* in 1946 in Germany and 1947 in France, publicly announced the "turn" in his philosophical work; in which case, he described *Being and Time* as too subjective, too concerned with how "man thinks to ask the question of Being".[45] This new stage in Heidegger represented a turning against the "self-assertion of the man" and an emphasis upon "man as the being that listens to Being, the ground of authentic thinking and speaking".[46]

Moreover Heidegger separated willing from thinking and interpreted the will negatively as the will to power,

> which he interpreted in terms of autocracy or the will to power and associated with technology's inevitably destructive domination. Rejecting the technological mode and rejecting the will, Heidegger had turned to thinking. Heidegger's view that willing and

thinking are necessarily in conflict was one that (Hannah) Arendt wanted to criticize, as she wanted to reject both his repudiation of willing in favor of thinking and his contention that thinking itself is a kind of acting.... For a moment, she felt, Heidegger had turned away from his preoccupation with Being to a concern for beings and for history—even for politics—and to the possibility that, in privileged eras, eras of transition, men can become "mindful of what is destined." The moment passed and Heidegger went on to repudiate willing, which in Arendt's terms, meant rejecting the possibilities of politics, of action that begins something new.[47]

The Letter on Humanism, more sympathetically interpreted perhaps, represents Heidegger's inherent mysticism and his alienation from his actions during 1933, which led him to a more radical fidelity to the question of Being and disassociation from the political context. But his dismissal of the humanist tradition cut him off from a return to the tradition of critical reflection and the effort to address this level of critique within his ontology.[48] Thus this juncture in his work removes him from conversation with contemporaries, who charge his ontology with an inability to address critically the distortions of tradition and authority on the level of historical existence.

After the war Ricoeur, like Arendt, takes the path of practical philosophy. He attends to symbol, myth and poetics, focussing upon the question of subjectivity, in terms of the phenomenology of will and indirect discourse. The legacy of the war and its horrors led him to a renewed attempt to comprehend finitude and guilt and to discover within the humanist tradition the resources for the enactment of a more authentic and ethical culture. While he accepts the Heideggerian dismissal of the Promethean subject,[49] he questions the subtle Romanticism of Heidegger's direct ontology.

But despite Ricoeur's implicit alienation from Heidegger the man, it is Heidegger's work, far more than Jaspers's, that serves as an enduring philosophical reference,[50] particularly in terms of Ricoeur's development of hermeneutics and the philosophy of the imagination. It is a dialectical relation, which can be described as one of kinship and conflict, in which both thinkers share a common legacy of inspiration and adaptation through their common mentor, Husserl, and their development of Kant's philosophy of the imagination in relation to hermeneutics through their grafting of phenomenology with hermeneutics. Ricoeur's dissatisfaction with Heidegger's ontological hermeneutics stems from what he recognizes as its failure to incorporate a critical level to hermeneutics, since it transcends altogether the exegetico-historical level of derivative hermeneutics.[51]

After the war Ricoeur returned to his career as a philosopher and, in view of the examples of Marcel, Mounier, and Jaspers, committed himself to a philosophy in search of a new humanity responsive to the problems of the day, particularly in terms of the relation between speaking and acting.[52] He renewed his study of Husserl, translating Husserl's *Ideas*, thus making Husserl's work more widely available in France. Ricoeur also joined the team of Mounier's *Esprit* and the Christian Socialist movement it represented. Ricoeur's creed and self-definition are reflected in the following statement published in the early 1950's:

> I look within the very act of speaking for this alternation between contact and distance that should be found in all responsible behavior of an 'intellectual' confronted with the same problem....the philosophical way of being present to my time seems to be linked to a capacity for reachieving the remote intentions and the radical cultural presuppositions which underlie what I earlier called the civilizing drives of our era.... I believe in the efficacity of reflection because I believe that man's greatness lies in the dialectic of work and the spoken word, saying and doing, signifying and making are intermingled to such an extent that it is impossible to set up a lasting and deep opposition between '*theoria*' and 'praxis'.[53]

His style of approaching the role of university professor, while not that of the remote or contemplative thinker, retains a strong affirmation of the reflective life, but at the service of action. The rupture of war brought home forcefully the need to understand the human condition, and to renew and discover its capacity to enact an ethical society.

> [W]e cannot afford to neglect political philosophy. When one has witnessed and taken part in the horrifying events that led to the hecatombs of concentration camps, to the terror of totalitarian regimes, and to nuclear peril, there can no longer be any doubt that the problematic of evil is also intertwined with the problematic of power. Nor can there be any doubt that the theme of *alienation*, running from Rousseau through Hegel to Marx, has some connection with the accusation of the old prophets of Israel.[54]

In France the blend of marxism, existentialism and psychoanalysis reshaped the intellectual constellation of the philosophical scene through a revival of the masters of suspicion: Marx, Nietzsche and Freud. In this context the existentialism of Sartre exemplified the post-war themes of nihilism and the death of God and the need to break with the dominance of the past and its traditions, while questioning the power of the future to redeem the absurdity of human existence. Although Ricoeur was sympathetic to existentialism, he was critical of its nihilistic and atheistic interpretations and its reduction of anthropology to finitude, as well as its radical disavowal of history and tradition. His work parallels Sartre's in that, like Sartre, he creatively develops Husserl's phenomenological method in relation to the imagination, while registering discomfort toward the influence of Heidegger.

Sartre represented an extreme reaction to Heidegger. Sartre defined freedom and the imagination[55] as ways of escape from the emptiness of existence. His work *Being and Nothingness* plays forth his nihilistic alternative to Heidegger's *Being and Time*. According to Sartre freedom functions most authentically as a decision of resistance over-against the absurdity of evil. Ricoeur seeks a path that affirms existence, in which the imagination[56] functions to mediate the disproportion of the human condition and to critique the *status quo* by projecting different ways of being in the world. Thus for Ricoeur the moment of the imagination's retreat leads back to existence and a renewed praxis.

His own life serves as a model for this development of the imagination for his imprisonment is analogous to an *epoche,* but one that did not lead to despair or a nihilistic definition of reality; rather he returns to consider the bond between thought and action. Thus his development of the imagination[57] leads back to action and a transformation of existence rather than to Sartrean escapism, in which case the imagination functions as resistance to a reality defined as absurd.

Ricoeur maintains the need to reappropriate the resources of history and tradition for the legacy of his ten years at the University of Strasbourg, teaching the history of philosophy[58] deepened his respect for the richness and variety of the repertoire of the history of philosophy. It also served to clarify and further differentiate his constructive reading of the history of philosophy, from Heidegger's deconstruction of it. As Ricoeur states:

> my experience as an historian of philosophy kept me from adhering to the Heideggerian idea of the unity of "Metaphysics"; instead I was struck—and bothered—by the singular nature of the philosophical works, and this raised the thorny problem of the unity of truth. In addition, this has made me resist all the more strongly the Heideggerian project of

"destroying classical ontology." In this respect I share with Gadamer the heightened sense of the continuity of the philosophical tradition, at least on the level of the great problems, despite the obvious discontinuity between the individual replies given to those problems by the great philosophers.[59]

The major philosophical endeavor that spans Ricoeur's career is the projected three volume work on the philosophy of the will. Merleau-Ponty's *Perception*, served as the model for Ricoeur's doctoral dissertation *The Voluntary and the Involuntary*,[60] the first volume of Ricoeur's phenomenology of freedom. The influence of Roman Ingarden's adaptation of the Husserlian method in relation to a phenomenology of literary expression is more evident in the second volume of Ricoeur's philosophy of freedom, that is *Finitude and Guilt*: (Part One: *Fallible Man* and Part Two: *The Symbolism of Evil*). It is in *Fallible Man* that Ricoeur begins to address his development of the philosophy of the imagination in relation to Kant and Husserl. This volume also is written as an implicit reply to Sartre's reduction of the human condition to finitude and the imagination to a strategy of escape from the absurdity of being.[61] Ricoeur proposes a dialectic between finitude and infinitude as more adequately describing the tension and disproportion structuring the human condition and freedom.[62] In the *Symbolism of Evil* he begins to make the turn to hermeneutics. Therefore the second volume of Ricoeur's phenomenology of the will: *Finitude and Guilt*[63] will serve as the chief text of the next chapter, along with pivotal essays from his collection *The Conflict of Interpretations*.

This chapter establishes the context of Ricoeur's philosophical background and the forces of history that served to alienate Ricoeur from Heidegger. But Heidegger's ontological hermeneutics endures as a prominent philosophical reference for Ricoeur's development of hermeneutics. Ricoeur draws upon Husserl and Kant, representatives of the tradition of critical reflection, as well as Dilthey with his quest for method. It is to their work that he returns in view of the masters of suspicion: Marx, Nietzsche and Freud. This study will note that Ricoeur is indebted to Heidegger's contribution to hermeneutics and the philosophy of the imagination, but Ricoeur is distinguished from Heidegger by his creative adaptation of the Kantian philosophy of the imagination with the Husserlian theory of intentionality. Ricoeur's focus for this development of the philosophy of the imagination is the functioning of symbolic/metaphoric language.

ENDNOTES OF CHAPTER TWO

[1]Paul Ricoeur, "Existence and Hermeneutics", trans. Kathleen McLaughlin in *Conflict of Interpretations* ed., Don Ihde (Evanston: Northwestern University Press, 1974), pp. 12-16.

[2]Ibid., p. 18.

[3]Ricoeur, "Hermeneutics and the Critique of Ideology", ed. and trans. John B. Thompson (Cambridge: Cambridge University Press, 1981), pp. 86-87.

[4]Ricoeur, "My Relation to the History of Philosophy", *Iliff Review*, 35(1978), p. 7. This relationship of kinship and conflict is exemplified through major works of Ricoeur, for example: from the early work *Fallible Man* to the *Conflict of Interpretations* (where he makes the turn to hermeneutics explicit and sets his agenda) to the more recent works *The Rule of Metaphor* and *Time and Narrative*.

[5]They share a common reference to Kant's development of the philosophy of the imagination. Ricoeur accepts Heidegger's Copernican revolution, that understanding is a mode of being, (which is based upon his radical interpretation of Kant's definition of the transcendental imagination) but Ricoeur seeks to validate and critique this ontology by taking the longer, indirect route to an ontological hermeneutics through an analysis of language, particularly symbol and metaphor, utilizing literary criticism, psychoanalysis and social and political philosophy of history. His development of the philosophy of the imagination is explicated in relation to symbol, metaphor and narrative. See *Fallible Man*, trans. Charles Kelbley (Chicago: Henry Regnery Co., 1965), p. 61 and pp. 66-71 and "Narrative and Time" *Critical Inquiry* (1980) pp. 7, 183ff.

[6]Ricoeur, *Freud and Philosophy*, trans. Denis Savage (New Haven: Yale University Press, 1970), pp. 35-36.

[7]"Existence and Hermeneutics", pp. 6-11.

[8]Herbert Spielgelberg, *The Phenomenological Movement* (The Hague: Martinus Nijhoff, 1960), II, p. 569.

[9]William Barrett, *Irrational Man: A Study in Existential Philosophy* (Garden City: Doubleday & Co., 1958), p. 241.

[10]Ibid., p. 9.

[11]Ricoeur, "Emmanuel Mounier: A Personalist Philosopher", in *History and Truth*, trans. Charles A. Kelbley (Evanston: Northwestern University Press, 1965), p. 134.

[12]"My Relation to the History of Philosophy", 5. See also *Irrational Man,* p. 173 and Don Ihde's *Hermeneutic Phenomenology* (Evanston: Northwestern University Press, 1971), p. 8.

[13]Ibid.

[14]Ricoeur, "Emmanuel Mounier", pp. 142-43.

[15]Ibid., p. 135.

[16]Ibid., pp. 5-7.

[17]Ibid., p. 5.

[18]Ricoeur, *Freedom and Nature: The Voluntary and the Involuntary,* trans. Erazim Kohak (Evanston: Northwestern University Press, 1966), p. 15.

[19]"My Relation to the History of Philosophy", pp. 5-6.

[20]Ibid., pp. 5-7.

[21]Elizabeth Young-Bruehl, *Hannah Arendt: For Love of the World* (New Haven: Yale University Press, 1982), p. 47.

[22]Ibid.

[23]George Steiner, *Martin Heidegger*, ed. Frank Kermode (New York: Penquin Books, 1980), p. 76. See also "General Introduction 'The Question of Being'" by David Farrell Krell (New York: Harper & Row, 1977), p. 17.

[24]Martin Heidegger, *Kant and the Problem of Metaphysics,* trans. James S. Churchill (Bloomington: Indiana University Press, 1962), pp. 133-208. See also, Ray L. Hart, *Unfinished Man and the Imagination* (New York: Herder & Herder, 1968), p. 236, n.86 and p. 316, n.4.

[25]*Hannah Arendt*, pp. 47-48.

[26]*Martin Heidegger*, p. 27. See also *Hannah Arendt*, p. 443.

[27]*Hannah Arendt*, pp. 64-65.

[28]*Irrational Man*, p. 32.

[29]*Hannah Arendt*, pp. 69-70 and p. 443.

[30]Ibid., p. 217.

[31]Ibid., p. 109, p. 506, n.39.

[32]Ibid., p. 218.

[33]Ibid., pp. 442-443.

[34]"General Introduction:'The Question of Being'", p. 28.

[35]Conversation with Ricoeur, Spring 1980. See also "My Relation to the History of Philosophy", p. 6.

[36]"My Relation to the History of Philosophy", pp. 5-6.

[37]"Phenomenology and Hermeneutics", in Hermeneutic and the Human *Sciences*, p. 116.

[38]"My Relation to the History of Philosophy", p. 6.

[39]*Hannah Arendt*, p. 218.

[40]"My Relation to the History of Philosophy", p. 9.

[41]Ibid., p. 6.

[42]Ibid. See also "Currents in French Phenomenology", p. 571.

[43]"My Relation to the History of Philosophy", p. 7.

[44]*Hannah Arendt*, p. 215.

[45]Ibid., p. 302.

[46]Ibid.

[47]Ibid., p. 445.

[48]"Hermeneutics and the Critique of Ideology", pp. 88-89.

[49]Ricoeur, *Freedom and Nature: The Voluntary and the Involuntary*, trans. Erazim V. Kohak (Evanston: Northwestern University Press, 1966), pp. 464-466.

[50]See above, note 4,

[51]"Existence and Hermeneutics", p. 10.

[52]Ricoeur, "Preface to the First Edition", *History and Truth*, p. 5.

[53]Ibid., pp. 4-5.

[54]Ricoeur, *Fallible Man*, rev. trans. Charles Kelbley (New York: Fordham, 1986), p. xlv.

[55]*Irrational Man*, p. 246.

[56]Jean-Paul Sartre, *The Psychology of Imagination*, (New York: Philosophical Library, 1948), pp. 262-262. See also Ray L. Hart, *Unfinished Man and the Imagination,* pp. 364-368 and Ricoeur, "Negativity and Primary Affirmation", in *History and Truth*, pp. 318-328.

[57]Mary Schaldenbrand, "Metaphoric Imagination: Kinship Through Conflict" in *Studies in the Philosophy of Paul Ricoeur*, ed. Charles E. Reagan (Athens: Ohio University Press, 1979), p.61.

[58]"My Relation to the History of Philosophy", p. 7.

[59]Ibid.

[60]Ibid.

[61]Charles A. Kelbley, "Introduction" to *History and Truth*, p. xix.

[62]*Fallible Man*, pp. 3-12.

[63]Ricoeur, *Finitude and Guilt: Fallible Man*, I. and *The Symbolism of Evil*, II (Boston: Beacon Press, 1967).

CHAPTER THREE

RICOEUR'S TURN TO HERMENEUTICS

Ricoeur's turn to hermeneutics is realized through his wager upon symbolic/ metaphoric[1] discourse as a critical and creative resource toward the founding of a hermeneutics that can counteract the false consciousness of the self and challenge the distortions of tradition and ideology.[2] Unlike Heidegger Ricoeur's focus remains directed upon the human condition as mediated by its societal, historical, cultural, religious and artistic expressions. Language (and at this early stage of his turn to hermeneutics) particularly, symbol[3] in its cosmic, onieric and poetic dimensions, is the prism he utilizes as a central key to the interpretation of the self and society.

I will argue it is by Ricoeur's correlation of the philosophy of the imagination with language, specifically symbolic and metaphoric discourse, that he is able to explicate a critical methodological dimension to hermeneutics in terms of the creativity of language. But while my focus is the philosophy of the imagination and language in Ricoeur's development of hermeneutics, the philosophy of the imagination remains a subterrenean theme in his work, which he defines indirectly and primarily through the philosophy of language and his use of dialectic. As Mary Schaldenbrand states:

> Remarking the need for a philosophy of imagination, Ricoeur implies its present absence. And yet, when I return to his major works, I find that all of them assign to imagining the pivot-function. Though represented as stages in a 'Philosophy of Willing,' they could as well be taken as stages in a developing philosophy of imagination. In effect, what Ricoeur calls for is already underway in his own work. Admittedly, taken as they stand, these major works by no means compose a systematic philosophy of imagining. But, when recovered and reinterpreted within the linguistic context of recent studies in metaphor, they confirm the judgment: from its beginning until now, the work of Ricoeur consistently develops the philosophic sense of imagination as 'mediating

function.' His work, while not achieving an explicit and systematic critique of imagination, puts us well on the way toward doing so.[4]

This development of the philosophy of the imagination in relation to symbolic/ metaphoric language, I propose, is pivotal to his explication of a critical hermeneutics left unfulfilled by Heidegger's ontological hermeneutics.

The order of discussion of this chapter is as follows: I will sketch Ricoeur's evaluation of the lack of a critical development of hermeneutics, in terms of his dialectical view of the history of hermeneutics from Schleiermacher and Dilthey to Heidegger and Husserl in his article "Existence and Hermeneutics" (in *The Conflict of Interpretations*).[5] We will uncover the relevance of the philosophy of the imagination and its relation to language to Ricoeur's discussion of the unresolved *aporias* of hermeneutics which hinder this critical development. The first *aporia* is the gap between the psychology of the imagination and language, the legacy of Schleiermacher and Dilthey. The second *aporia* is between epistemology and ontology, the heritage of Heidegger's ontological development of hermeneutics. My argument will be that Ricoeur's strategy to resolve these aporias lies in uniting the philosophy of the imagination to language (particularly equivocal language) through his return to the earlier Husserl's theory of intentionality. This grafting of phenomenology to hermeneutics is the longer route, which he regards as necessary to found a critical hermeneutics in light of Heidegger's fundamental hermeneutics.

After setting forth Ricoeur's agenda, I will turn back to his earlier work, *Fallible Man*.[6] Here I will show Ricoeur presents his early phenomenological development of the philosophy of the imagination in relation to Husserl's theory of intentionality and Kant's philosophy of the imagination. *Fallible Man* addresses his dissatisfaction with Heideggerian ontology's direct identification of the imagination with time. Ricoeur's adaptation of Husserl and Kant leads him to unite the imagination with language as its indirect expression.

Finally we will return to Ricoeur's philosophical discussion of his turn to hermeneutics in the *Conflict of Interpretations*, and the significance of the prior work to this stage. His regrafting of hermeneutics to phenomenology, in terms of the early Husserl as well as Hegel's phenomenology of spirit, requires a critique of the *cogito* and of claims to absolute knowledge. Here he makes the return route to epistemology and regional hermeneutics in relation to the horizon of Heidegger's ontological hermeneutics and the post-war absorption with Freudian psychoanalysis.

I

Heidegger serves as a major, though alienated, partner to Ricoeur's endeavor to found a critical hermeneutics in terms of the connection between symbolic/metaphoric discourse and the philosophy of the imagination. Heidegger's task was to reappropriate the forgotten question of Being and to break from the subject/object dualism of the neo-Kantian framework of general hermeneutics and its obsessive emulation of the scientific method. In part through his creative adaptation of Kant's philosophy of the transcendental imagination,[7] in which case understanding is redefined as a mode of being, he established the priority of being-in-the-world to subjectivity and objectivity. As Ricoeur states:

> He wanted to retrain our eye and redirect our gaze; he wanted us to subordinate historical knowledge to ontological understanding, as the derived form of a primordial form. But he gives us no way to show in what sense historical understanding, properly speaking, is derived from this primordial understanding. Is it not better, then, to begin with the derived forms of understanding and to show in them the signs of their derivation? This implies that the point of departure be taken on the same level on which understanding operates, that is, on the level of language.[8]

Heidegger's ontological hermeneutics transcended the limitations of the psychological definition of the imagination, which undermined the prior hermeneutics of Schleiermacher and Dilthey. But Ricoeur recognizes that the omission of this fundamental hermeneutics is its failure to address the validity of the prior concern for method and critique that arose at the historical-exegetical level of texts, defined by Dilthey as expressions of life.

The post-war situation cried out for critique, for an analysis of the distortions of power and hence resurrected the masters of suspicion[9] of the Cartesian heritage: Marx, Nietzsche and Freud. Their diverse hermeneutics of suspicion of the self and society; utilize the resources of indirect discourse over against the subjectivist philosophy of consciousness.

> [T]he intention they had in common, ...[is] to look upon the whole of consciousness primarily as 'false' consciousness. They thereby take up again, each in a different manner, the problem of the Cartesian doubt, to carry it to the very heart of the Cartesian stronghold. The philosopher trained in the school of Descartes knows that things are doubtful...but he does not doubt that...in consciousness meaning and consciousness of meaning coincide. Since Marx, Nietzsche and Freud, this too has become doubtful. After the doubt about things, we have started to doubt consciousness.[10]

Thus while Heidegger replaced the belief in a presuppositionless starting point with the insight that we always begin from within a context and set of presuppositions, the post-war renewal of Nietzsche, Marx and Freud offered a set of methods to critique the cogito and its presuppositions. However their strategies arise at the level of interpreting historical being and consciousness through a reduction of symbolic discourse, a level of critique contrary to Heidegger's appropriation of Being in terms of fundamental ontology and his later turn[11] to poetic discourse as the place of manifestation of Being. Overall the reductive hermeneutics of the masters of suspicion stand in opposition to "any hermeneutics understood as the recollection of meaning and as the reminiscence of Being",[12] particularly the phenomenology of the sacred. Ricoeur adds "at issue in this controversy is the fate of what I shall call, for the sake of brevity, the mytho-poetic core of imagination",[13] that is, the upsurge of the possible over against the ascesis of the real.

For Ricoeur the forgotten question is how to reappropriate the indirect meaning of the symbolic, and its reference to existence, in a way that is not simply reductive, but allows for an appropriation of meaning that both recovers and invents new ways of being in the world, while challenging *status quo* interpretations of the self and society. Thus following upon Heidegger in this post-war context with its need for a hermeneutics of suspicion, the route to being that Ricoeur wagers upon is indirect and through the critical mediation of equivocal forms of discourse that refer to historical being and the sacred.

Ricoeur's contribution to the hermeneutical debate coincides with his capacity to act as one who reconciles by seeking kinship within the conflicts of the philosophical tradition. He makes the return route to epistemology, employing the breakthrough of Heidegger's ontological hermeneutics, seeking to reconcile the contributions of what is best at the fundamental and derivative levels of hermeneutics.

In order to answer Dilthey's quest for method after the critique of objectivism and the scientific method by Husserl, Ricoeur turns to the philosophy of language as a more fitting model. He uses Kant and Hegel in light of the masters of suspicion to foster a regrafting of hermeneutics upon the phenomenological method that attends to the exegesis of equivocal language. Considering this regrafting, initiated in light of Heidegger's prior grafting, I will show that while in general Ricoeur agrees with Heidegger's Copernican revolution, Ricoeur disagrees with the directness of Heidegger's ontological interpretation of the Kantian philosophy of the transcendental imagination. Ricoeur's development of the imagination is distinguished from Heidegger's by his adaptation of the Kantian philosophy of the transcendental and creative imagination to the Husserlian theory of intentionality, in relation to equivocal language.

His approach to the sacred is consistent with the influence of his early mentor Gabriel Marcel, who refused to identify God with Being in the development of his concrete ontology. For Ricoeur the equivocity of Being is spoken through the symbolic, particularly through the symbolism of the sacred. But such symbolism remains ambivalent and in need of a hermeneutics of suspicion, as well as appropriation and transformation, inasmuch as it is conveyed through a human, fallible community, always merely approaching the enactment of a just society. It is Ricoeur's wager that it is the "symbol giving rise to thought"[14] that projects a just society's conditions of possibility through the creative imagination, eliciting an interpretation that potentially disrupts and stretches the self towards authenticity through innovation and critique.

Ricoeur sets out to develop a critical hermeneutics, in light of Heidegger's Copernican revolution by grafting the hermeneutic problem onto the phenomenological method through the focus of equivocal language. While questions of method and critique are lost from view by Heidegger's version of ontological hermeneutics, Ricoeur identifies the latter as the central task of contemporary hermeneutics. In the articles "The Task of Hermeneutics" and "Existence and Hermeneutics"[15] he evaluates what is gained and lost from view by Heidegger through comparison with the prior development of hermeneutics in Schleiermacher and Dilthey. Ricoeur uncovers a set of *aporias* left unresolved by the shift from regional hermeneutics to general hermeneutics and from epistemology to ontology. He seeks to overcome these aporias by making the return route from ontology to epistemology via the philosophy of language and a regrafting of hermeneutics to the phenomenological method of the early Husserl. My purpose in this section is to show that the definition of the philosophy of the imagination and its relation to language underlies these *aporias* and to expound Ricoeur's grafting of phenomenology to hermeneutics by way of Heidegger's depsychologizing of the imagination.

Ricoeur's agenda to mediate these *aporias* will be realized through his alignment of the philosophy of the imagination with language, in which case his grafting of the phenomenological method to hermeneutics focusses from the beginning upon language, particularly equivocal language. He begins his review with exegesis,[16] as representative of the earliest stage of hermeneutics, and recovers through this review a kinship between the emerging definition of hermeneutics and the much later development of phenomenonological method.

Because exegesis is planted within the context of a tradition, community and language, which imply presuppositions, the need for interpretation arises. Since phenomenology implies a going back to things to phenomena to the mediation of experience, it speaks to this exegetical level of the problem of hermeneutics. But Ricoeur's adaptation of phenomenology breaks with the Husserlian ideal[17] of univocal language by applying the phenomenological method to the modes of comprehension of equivocal forms of speech such as symbol, myth and metaphor. He notes that Aristotle's definition of hermeneutics includes all meaningful discourse; "meaningful discourse is *hermeneia*, 'interprets' reality, precisely to the degree that 'it says something *of* something'".[18] He allies the latter to the Husserlian definition of phenomenology by adding "discourse is *hermeneneia* because a discursive statement is a grasp of the real by meaningful expressions, not a selection of so-called impressions coming from things themselves".[19] This definition points to the bond between experience and language, in which interpretation is grounded in the very act of speech. But exegesis of equivocal forms of speech makes demands on traditional philosophy insofar as this type of exegesis raises questions of meaning and signification that cannot be satisfied by the logic of argumentation established by the *Metaphysics* of Aristotle.

> [E]xegesis implies an entire theory of signs and significations, as we see, for example, in Augustine's *De doctrina christiana.* More precisely, if a text can have several meanings, for example a historical meaning and a spiritual meaning, we must appeal to a notion of signification that is much more complex than the system of so-called univocal signs required by the logic of argumentation. And finally, the very work of interpretation reveals a profound intention, that of overcoming distance and cultural differences and of matching the reader to a text which has become foreign, thereby incorporating its meaning into the present comprehension a man is able to have of himself...hermeneutics involves the general problem of comprehension. And, moreover, no noteworthy interpretation has been formulated which does not borrow from the modes of comprehension available to a given epoch: myth, allegory, metaphor, analogy, etc.[20]

Ricoeur's reference to equivocal language stretches the traditional interpretation of Aristotle's definition of hermeneutics and subverts Husserl's confinement of phenomenology to univocal discourse, thus this preliminary grafting of phenomenology with hermeneutics changes the stock.[21]

The development of philology and history along with the advent of the Enlightment and Romanticism mark the next major stage of hermeneutics that Ricoeur addresses, that is, the contribution of Schleiermacher and Dilthey. As Ricoeur states:

> exegesis could lead to a general hermeneutics only by means of a second development, the development of classical philology and the *historical sciences* that took place at the end of the eighteenth century and the start of the nineteenth century. It is with Schleiermacher and Dilthey that the hermeneutic problem becomes a philosophic problem.[22]

But the development from regional hermeneutics to general hermeneutics by Schleiermacher poses an advance for hermeneutics, as well as an *aporia*[23] (that is continued by his follower Dilthey), for it is with Schleiermacher that the role of the philosophy of the imagination and its relation to language first enters the development of hermeneutics. He is influenced by the renewal of poetic language by Romanticism and its challenge to the reign of neo-classical rhetoric. This period marks a rebirth of equivocal forms of discourse and a new emphasis on creativity that calls into question the ideal of univocal interpretation. This brings with it attention to the creativity of the artist rather than to the imitation of nature.

Schleiermacher, influenced by Kant's *Critique of Pure Reason*, asks what are the operations of understanding common to the two great branches of hermeneutics, biblical exegesis and philology. But his further innovation is to follow the lead of Romanticism and its advocacy of the poetic imagination of the author as the model to define the interpretive act of understanding. As Ricoeur states:

> Hermeneutics could not add to Kantianism without taking from Romantic philosophy its most fundamental conviction, that mind is the creative unconscious at work in gifted individuals. Schleiermacher's hermeneutical programme thus carried a double mark: *Romantic* by its appeal to a living relation with the process of creation, *critical* by its wish to elaborate the universally valid rules of understanding. Perhaps hermeneutics is forever marked by this double filiation—Romantic and critical, critical and Romantic. The proposal to struggle against misunderstanding in the name of the famous adage 'there is hermeneutics where there is misunderstanding' is critical; the proposal 'to understand an author as well as and even better than he understands himself' is Romantic.[24]

Kant is also the philosopher who gives a renewed definition to the philosophy of the imagination in the First and Third Critique.[25] But Schleiermacher seeks to overcome the limitations of Kant's definition of the imagination, specifically his narrow notion of experience in the First Critique, and particularly the lack of any basis in experience for the creative imagination in the Third Critique, which projects aesthetic and religious symbols. Schleiermacher, as a theologian, particularly sought to overcome Kant's reduction of the credibility of religious symbolism, by broadening the definition of experience to include religious and aesthetic experience. Thus Schleiermacher's development of hermeneutics relies more upon Romanticism's notion of the empathetic imagination, by its aim to replicate the creative experience of the author, than upon Kant's definition of the creative imagination, defined in the Third Critique as the creative representations of genius with no basis in experience and to which no concept is equal.

The early Schleiermacher linked the act of understanding with language as the vehicle of understanding, but his later development of hermeneutics separated understanding and language as the subjective and objective levels of hermeneutics that must be practiced separately. Thus Ricoeur recognizes a central *aporia* framed by Schleiermacher, that is the division between the text and the mind of the author. The critical and creative dimensions of hermeneutics are separate acts of interpretation, which cannot be practiced together and the psychological takes precedence over the critical. As Ricoeur comments:

> it can be seen that, in the notes on hermeneutics which were never transformed into a finished work, Schleiermacher left his descendants with an *aporia* as well as an initial sketch. The problem with which he grappled is that of the relation between two forms of interpretation: 'grammatical' interpretation and 'technical' interpretation....................
>
> ....
>
> Grammatical interpretation is based on the characteristics of discourse which are common to a culture, technical interpretation is addressed to the singularity, indeed to the genius, of the writer's message. Now although the two interpretations have equal status they cannot be practised at the same time. Schleiermacher makes this clear: to consider the common language is to forget the writer; whereas to understand an individual author is to forget his language, which is merely passed over...................
>
> ....
>
> The proper task of interpretation is accomplished in this second interpretation. What must be reached is the subjectivity of the one who speaks, the language being forgotten. Here language becomes an instrument at the service of individuality. This interpretation is called 'positive', because it reaches the act of thought which produced the discourse.[26]

Thus the primary act of interpretation leads beyond language to identification with the mind of the author in order to reach the experience in back of the text. Understanding is defined as re-experiencing the creative imagination of the author, through the empathetic imagination of the reader. Thus the psychology of the imagination defines the act of interpretation. Ricoeur adds:

The difficulty of reconciling the two hermeneutics is thus complicated by superimposi-
tion of a second pair of opposites, *divination and comparison,* upon the first pair,
grammatical and technical.... Elsewhere I argue that this obstacle can be overcome
only by clarifying the relation of the work to the subjectivity of the author and by
shifting the interpretative emphasis from the empathetic investigation of hidden
subjectivities towards the sense and reference of the work itself. But first it is necessary
to push the central *aporia* of hermeneutics further by considering the decisive
development which Dilthey achieved in subordinating the philogical and exegetical
problematic to the problematic of history. It is this development, in the sense of a
greater *universality,* which prepares the way for the displacement of epistemology
towards ontology, in the sense of a greater *radicality.* [27]

Dilthey's emphasis upon history also facilitates Heidegger's return to Kant's
definition of the transcendental imagination, in which case Heidegger redefines
understanding as a mode of being, projecting time in terms of the dialectic of
past/present/future constituting the horizon of *Dasein.*

The development of history as a science, a major achievement of nineteenth
century German culture, marked the stage at which the human sciences and the
study of the cultural expressions of humanity, apart from nature and the science
of nature, began to come into their own as a new domain of knowledge.[28]
Dilthey is the author of the pact between history and hermeneutics. He
radicalized Schleiermacher's general hermeneutics by moving from the general
rules of interpreting texts to the problematic of interpreting history as one great
text, as the great document of the human condition.[29] This development of
hermeneutics also replies to the Kantian gap between physics and ethics, as well
as the abstractness of the Kantian subject. But since the major philosophical
influences of Dilthey's period[30] are neo-Kantianism and positivism, he was led
to seek a solution on the level of epistemology and its reform. He sought a
validity to the method of the human sciences equal to the method of the natural
sciences and its criteria of objectivity. As Ricoeur states:

Posed in these terms, the problem was epistemological; it was a question of elaborating
a critique of historical knowledge as solid as the Kantian critique of the knowledge of
nature and of subordinating to this critique the diverse procedures of classical
hermeneutics.... But the resolution of the problem exceeded the resources of mere
epistemology.[31]

Dilthey continued to rely upon the psychology of the imagination in keeping with Schleiermacher, and thus the division between understanding and language. For Dilthey the human sciences and the natural sciences represented two distinct epistemological domains,[32] in which understanding characterized the former, while explanation defined the chief trait of the latter. But as Ricoeur notes:

> It is in the sphere of psychology that Dilthey searches for the distinctive feature of understanding. Every *human science*—and by that Dilthey means every modality of the knowledge of man which implies an historical relation presupposes a primoridal capacity to transpose oneself into the mental life of others. For in natural knowledge, man grasps only phenomena distinct from himself, the fundamental 'thingness' of which escapes him. In the human order, on the other hand, man knows man; however alien another man may be to us, he is not alien in the sense of an unknowable physical thing. The difference of status between natural things and the mind dictates the difference of status between explanation and understanding. Man is not radically alien to man because he offers signs of his own existence..
> ....
> Dilthey still belongs to the generation of neo-Kantians for whom the pivot of the human sciences is the individual, considered, it is true, in his social relations, but fundamentally singular. It follows that the foundation of the human sciences must be psychology, the science of the individual acting in society and in history.[33]

Dilthey's major advance beyond Schleiermacher lies in his notion of the "expressions of life", which supercedes Schleiermacher's emphasis upon experience. The "expressions of life" are the texts, monuments and works of art which manifest the interconnection of history.

> The key to the critique of historical knowledge, which was painfully missing in Kantianism, is to be found in the fundamental phenomenon of *interconnection,* by which the life of others can be discerned and identified in its manifestations. Knowledge of others is possible because life produces forms, externalises itself in stable configurations...
> ....
> The organised systems which culture produces in the form of literature constitute a secondary layer, built upon this primary phenomenon of the teleological structure of the productions of life.[34]

Dilthey makes an advance upon Schleiermacher in that he recognizes it is not possible to transpose oneself into another and grasp the mental life of others in its immediate expressions through the empathetic imagination. According to Dilthey the goal instead is to reproduce it through the interpretation of objectified signs. So Dilthey moves toward overcoming the gap between imagination and language in terms of his notion of "expressions of life" as manifesting the interconnections of history. Like Schleiermacher philology provides the objective stage of understanding. But Dilthey continued to subordinate the hermeneutical problem to the psychology of replicating the experience in back of the text. In the age of positivism, experimental knowledge remained the dominant criterion for objectivity.

> Dilthey's work even more than Schleiermacher's, brings to light the central *aporia* of a hermeneutics which subsumes the understanding of texts to the law of understanding another person who expresses himself therein. If the enterprise remains fundamentally psychological, it is because it stipulates as the ultimate aim of interpretation, not *what* a text says, but *who* says it. At the same time the object of hermeneutics is constantly shifted away from the text, from its sense and its reference, towards the lived experience which is expressed therein.[35]

As Ricoeur adds describing Gadamer's critique of Dilthey:

> [Dilthey's] point of departure remains the consciousness of self as master of itself. With Dilthey subjectivity remains the last reference.... History precedes me and my reflection. I belong to history before belonging to myself. Now Dilthey could not understand this because his revolution remained an epistemological one and because his reflexive criterion prevailed over his historical consciousness.[36]

After 1900[37] Dilthey relied more on Husserl's theory of intentionality to support his notion of interconnection and structured meaning expressed through written works. Husserl's theory of intentionality established the property of intending an identifiable meaning. "Mental life itself cannot be grasped, but we can grasp what it intends—the objective and identical correlate in which mental life surpasses itself."[38]

Dilthey perfectly perceived the crux of the problem: namely that life grasps life only by the mediation of units of meaning which arise above the historical flux. Here Dilthey glimpsed a mode of transcending finitude without absolute knowledge, a mode which is properly interpretative. Thereby he indicated the direction in which historicism could overcome itself, without invoking a triumphant coincidence with some sort of absolute knowledge.[39]

A further contribution of Husserl to the hermeneutic problem is his challenge to objectivism and the notion that the natural sciences pose the only valid methodological model[40] for the human sciences. The last phase of his phenomenology clears the way for Heidegger's ontology of understanding by uncoverng a level of experience prior to the subject/object dualism central to neo-Kantianism.

The *aporia* between the psychology of the imagination and language emerges as the central limitation which the neo-Kantian epistemology influencing both Schleiermacher and Dilthey, combined with the dominance of positivist criteria, could not overcome. While Dilthey was limited by his subjectivism, his emphasis on texts as expressions of life and his later use of Husserl's theory of intentionality to define the transcendent character of meaning are the insights Ricoeur retrieves in his effort to overcome the *aporia* between language and the philosophy of the imagination.

Both Dilthey and Husserl prepare the way for the shift from epistemology to ontology, in which case understanding is redefined by Heidegger as a mode of being through a retrieval of Kant's definition of the transcendental imagination. At this final stage of Ricoeur's review of the development of hermeneutics he assesses Heidegger's achievement and his own agenda for hermeneutics. He comments:

There are two ways to ground hermeneutics in phenomenology. There is the short route...and the long route, the one I propose to travel. The short route is the one taken by an *ontology of understanding*, after the manner of Heidegger. I call such an ontology of understanding the "short route" because, breaking with any discussion of *method*, it carries itself directly to the level of an ontology of finite being in order there to recover *understanding*, no longer as a mode of knowledge, but rather as a mode of being.... Before saying why I propose to follow a more roundabout, more arduous path, starting with linguistic and semantic considerations, I wish to give full credit to this ontology of understanding.... The doubt I express...is concerned only with the possibility of the making of a direct ontology, free at the outset from any methodological requirements and consequently outside the circle of interpretation whose theory this ontology formulates.[41]

Heidegger's ontological hermeneutics delivers hermeneutics from the limitations of the psychology of the imagination. He revolutionizes hermeneutics through a radical adaptation of Kant's philosophy of the transcendental imagination,[42] in which case understanding is defined as a mode of being breaking with the subject/object dualism of neo-Kantianism.

Dilthey linked the question of understanding to the problem of the other person; how to gain access to another mind was a problem that dominated all of the human sciences, from psychology to history. Now it is remarkable that, in *Being and Time*, the question of understanding is wholly severed from the problem of communication with others...
....
The foundations of the ontological problem are sought in the relation of being with the world and not in the relation with another...
....
This shift of the philosophical locus is just as important as the movement from the problem of method towards the problem of being. The question of the *world* takes the place of the question of the *other*. In thereby making understanding *worldly,* Heidegger *de-psychologizes* it.[43]

But his ontological hermeneutics transcends altogether the exegetico-historical problems of interpreting texts. Heidegger breaks entirely with epistemology and redefines hermeneutics as ontology. But as Ricoeur notes:

the *aporia* is not resolved but merely displaced elsewhere and thereby aggravated. It is no longer between two modalities of knowing *within* epistemology, but it is *between* ontology and epistemology taken as a whole. With Heidegger's philosophy, we are always engaged in going back to the foundations, but we are left incapable of beginning the movement of return which would lead from the fundamental ontology to the properly epistemological question of the status of the human sciences. Now a philosophy which breaks the dialogue with the sciences is no longer addressed to anything but itself. Moreover, it is only along the return route that we could substantiate the claim that questions of exegesis and, in general, of historical critique are *derivative*. So long as this derivation has not been undertaken, the very movement of transcendence towards questions of foundation remains problematic...

....

For me, the question which remains unresolved in Heidegger's work is this: *how can a question of critique in general be accounted for from within the framework of a fundamental hermeneutics?*[44]

Ricoeur's strategy is to return to Husserl, in light of Heidegger's achievement and to retrieve the contribution of the early Husserl's method. It is the later Husserl that is closer to Heidegger and prepares the way for his overcoming of the subject/object dualism, characteristic of neo-Kantianism, through his retrieval of the transcendental imagination. As Ricoeur states:

Husserl's final phenomenology joins its critique of objectivism to a positive problematic which clears the way for an ontology of understanding. This new problematic has as its theme the *Lebenswelt*, the "life-world," that is, a level of experience anterior to the subject-object relation, which provided the central theme for all the various kinds of neo-Kantianism.[45]

But Ricoeur notes it is against the early Husserl that the ontology of understanding of Heidegger is erected,[46] particularly against its subjectivist focus, the basis of Husserl's theory of intentionality and meaning. Ricoeur adds:

And if the later Husserl points to this ontology, it is because his effort to reduce being failed and because, consequently, the ultimate result of phenomenology escaped the initial project. It is in spite of itself that phenomenology discovers, in place of an idealist subject locked within its system of meanings, a living being which from all time has, as the horizon of all its intentions, a world, the world.[47]

Heidegger's depsychologizing of the philosophy of the imagination is central to the emergence of contemporary hermeneutics and its overcoming of the Cartesian notion of the world as view and the dualism of subject and object. Understanding is redefined through this interpretation of the imagination, from replicating the creativity of the mind of the author to viewing understanding as constitutive of existence. He explicates the anticipatory structure of understanding as fore-having, fore-understanding, and fore-conception.[48] His Copernican revolution transcends the psychological definition of the imagination which limited Dilthey's hermeneutics, as well as his adherence to objectivist criteria. But the legitimate concerns of Dilthey for method and critical reflection at the level of texts and historical beings are left unaddressed, since Heidegger's project attends to primordial being and is preoccupied with the deconstruction of classical metaphysics, in pursuit of the question of Being. He never makes the return route to reform the reflective tradition in relation to this direct ontology. As Ricoeur adds:

> the recognition of a critical instance is a vague desire constantly reiterated, but constantly absorbed, within hermeneutics. From Heidegger onwards, hermeneutics is wholly engaged in *going back to the foundations*, a movement which leads from the epistemological question concerning the conditions of possibility of the human sciences to the ontological structure of understanding ....
> ....
> For it is in the movement of derivation that the link between pre-understanding and prejudice becomes problematic and the question of critique is raised afresh, in the very heart of understanding.[49]

Thus there is an absence of a practical hermeneutics of suspicion, at the level of historical being, since this hermeneutics of the appropriation of the question of Being is not focussed upon these questions. The relation between primordial being and historical being is not addressed because of Heidegger's drive to inquire into Being. Heidegger's work is vulnerable to charges of an implicit and unquestioning assent to tradition and authority, since he does not attend to the problem of how to distinguish between authentic and inauthentic expressions of tradition and the authority of institutions, to which *Dasein* belongs and through which it interprets and projects its horizon of being-in-the-world.

Ricoeur, in keeping with Heidegger, develops the Kantian philosophy of the imagination, but in relation to language and a problematic of reflection and existence. It is this move which, as a consequence, enables him to retrieve the concerns of Dilthey for critical reflection at the level of the philosophy of language. Like Heidegger Ricoeur grafts phenomenology to hermeneutics but through an adaptation of the early Husserl's theory of intentionality and *epoche*, rather than at the level of the later Husserl's theory of the "Life-world", which distinguishes Ricoeur's development of the philosophy of the imagination in relation to hermeneutics from that of Heidegger.

> [T]he semantic approach keeps hermeneutics in contact with methodologies as they are actually practiced and so does not run the risk of separating its concept of truth from the concept of method. Moreover, it assures the implantation of hermeneutics in phenomenology at the level at which the latter is most sure of itself, that is, at the level of the theory of meaning developed in the *Logical Investigations*. Of course, Husserl would not have accepted the idea of meaning as irreducibly nonunivocal. He explicitly excludes this possibility in the First Investigation, and this is indeed why the phenomenology of the *Logical Investigations* cannot be hermeneutic. But, if we part from Husserl, we do so within the framework of his theory of signifying expressions; it is here that the divergence begins and not at the uncertain level of the phenomenology of the *Lebenswelt*.[50]

By uniting Husserl's theory of intentionality with the problem of equivocal language and hermeneutics, Ricoeur retains historical being and its works as the focus of his hermeneutics. On the other hand he separates himself from Husserl's idealist interpretation by taking up a critique of the reflective tradition in relation to symbolic discourse.

The later work of Heidegger makes the turn to language and recognizes language as the house of Being, but at this point poetic discourse appears to merge with philosophic discourse. Moreover this ontology continues to transcend altogether the critical historical problems of interpreting texts, concommittantly casting aside the value of the humanist tradition with its focus upon self-understanding through understanding others.

While Heidegger's direct ontology identifies the imagination with time, Ricoeur at the derivative level of historical hermeneutics will endeavor to develop the critical dimension of hermeneutics by attending to the objectification of the creative imagination in works of language, which display the configuring of time through symbol and myth. At this stage he retrieves the Romantic recognition of poetic language in terms of symbolic discourse and wagers upon its potential to instruct the hermeneutical process at the level of philosophic discourse, specifically to reform the tradition of the *cogito* and critical reflection, represented by Descartes, Kant, Hegel, Dilthey and Husserl. This is an undertaking that Heidegger's short route to ontology, by breaking with epistemology, does not bother to readdress.

In summary Ricoeur identifies and differs from Heidegger in various ways. Because of his commitment to this longer route, Ricoeur adheres to a truncated ontology, retaining as his focus symbolic language and the subject, rather than the direct ontology of Heidegger and the question of Being. Like Heidegger Ricoeur utilizes Kant's philosophy of the imagination, but he focusses primarily upon the creative imagination and its subversive power within the circle of interpretation, assuming Heidegger's redefinition of the transcendental imagination as the anticipatory structure of understanding, but seeking to validate and to develop its subversive trajectory through the objectification of language.

Ricoeur, like Heidegger, grafts phenomenology to hermeneutics, but by returning to the early Husserl of the *Cartesian Meditations* and *The Logical Investigations* rather than the later Husserl of the *Crisis*. His approach to the history of philosophy is constructive rather than deconstructive. He seeks to retrieve it as a repertoire that he reads dialectically, in light of the contemporary horizon and in view of Heidegger's critique of classical metaphysics the *cogito* and the world-as-view. This return route demands instead a critique directed at the reflective tradition,[51] seeking its transformation and reappropriation as concrete reflection. Thus as Heidegger was preoccupied with the critique of classical metaphysics, the *cogito* and the world-as-view, before making the fuller turn to language, Ricoeur at this stage is preoccupied with a critique of the reflective tradition and the *cogito*, but does so in order to rehabilitate the subjectivist tradition in relation to the priority of the hermeneutic circle before attending more precisely to the philosophy of language. Thus he maintains at the forefront of his hermeneutics the problem of self-understanding, (rather than the question of Being), and the ongoing task of overcoming false consciousness by attention to indirect discourse, particularly symbol.

While they both make the turn to language, Ricoeur attends to written language and texts, retaining continuity with the eighteenth and nineteenth century authors of hermeneutics, Schleiermacher and Dilthey and on the other hand utilizing and accepting the methods and advances of twentieth century semiotics, literary criticism, and Anglo-American philosophy of language. Finally he maintains the discontinuity and interplay between poetic discourse and philosophic discourse within hermeneutics, a distinction which he contends is blurred[52] by the radicalism of the later Heidegger.

At this stage Ricoeur's development of a critical hermeneutics is advanced by his grafting of hermeneutics to phenomenology at the level of understanding and its objectification through indirect language. Thus he seeks to wed Dilthey's definition of texts as the "expressions of life" to Husserl's phenomenological theory of intentionality and *epoche*. But this grafting is made in view of the horizon of Heidegger's reformulation of the hermeneutic circle as the anticipatory structure of understanding, which represents the depsychologizing of the imagination and subversion of the subject/object dualism of neo-Kantian epistemology. This Heideggerian breakthrough lays the groundwork for Ricoeur's return to the advances in the area of the mediation of experience and transcendence of subjectivity represented by Dilthey's "expressions of life" and Husserl's theory of intentionality and *epoche*.

The claim of this chapter is that Ricoeur's uniting of phenomenology at the level of the earlier Husserl's theory of signification in relation to equivocal language and the creative imagination is central to his development of a critical and creative dimension of hermeneutics. This uniting of phenomenology to hermeneutics can more adequately address: Dilthey's concern for objectivity and critically validate from within the hermeneutical circle and Heidegger's redefinition of the imagination as the anticipatory structure of understanding, through its expression and objectification in works of language. The method-ological model shifts from the natural sciences to the philosophy of language and away from psychology and the tenets of positivism.

It is Ricoeur's uniting of the philosophy of the imagination with the functioning of symbolic language, as opposed to the psychology of the author, that is pivotal to his development of a critical hermeneutics, which can integrate the Romantic recognition of the creativity of language with the Enlightenment advocacy of critical reflection and method. The achievement of his grafting of phenomenology to hermeneutics at this early stage is the identification of the mediating function of symbolic language with the objectification of the creative imagination, explicated through his adapation of Husserl's theory of intentionality in relation to symbolic language.

Later we will see that this adaptation of Husserl's theory of intentionality and *epoche* forms the basis for Ricoeur's explication of a moment of critical distanciation within the hermeneutical circle of understanding at the level of general hermeneutics gained through his fuller turn to language and his development of a theory of metaphor and texts. Thus at this later stage he will be equipped to address more adequately the absence of a critical development of hermeneutics by Heidegger and his follower Gadamer and to retrieve Dilthey's quest for method.

II

Fallible Man forms the first part of the second volume of Ricoeur's philosophy of freedom, under the title *Finitude and Guilt*. In turning back to this earlier work of Ricoeur's, my intention is to draw out the centrality of the philosophy of the imagination to *Fallible Man's* structure and to describe Ricoeur's linguistic development of the philosophy of the imagination, insofar as it is relevant to his turn to hermeneutics and overcoming of the two aporias sketched above. *The Symbolism of Evil* (the sequel to *Fallible Man)* examines the problem of evil through the narrative texts of symbol and myth, which mediate the complexity of evil.

Both Ricoeur and Heidegger make use of Kant's philosophy of the imagination in relation to phenomenology and the development of hermeneutics. In *Fallible Man* Ricoeur refers to Heidegger's *Kant and the Problem of Metaphysics*.[53] I will point out that his dissatisfaction with Heidegger's adaptation at this stage is consistent with his later wager to develop a critical hermeneutics by taking the longer indirect route through attention to the philosophy of language. Here he begins by establishing a correlation between the philosophy of the imagination and the intentionality of language. Heidegger's contribution to hermeneutics is made at the level of fundamental ontology, while Ricoeur's is characterized by a longer route that seeks to return from ontology to epistemology, attending to the derivative level of equivocal language.

Fallible Man, written prior to Ricoeur's turn to hermeneutics, centers upon a description of the human condition, which sets out to avoid a reduction of fallibility and fault to a condition of finitude, the position of Jaspers and Sartre. Instead (borrowing from Descartes) Ricoeur seeks to describe the human condition as a dialectic of finitude and infinitude.[54] In Husserlian fashion he brackets fault and endeavors to portray an anthropology, abstracted from the problem of evil, in which fallibility arises as a possibility due to the disproportion he uncovers and the fragile modes through which the self mediates this disproportion in a third term. This work is in keeping with the concrete ontology of his mentor Marcel and the effort to decenter the *cogito. Fallible Man* exemplifies the brand of French existentialist phenomenology, which applies the Husserlian method to existentialist themes.

Kant's development of the philosophy of the productive imagination in *The Critique of Pure Reason* is prominent in *Fallible Man,* while Kant's definition of the creative imagination in *The Critique of Judgment* under lies *The Symbolism of Evil,* in which Ricoeur practises the turn to hermeneutics. As Ricoeur states:

> Kant...is without a doubt the philosopher who has never ceased to inspire me and to provoke me. I have always recognized in him the philosopher who joins a precise architectonic of the power of thought to an intransigent sense of the limits involved. When I started off along the path of symbolical interpretation, it was in Kant that I found the suggestion of uniting the investigation of schematism, hence of productive imagination, with the elaboration of limiting concepts, that is, of concepts which at once express the work of reason beyond understanding and prevent understanding from locking sense within fixed and closed determinations. Of all the works the one that is most strongly marked by Kant...is *Fallible Man.* The idea of a disproportion between the level of thought and that of feeling, and the idea of a fragile and hidden mediation in a third term, the imagination, both these ideas derive directly from Kant.[55]

In *Fallible Man* Ricoeur's reading of Kant in relation to Husserl gives the Kantian schema a linguistic turn. I will delineate this by focussing upon the

second chapter of *Fallible Man*, "The Transcendental Synthesis", in which
Ricoeur makes use of Kant's transcendental/productive imagination in relation
to Husserl's phenomenology. He also notes his dissatisfaction with Heidegger's
identification of Kant's philosophy of the transcendental/productive imagination
with time.

Kant's philosophy of the productive imagination, as a synthesizing act that
mediates between understanding and experience as the "third term", serves as
the model for the anthropology Ricoeur sketches in *Fallible Man*. Humanity
constitutes itself through mediating the disproportion of the self. He describes
this anthropology as follows:

> he is intermediate within himself, within his *selves*. He is intermediate because he is a
> mixture, and a mixture because he brings about mediations. His ontological characteris-
> tic of being-intermediate consists precisely in that his act of existing is the very act of
> bringing about mediations between all the modalities and all the levels of reality within
> him and outside of him. That is why we shall not explain Descartes by Descartes, but
> by Kant, Hegel and Husserl: the intermediacy of man can only be discovered via the
> detour of the transcendental synthesis of the imagination, or by the dialectic...of
> significance and presence, of the Verb and the Look.[56]

The first chapter ("The Pathique of 'Misery' and Pure Reflection") prefaces
this reflection with a meditation on the myth of *melange* and the rhetoric of
misery. Thus Ricoeur's description of a divided self is established by first
referring to these pre-philosophic, poetic narratives, which influenced the
philosophy of Plato, Kierkegaard and Pascal.[57] His reference to a repertoire of
philosophers is creative and consciously unorthodox. Chapter two establishes
at the level of knowing the model for subsequent chapters of a disproportion that
is mediated by a third term, the imagination. The anthropology of *Fallible Man*
is developed through the spheres of knowing, acting and feeling, in which case
Ricoeur sets out to deepen the tradition of reflection, from pure reflection to
concrete reflection. The self mediates its disproportion through exterior works
and interiorizes the meaning of the self through feeling. As Ricoeur states:

> [I] look within the power of knowing for man's most radical disproportion. From it I
> seek a clue to the exploration of all the other modalities of man as intermediate: what

was mélange and misery for the pathetic comprehension of man will be called "synthesis" in the object; the problem of the intermediate will become that of the "third term" which Kant called "transcendental imagination" and which is discovered reflectively *on* the object ....
....

[T]ranscendental reflection based on the subject can...serve as a guide...for I can reflect on the new forms presented by man's non-coincidence with himself in the orders of action and feeling only in terms of the disproportion between Reason and Sensibility, or, as we shall presently, and more accurately express it, between the Word and Perspective. Likewise if we take the mediation of the transcendental imagination as a model, we can understand the new forms that the intermediary or mediating function acquires in the practical and affective order...
....

But...in man's precomprehension of himself there is a wealth of meaning that reflection is unable to equal. This residue of meaning will force us to attempt an entirely different approach in Book II: no longer by pure reflection but by an exegesis of the fundamental symbols in which man avows the servitude of his free will.[58]

Before turning to Ricoeur's adaptation of Kant to Husserl in *Fallible Man,* let us consider Kant's definition of the transcendental, productive imagination as set forth in his *Critique of Pure Reason.* His definition of the imagination as a transcendental synthetic activitives the imagination a cognitive significance it lacked prior to Romanticism. Kant defines the transcendental imagination as the synthesis between the understanding and sensibility in the "third term" of the schema. It constitutes the unity of consciousness, which allows for objective experience. As he states:

Obviously there must be a third thing, which is homogeneous on the one hand with the category, and on the other hand with the appearance, and which thus makes the application of the former to the latter possible. This mediating representation must be pure, that is, void of empirical content, and yet at the same time, while it must in one respect be *intellectual*, it must in another be *sensible*. Such a representation is the *transcendental schema* .[59]

This transcendental definition of the imagination implies that "our ordered world, and the possibility of understanding any part of it, depends on the existence of this synthesizing activity."[60] Moreover for Kant the schema which connects the understanding and sensibility is the structure of the schematizing activity of imagination in time. Time is the structure of consciousness to which all our experiences are subject. Since time as conceived by Kant "is universal and pure, it can connect up with the pure concepts (the catergories); and since it organizes all representations, it is connected to our perceptions. It can serve, therefore, as the mediating link between concepts and percepts".[61]

But Kant also states that this "third term" is not directly available for analysis. "This schematism of our understanding, in its application to appearances and their mere form, is an art concealed in the depths of the human soul, whose real modes of activity nature is hardly ever to allow us to discover, and to have open to our gaze."[62]

Let us now turn to Ricoeur's adaptation of Kant in relation to Husserl. The structure of the second chapter of *Fallible Man* follows a regressive dialectical pattern. Ricoeur moves from "finite perspective" to "infinite verb" to "pure imagination" in which the latter designates the third term, the synthesizing act that mediates a unity between the opposition between "finite perspective" and "infinite verb" at the level of knowing. This regression reveals the priority of the pure imagination to the prior levels.

The finite perspective of the body, opens the subject onto the world. As Ricoeur states:

> [M]y perceiving body is not only my openness onto the world, it is also the "here from where" the thing is seen ....
> ....
>
> Primal finitude consists in *perspective* or *point of view*. It affects our primary relation to the world which is to "receive" objects and not to create them.... It is rather a principle of narrowness or, indeed, a closing within the openness.[63]

Moving to the second stage of this dialectic Ricoeur describes the "infinite verb" as trangressing the finitude of perspective, through the intentionality of language. Through language the subject signifies the thing as a whole, beyond the narrowness of the side perceived. As Ricoeur puts it:

I anticipate the thing itself by relating the side that I see to those that I do not see but which I *know*. Thus I judge of the entire thing by going beyond its given side into the thing itself. This transgression is the intention to signify ....

....

Therefore, I am not merely a situated onlooker, but a being who intends and expresses as an intentional transgression of the situation. As soon as I speak, I speak of things in their absence and in terms of their nonperceived sides.... In being born I enter into the world of language which precedes me and envelops me. The mute look is caught up in speech which articulates the sense of it.[64]

This regressive analysis reveals the priority of speech to percept. The synthesis of "finite perspective" and "infinite verb" brings Ricoeur to the notion of "pure imagination", the third term that mediates "meaning" and "appearance" upon the objectivity of the thing. The thing is the unity which is realized in a correlate of speech and point of view.[65] Here Ricoeur also parts from Kant's epistemology. As he states:

Kant reduced the scope of his discovery to the restricted dimensions of an epistemology.... But criticism is more than epistemology.... [The real *a priori* synthesis] consists in the things objectival character...namely, that property of being thrown before me, at once given to my point of view *and* capable of being communicated in a language comprehensible to any rational being. The objectivity of the object consists in a certain expressibility adhering to the appearance of anything whatsoever.[66]

At this point he indicates his agreement with Heidegger's Copernican revolution.

This objectivity is neither in consciousness nor in the principles of science; it is rather the thing's mode of being. It is the ontological mode of those "beings" which we call things. Heidegger—whom we shall eventually refuse to follow—is right in saying that the Copernican revolution is first of all the return from the ontic to the ontological, i.e., from the "thing," considered as a "being" among "beings"...to its ontological constitution. Objectivity indicates this synthetic constitution itself as a uniting of meaning to presence. In order for something to be an object, it must conform to this synthetic constitution: "Ontic truth conforms necessarily to ontological truth. There again is the legitimate interpretation of the meaning of the 'Copernican revolution'."[67]

But Ricoeur disagrees with Heidegger's reduction of the "third term" to time, since Ricoeur asserts with Kant that this "third term" is obscure and is not open to direct reflection. He adds, "[t]o say that time is the unity of that duality is to name the difficulty as well as to situate it—which is not nothing—but it does not solve it".[68] Rather it is through language that Ricoeur seeks to explicate the synthesizing activity of the productive imagination as its indirect objectification. "[Kant] could not draw this order from time itself, but on the contrary had to determine time by the category. We can only upset the problem by throwing out what constitutes the essence of rationality, namely an articulate discourse."[69]

Ricoeur's interpretation is creative, since he reads Kant in relation to Husserl's theory of intentionality. He replaces Kant's terms "understanding" and "sensibility" with "meaning" and "appearance". His analyses conjoin schematizing imagination to linguistic functions constitutive of discourse as "saying something of something".[70] The constitution of the self is projected through the works, which testify to the effort and desire to be, mediating the project of the person. "Now this world of persons expresses itself through the world of things by filling it with new things which are human works".[71]

> [T]he person is primarily a project that I represent to myself, which I set before me and entertain, and that this project of the person is, like the thing but in an entirely irreducible way, a "synthesis" which is effected...
>
> ....
>
> Man appeared to us as a being stretched between the this-here-now, the certainty of the living present and the need to complete knowledge in the truth of the whole. By whatever name this primordial duality is called—opinion and science, intuition and understanding, certainty and truth, presence and sense—it forbids us to formulate a philosophy of perception prior to a philosophy of discourse and forces us one to work them out together, one with the other, one by the other.[72]

Thus like Heidegger Ricoeur utilizes Kant's philosophy of the imagination, but addressed to the mediation of the disproportion of the self. The self projects and overcomes its disproportion through language and diverse literary works that testify to the effort and desire to be understood as the third term. His route to ontology is indirect, while Heidegger's is direct, since his interpretation of Kant's philosophy of the imagination directly identifies the "third term" of the imagination with time; in which case, understanding is redefined as a mode of being. Heidegger's effort was to break from the dualism of subjectivity and objectivity, and Kant's definition of the imagination as the "third term" is Heidegger's route to his radical reversal from epistemology to fundamental ontology. It precedes the subject/object differentiation. Language is secondary in *Being and Time* while after the "turn" language is recognized as the house of being. Ricoeur's commentary on Heidegger in *Fallible Man* is directed to *Being and Time* and does not take into account the ramifications of Heidegger's later turn to language.

While Ricoeur accepts the Copernican reversal of Heidegger, in which he establishes the priority of being to subjectivity, he differs with Heidegger's direct identification of the imagination's third term with time. In contrast with Heidegger, Ricoeur's use of phenomenology relies upon the early Husserl of the *Logical Investigations* and his theory of intentionality rather than the later Husserl of the "life-world". Ricoeur's adaptation of Kant's philosophy of the imagination develops it in relation to language. This leads Ricoeur to a different interpretation of Kant's "third term". Instead Ricoeur seeks to approach the "third term" indirectly through its objectification in language. This anthropology decenters the *cogito* through sketching the dialectical character of self-appropriation in terms of the mediating activity of the imagination.

Part 2 of *Finitude and Guilt: The Symbolism of Evil* removes the brackets surrounding "fault" and approaches the problem of evil through an exegesis of the symbols and myths of the western tradition that tell of the beginning and end of evil through these multivalent narratives. Kant's philosophy of the creative imagination is most evident in the "Conclusion" to *The Symbolism of Evil* through the aphorism "the symbol gives rise to thought".

The Symbolism of Evil explores the symbols and myths of evil by following the intentionality of the symbols. This work in practice makes the turn to hermeneutics. The development of the imagination in *The Symbolism of Evil* is to move from language as the objectification of the mediating imagination in *Fallible Man* to the creative imagination and its objectification in the poetic language of symbol and myth. This language represents a communal mediation of the opacity of existence, particularly evil. As Ricoeur states in the later work, *Freud and Philosophy*:

> the problem of evil forces us to return from Hegel to Kant—that is to say, from a dissolution of the problem of evil by dialectic to the recognition of evil as something inscrutable, and hence as something that cannot be captured in a total and absolute knowledge. Thus the symbols of evil attest to the unsurpassable character of all symbolism; while telling us of the failure of our existence and of our power of existing, they also declare the failure of systems of thought that would swallow up symbols in an absolute knowledge.[73]

Myths, as narratives, introduce a temporal dimension to this process of mediation. A dialectic between the archeology and teleology of the symbols guides Ricoeur's reading of these narratives. Although there is a developmental structure to Ricoeur's examination of these myths from the archaic expressions of stain and defilement to the more self-conscious expressions of guilt, the archaic remains at work in these more developed types and is not simply reduced by the later myths.

The "Conclusion" to *The Symbolism of Evil* meditates upon Kant's aphorism from the Third Critique, that is, "the symbol gives rise to thought" to which no concept is equal. This marks Ricoeur's conscious turn to hermeneutics through a focus upon symbolic discourse and its structure of double intentionality. As Ricoeur states in the "Preface" to Fallible Man: "'The symbol gives thought.' That text is the pivotal point of the whole work. It shows how we can both respect the specific nature of the symbolic world of expressions as well as think, not at all "behind" the symbol, but "starting from" the symbol."[74] He outlines the possibility of a creative interpretation that does not reduce the symbols but seeks to respect their multiplicity of meaning particularly as innovators of meaning. It is the deciphering of this creativity as a guide to the process of interpretation that opens the way to a the development of a critical hermeneutics. The Copernican reversal is no longer to see the symbol as a less rational mode of comprehension, but as a key to the process of mediation of the self and reality. The interpretation of symbol and myth at work in *The Symbolism of Evil* follows the intentionality of the symbols and myths dialectically through an adaptation of Hegel. It is not a psychological interpretation, which seeks to go in back of the text to replicate the experience behind it, but instead it follows the intentionality projected before the text and its world. Self-understanding comes last via the symbol rather than through an empathetic identification with the mind of the author: "...mediating requires entry into their meaning-movement. Only as drawn and conducted by them is the subject of evil and fault able to span the extremes...they are the extremes of evil from its utmost point of exteriority to its inmost point of interiority."[75] Thus *The Symbolism of Evil* goes beyond the Romantic view of the psychology of the imagination, which limited the work of Schleiermacher and Dilthey.

Mary Schaldenbrand notes the advance made in the philosophy of the imagination by Ricoeur in the *Symbolism of Evil* extending the development of the imagination in *Fallible Man:*

> *The Symbolism of Evil* affirms imagining as mediation. But it makes new and important gains. Now the mediating schematism includes, in addition to a transcendental function, the poetic function. Now, too, the linguistic schema extends beyond the noun and the verb to text.... Ricoeur dares to say:"Life is a symbol, an image, before being experienced, and lived." For, indeed, "One lives only what one imagines...."[76]

This correlation of the Kantian philosophy of the imagination to the phenomenon of symbolic/metaphoric language, in light of Heidegger's Copernican revolution, then opens the way to overcome the first *aporia* that Ricoeur sketched above in his review of the history of hermeneutics, that is the separation between language and the psychological definition of the imagination. Ricoeur retrieves the Romantic revival of poetic language, but now in relation to a philosophy of the imagination which is depsychologized and bonded to the philosophy of language, particularly through Husserl's theory of meaning and intentionality. The effort to develop a critical hermeneutics and overcome the second aporia between ontology and epistemology will be made through his fuller turn to language and development of the theory of metaphor, which will further refine his definition of the philosophy of the imagination and add precision to his understanding of the functioning of symbolic discourse.

III

Let us now return to Ricoeur's discussion of his agenda for hermeneutics in *The Conflict of Interpretations*. As he makes the return route by grafting phenomenology to hermeneutics through the earlier Husserl, he also seeks to critique the *cogito*. The focus of his hermeneutics is symbolic language. Symbol and interpretation are defined correlatively in his article "Existence and Hermeneutics" as follows:

> I define "symbol" as any structure of signification in which a direct, primary, literal meaning designates in addition, another meaning which is indirect, secondary and figurative and which can be apprehended only through the first.... Interpretation...is the work of thought which consists in deciphering the hidden meaning in the apparent meaning, in unfolding the levels of meaning implied in the literal meaning. In this way I retain the initial reference to exegesis, that is, to the interpretation of hidden meanings. Symbol and interpretation thus become correlative concepts; there is interpretation wherever there is multiple meaning, and it is in interpretation that the plurality of meanings is made manifest.[77]

The primacy of the subject and consciousness are displaced by the axis of language. As Ricoeur adds: "It is first of all and always in language that all ontic or ontological understanding arrives at its expression. It is thus not vain to look to semantics for an *axis* of reference for the whole of the hermeneutic *field*."[78] The grafting of phenomenology to hermeneutics changes the stock in that Husserl's idealization of univocal meaning is replaced by Ricoeur's attention to symbolic discourse. By joining these multivocal meanings to self-knowledge, Ricoeur decenters the *cogito*, a cornerstone of Husserl's *Logical Investigation*. As he states:

> We have already seen how the introduction of ambiguous meanings into the semantic field forces us to abandon the ideal of univocity extolled in the *Logical Investigations*. It must now be understood that by joining these multivocal meanings to self-knowledge we profoundly transform the problematic of the *cogito*...
> ....
> Reflection is blind intuition if it is not mediated by what Dilthey called the expressions in which life objectifies itself. Or, to use the language of Jean Nabert, reflection is

nothing other than the appropriation of our act of existing by means of a critique applied
to the works and the acts which are the signs of this act of existing. Thus reflection is
a critique, not in the Kantian sense of a justification of science and duty, but in the sense
that the *cogito* can be recovered only by the detour of a decipherment of the documents
of life. Reflection is the appropriation of our effort to exist and of our desire to be by
means of works which testify to this effort and this desire. [79]

But Ricoeur deepens this critique of the *cogito*. He does this by way of the
reductive hermeneutics of Freud's psychoanalysis and read over against the
recollective hermeneutics of his phenomenology of the sacred by way of his
adaptation of Hegelian teleology.

This commitment to a longer return route through regional hermeneutics leads
Ricoeur at this stage to an engagement with the conflict between Freudian
psychoanalysis and the phenomenology of the sacred. The symbol serves as the
axis of reference for the critique of the subjective tradition and mediation of a
hermeneutics of suspicion and of appropriation. The constitution of the subject,
in relation to narrativity, is brought to the fore in terms of the temporal mediation
of the symbolic as manifested by the conflicting hermeneutics. The reduction of
the symbolic by the archeology of Freudian psychoanalysis is dialectically
countered through the projective reading of the symbolic by Ricoeur's adaptation
of the teleology of the Hegelian hermeneutics of the Spirit as well as the
eschatology of the sacred. From the perspective of philosophical hermeneutics,
Ricoeur mediates these regional interpretations dialectically, arbitrating their
absolutist claims thereby transforming and limiting the philosophical parameters
of the reflective tradition.

We will not discuss Ricoeur's work *Freud and Philosophy* in detail, but only
in a summary fashion. He counters Freud's reductive interpretation of the
symbolic by reading it in relation to Hegel's teleology of the symbolic. Freud's
hermeneutics of suspicion establishes that we begin with false consciousness.
This reductive hermeneutics uncovers the distortions of desire through the
archeology of the unconscious, which the symbol masks. But in turn Ricoeur via
Hegel reads the symbol teleologically, as also projecting the growth of
consciousness. A kinship between the archeology and teleology of the symbol
is recovered through this dialectical reading. But Hegel is limited by Kant. So as

Ricoeur critiques absolute idealism, he also nullifies the movement of interpretation toward absolute knowledge. As Ricoeur states:

> The existence that psychoanalysis discovers is that of desire; it is existence as desire, and this existence is revealed principally in an archaeology of the subject. Another hermeneutics—that of the philosophy of spirit,...suggests another manner of shifting the origin of sense, so that it is no longer behind the subject but in front of it...a hermeneutics representing the prophecy of consciousness. In the final analysis this is what animates Hegel's Phenomenology of Spirit...its mode of interpretation is diametrically opposed to Freud's. Psychoanalysis offered us a regression toward the archaic; the phenomenology of spirit offers us a movement in which each figure finds its meaning, not in what precedes but in what follows.... But what is important for our intention is that this teleology, just like Freudian archeology, is constituted only in the movement of interpretation, which understands one figure through another figure.... It is the task of this hermeneutics to show that existence arrives at expression, at meaning, and at reflection only through the continual exegesis of all the significations that come to light in the world of culture. Existence becomes a self...only by appropriating this meaning, which first resides "outside," in works, institutions, and cultural monuments in which the life of the spirit is objectified.[80]

A fundamental motif of Ricoeur's turn to hermeneutics is to read poetic/symbolic discourse and the classic repertoire of philosophic discourse in tension with one another as separate domains of discourse. In keeping with his adaptation of the phenomenological method to the hermeneutic problem, poetic/symbolic discourse is given greater weight, as the primary discourse which instructs and redefines the parameters and presuppositions of the reflective tradition. Thus he transforms the reflective tradition through his turn to hermeneutics.

Dialectic is pivotal to Ricoeur's philosophical method and a component of his developing philosophy of the imagination, as it functions on the level of philosophic reflection. He correlates and grounds this use of dialectic through his analysis of the rule of symbolic/metaphoric language. As Mary Schaldenbrand delineates this dialectical method:

> a field is sketched out between polar extremes; oppositions are set in sharpest relief;
> then beneath and within oppositions, hitherto hidden exchanges and reciprocities are

brought to light; in the end, what first appeared external and opposed is shown to be mutually inherent and solidary. What could more aptly describe this dynamic than the formula: 'kinship in conflict'?[81]

This method is maintained and refined through his turn to hermeneutics and development of a critical hermeneutics. At this early stage his retrieval of the work of Schleiermacher and Dilthey is mediated through the dialectic of Husserl and Heidegger at the forefront, as well as that of Kant and Hegel at the level of the return to regional hermeneutics and transformation of the reflective tradition. This venture of seeking kinship within conflict is carried forward as he mediates the conflicting hermeneutics of Freudian psychoanalysis and the sacred through their common reference to the symbol and decentering of subjectivity.

Symbol and interpretation are defined correlatively at this early stage of Ricoeur's development of hermeneutics. This is in keeping with the traditional correlation between rhetoric and hermeneutics, that is, that the rules of creating speech serve to inform the rules of interpreting speech, except that here, following the Romantic turn, poetics, in terms of the symbol, replaces the influence of neo-classic rhetoric and its idealization of univocal expression on the development of hermeneutics. Ricoeur's use of method is informed by Aristotle's development of rhetoric, particularly the strategy of dialectic, which has its roots in Aristotle's philosophical treatise on rhetoric. But for Ricoeur dialectic corresponds to and translates the rule of symbol to the level of philosophical hermeneutics.

Like symbol dialectic is a coefficient of Ricoeur's engagement of the philosophy of the imagination with his turn to hermeneutics and his effort to develop a critical hermeneutics. Dialectic emerges as the creative and critical counterpart of symbolic discourse at the level of philosophic discourse, functioning both as a strategy of innovation and limitation over against the absolutist claims of the reflective tradition. This notion of dialectic (a post-Hegelian/Kantian hybrid) functions, in relation to symbolic discourse and the hermeneutical circle, as a limit concept that undercuts the reflective tradition's assumption of knowledge as presuppositionless and metaphysically absolute.

At this early stage of Ricoeur's turn to hermeneutics, his emphasis is upon a critique of the reflective tradition, through which he anchors self-understanding in relation to the hermeneutical circle of the archeology/teleology/eschatology of the symbolic, in which case the symbolic is pivotal to uncovering the kinship of the conflicting hermeneutics. He establishes, through the overdetermination of the symbol a dialectic between the past (archeology) and the future (teleology /eschatology). The correlative relationship between symbol and interpretation will be given greater precision through Ricoeur's later development of the theory of metaphor and the philosophy of the imagination at which point he moves from the level of regional hermeneutics to general hermeneutics. Thus Ricoeur first returns to epistemology and regional hermeneutics, in view of Heidegger's ontological hermeneutics, to draw out its implications at the methodological level. He develops the philosophy of the imagination in relation to language, in which case symbol and myth mediate the disproportion of the self. By returning to epistemology he takes on a critique of the reflective tradition and the *cogito* in order to retrieve Husserl's theory of intentionality at the service of interpretation of symbolic discourse.

In conclusion his grafting of hermeneutics to phenomenology (as differentiated from that of Heidegger) transforms Husserl's idealist position on the *cogito*. Freudian psychoanalysis of the symbolism of the psyche is read in relation to Ricoeur's development of the phenomenology of the symbolism of the sacred and Hegelian teleology. These are the conflicting hermeneutics he seeks to mediate through the overdetermination[82] of the symbol, again evoking the structuration of time in relation to the imagination but through the dialectic of archeology and teleology of the symbol. Freed by Heidegger from Schleiermacher's and Dilthey's psychology of the imagination, Ricoeur is able to retrieve their focus upon texts as the expressions of life through his adaptation of Husserl's theory of intentionality to equivocal language and the Kantian philosophy of the imagination. The symbol replaces subjectivity as the axis of interpretation, establishing the first stage of his pathway to a critical hermeneutics through a re-definition of reflection as concrete reflection.

This transformation of consciousness as a hermeneutical task prepares the way for the next stage of Ricoeur's fuller turn to language and his development of the theory of metaphor, which in the next chapter I will show gives greater precision to the correlation between the creative imagination, language and the subversive power of poetic discourse for a general hermeneutics. The latter can respond more adequately to Dilthey's quest for method and compensate for the implicit romanticism of Gadamer's general hermeneutics, the heritage of Heidegger.

ENDNOTES OF CHAPTER THREE

[1]Paul Ricoeur, "Existence and Hermeneutics", trans. Kathleen McLaughlin in *Conflict of Interpretations* ed., Don Ihde (Evanston: Northwestern University Press, 1974), pp. 12-16.

[2]Ricoeur, "Hermeneutics and the Critique of Ideology", ed. and trans. John B. Thompson in *Hermeneutics and the Human Sciences* (Cambridge: Cambridge Univerisity Press, 1981).

[3]Ricoeur, *The Symbolism of Evil*, trans. Emerson Buchanan (Boston: Beacon Press, 1967), pp. 11-18.

[4]Mary Schaldenbrand, "Metaphoric Imagination: Kinship Through Conflict" in *Studies in the Philosophy of Paul Ricoeur*, ed. Charles E. Reagan (Athens: Ohio University Press, 1979), pp. 58-59.

[5]"Existence and Hermeneutics", pp. 3-24 and "The Task of Hermeneutics" in *Hermeneutics and the Human Sciences*, pp. 43-62.

[6]Ricoeur, *Fallible Man*, rev. trans. Charles Kelbley (New York: Fordham, 1986).

[7]Martin Heidegger, *Kant and the Problem of Metaphysics*, trans. James S. Churchill (Bloomington: Indiana University Press, 1962), pp. 133-208. See also Ray L. Hart, *Unfinished Man and the Imagination* (New York: Herder & Herder, 1968), p. 236, n. 86 and p. 316, n. 4.

[8]"Existence and Hermeneutics", p. 10.

[9]Ricoeur, *Freud and Philosophy,* trans. Denis Savage (New Haven: Yale University Press, 1970), pp. 35-36.

[10]Ibid., p. 33.

[11]Ricoeur, "Heidegger and the Subject" in *Conflict of Interpretations,* p. 224.

[12]*Freud and Philosophy,* p. 35.

[13]Ibid.

[14]*The Symbolism of Evil,* pp. 347-357.

[15]See note 5 above.

[16]"Existence and Hermeneutics", pp. 3-4.

[17]Ibid., p. 17.

[18]Ibid., p. 4.

[19]Ibid.

[20]Ibid.

[21]Ibid., p. 17. .

[22]Ibid., p. 5.

[23]Ricoeur, "The Task of Hermeneutics", p. 46.

[24]Ibid., p. 46.

[25]Immanuel Kant, *The Critique of Pure Reason,* trans. Norman Kemp Smith (New York: St. Martin's Press, 1929) and *Critique of Judgment,* trans. J. H. Bernard (New York: Hafner Press, 1951); also see Mark Johnson, *The Body in the Mind* (Chicago: University of Chicago Press, 1987), pp. 147-166.

[26]"The Task of Hermeneutics", pp. 46-47.

[27]Ibid., pp. 47-48.

[28]Ibid., p. 49.

[29]Ibid., p. 48.

[30]Ibid., p. 50.

[31]"Existence and Hermeneutics", p. 5.

[32]"The Task of Hermeneutics", p. 49.

[33]Ibid.

[34]Ibid., p. 50.

[35]Ibid., p. 52.

[36]Ricoeur, "The Task of Hermeneutics" in *Exegesis,* ed. F. Bovon & G. Rouiller (Pittsburgh: Pickwick Press, 1978), pp. 292-293.

[37]"The Task of Hermeneutics" in *Hermeneutics and the Human Sciences*, p. 50.

[38]Ibid.

[39]Ibid., p. 53.

[40]"Existence and Hermeneutics", p. 8.

[41]Ibid., p. 6.

[42]Heidegger, *Kant and the Problem of Metaphysics.*

[43]"The Task of Hermeneutics", pp. 55-56.

[44]Ibid., p. 59.

[45]"Existence and Hermeneutics", p. 8.

[46]Ibid., p. 8.

[47]Ibid., p. 9.

[48]"The Task of Hermeneutics", p. 58.

[49]Ricoeur, "Hermeneutics and the Critique of Ideology" in *Hermeneutics and the Human Sciences,* pp. 88-89.

[50]"Existence and Hermeneutics", p. 15.

[51]Ibid., p. 16.

[52]*The Rule of Metaphor*, trans. Robert Czerny (Toronto: University of Toronto Press, 1977), p. 311.

[53]Ricoeur, *Fallible Man*, p. 39.

[54]Ibid., p. 3.

[55]Ricoeur, "My Relation to the History of Philosophy", *Iliff Review,* 35(1978),8.

[56]*Fallible Man*, p. 3.

[57]Ibid., pp. 8-15.

[58]Ibid. pp. 5-6.

[59]Kant, *The Critique of Pure Reason*, p. 181.

[60]Johnson, p. 151.

[61]Ibid., p. 153.

[62]Ibid. p. 183.

[63]*Fallible Man*, p. 21, p. 24.

[64]Ibid., pp. 26-27.

[65]Ibid., p. 58.

[66]Ibid., pp. 38-39.

[67]Ibid., p. 39.

[68]Ibid., p. 43.

[69]Ibid., p. 44.

[70]Schaldenbrand, p. 62.

[71]*Fallible Man,* p. 48.

[72]Ibid., pp. 69-70, p. 92.

[73]*Freud and Philosophy*, p. 527.

[74]*Fallible Man*, p. xliv.

[75]Schaldenbrand, p. 63.

[76]Ibid., 64 and *The Symbolism of Evil*, p. 278.

[77]"Existence and Hermeneutics", pp. 12-13.

[78]Ibid., p. 11.

[79]Ibid., pp. 17-18.

[80]Ibid. p. 22.

[81]Schaldenbrand, p. 79.

[82]*Freud and Philosophy*, pp. 341-342. Ricoeur adopts the term "overdetermin-ation" to refer to the richness of the symbol and its capacity through the act of interpretation to convey both the trajectory of the archeology and the teleology of consciousness.

CHAPTER FOUR

THE RULE OF METAPHOR AND THE PHILOSOPHY OF THE IMAGINATION

Ricoeur's long route to develop a critical hermeneutics leads him from the level of derivative hermeneutics to general hermeneutics and from a focus upon the symbol as the axis of interpretation, to a focus upon the text and the rule of metaphor. In this chapter I will argue that Ricoeur's development of the theory of metaphor and the philosophy of the creative imagination facilitates his explication of a critical hermeneutics, in terms of the creativity of language.

Ricoeur's mediation of the debate between Gadamer and Habermas at the level of general hermeneutics, serves a role similar to his address in the prior chapter of the conflict (at the level of derivative hermeneutics) between Hegelian phenomenology and Freudian psychoanalysis. True to the dialectical character of his philosophical method, at this stage, Ricoeur continues to draw upon the Romantic and Enlightenment traditions in his effort to define a new phase of hermeneutics, as a hermeneutics of the power-to-be, which can incorporate a hermeneutics of suspicion as the counterpart to a hermeneutics of appropriation at the level of general hermeneutics. This critical hermeneutics is based upon the rule-governed creativity of metaphor, as directive of the interpretation of the text by the reader.

The order of discussion of this chapter will be first to define the problematic of a critical hermeneutics as Ricoeur delineates this question in terms of the debate between Gadamer and Habermas and Ricoeur's own decision to focus upon metaphor and poetic texts. Second I will discuss his elaboration of the theory of metaphor, at the level of the sentence and fiction and its correlation to the philosophy of the creative imagination. Finally I will argue that the rule of metaphor as correlated to the mimetic and subversive power of the imagination is key to his development of a critical theory of interpretation. It is the ground of his exposition of a dialectic between understanding and distanciation in terms of the dialectic of *Mimesis₁*, *Mimesis₂* and *Mimesis₃* which overcomes Gadamer's disjunction between distanciation and understanding and rejoins "belonging" to the Heideggerian anticipatory structure of understanding as the power-to-be. In turn this development of the philosophy of the imagination in relation to the rule of metaphor, recovers a critical moment within the hermeneutic circle that responds to Habermas's demand for a critique of ideology by demonstrating the subversive power of the imagination at work in poetic texts, through the dialectic of the sedimentation and innovation of a living tradition.

I

In this section I will follow Ricoeur's discussion of the debate between Gadamer and Habermas in his article: "Hermeneutics and the Critique of Ideology"[1], and Ricoeur's dialectical mediation of this conflict in pursuit of his agenda to explicate a critical hermeneutics. Gadamer's hermeneutics of tradition and Habermas's critique of ideology, represent opposing philosophical traditions that Ricoeur endeavors to incorporate into his development of hermeneneutics. While Gadamer is influenced by German Romanticism, Heidegger's ontology and Dilthey's historical hermeneutics, Habermas is shaped by the Enlightenment tradition of critical reflection, the Frankfurt School and its post-Marxist critique of ideology. Gadamer speaks for a hermeneutics of the renewal of culture and tradition and an ontological avowal of its historical conditions, while Habermas calls for a critique of false consciousness, in terms of a philosophy of communi-cative action that discloses the hidden exercise of oppression and violence sustained by a distorted communication. The thrust of this position is toward the future as the place of restoration and as the antidote to the broken communica-tion of the past.

In Gadamer Ricoeur discovered both a master and ally,[2] because Gadamer, like Ricoeur, undertakes the descending dialectic from Heidegger's ontological reconstitution of hermeneutics to the derivative hermeneutics of the human sciences and questions of historicity and method.[3] But unlike Ricoeur, he does not honor Dilthey's quest for method, rather he views it as an obstacle to be overturned. His concern is to apply the Heideggerian shift to ontology to the questions of historicity, and in so doing to overcome the limitations of Dilthey's dualistic epistemology by establishing the priority of "belonging"[4] (Gadamer's transcription on the level of historical hermeneutics of Heidegger's term "being-in-the world") to the problematic of subjectivity and objectivity.

The axis of Gadamer's hermeneutics is historical consciousness,[5] rather than the text[6] as in Ricoeur's case. Gadamer continues Heidegger's development of the transcendental imagination, in relation to temporality, at the level of historicity, while Ricoeur develops the correlation between the creative imagination and metaphor at the level of texts, as expressive of the *mimesis* of action through works of fiction.

Gadamer's adherence to Romanticism and his adaptation of Heideggerian ontology to the historical dimension of hermeneutics lead him to profess that misunderstanding is overcome through recourse to the dialogue which we are, and to the retrieval of consensus. His emphasis is upon the human sciences that attend to the reappropriation of culture and tradition. Gadamer's hermeneutics offers a positive evaluation of prejudice,[7] tradition and authority as structures of "belonging".

> 'Dilthey was unable to free himself from the traditional theory of knowledge.' (WM 261; TM 245) Dilthey still begins from self-consciousness; for him, subjectivity remains the ultimate point of reference..
> ....
> It is thus against Dilthey, as well as the constantly resurging *Aufklärung,* that Gadamer proclaims: 'the prejudices of the individual, far more than his judgments, constitute the historical reality of his being' (TM 245). The rehabilitation of prejudice, authority and tradition will thus be directed...against the criteria of reflection.[8]

Thus Gadamer explicates his definition of hermeneutics as ontological in opposition to Dilthey's dualistic epistemology, and his adaptation of the methods and standards of objectivity in the natural sciences to the human sciences. Dilthey designates the human sciences as the sphere of subjectivity and understanding, while the natural sciences are defined as the sphere of objectivity and explanation.[9]

> History precedes me and my reflection; I belong to history before I belong to myself. Dilthey could not understand that, because his revolution remained epistemological and his reflective criterion prevailed over his historical consciousness..................
> ....
> Only a fundamental upheaval which subordinates the theory of knowledge to ontology can bring out the real sense of the *Vorstruktur des Verstehens*—the forestructure (or structure of anticipaton) of understanding—which is the condition for any rehabilitation of prejudice.[10]

While it is the failure of Dilthey's quest for method that Gadamer seeks to refute, he remains profoundly faithful to Dilthey by making history and historicity the primary experience of hermeneutics.

Instead of a reversal from objectivity to subjectivity, a revolution of thought is required and this is the great contribution of Heidegger's Copernican revolution. Heidegger's ontological redefinition of the hermeneutic circle in terms of the forestructure of understanding that precedes all subject/object dualisms is utilized by Gadamer to reformulate Dilthey's historical hermeneutics as foundational to the human sciences. Gadamer recovers the positive significance of prejudice, tradition and authority as structures of pre-understanding. He exemplifies the primary hermeneutical experience of "belonging" through the sphere of aesthetics, history and language.[11] This is in opposition to the alienating distanciation of the method of science, which according to Gadamer conceals the priority of "belonging" over judgment and objectification. It is the Cartesian tradition of judgment[12] that is destructive of a recognition of the hermeneutic circle and the priority of prejudice, tradition and authority.

Ricoeur focusses upon Gadamer's notion of "historical efficacy"[13] as crystallizing his phenomenological retrieval of prejudice, tradition and authority. It represents the major contribution of Gadamer's historical hermeneutics defined as foundational for the human sciences. Historical efficacy means that we are always situated in history and cannot make the past into an object. The tension between the other and oneself is unsurpassable in the dialectic of past, present and future. The epistemological implications are that a science free from prejudices is impossible. Thus Gadamer critiques the possibility of critique, since according to this explication of the priority of "belonging", the possibility of a presuppositionless point of view is denied. There is no cognitive overview or Hegelian type situation that constricts us absolutely. In Gadamer's hermeneutics, the primary experience is this awareness of historicity, over against the alienating distanciation of objectivity and method, which conceals the prior historical moment, in advance of the moment of reflection. But Gadamer's hermeneutics, in its radical critique of critique continues Dilthey's dichotomy between understanding and explanation. As Ricoeur points out, the more accurate title of Gadamer's hermeneutics is *Truth OR Method*.[14]

Thus according to Ricoeur, Gadamer offers an avenue of return to the questions of Dilthey's historical hermeneutics, leading across the spheres of aesthetics, history and language, freed now from the psychologism of Dilthey's hermeneutics, but bereft of a hermeneutics of suspicion, due to Gadamer's radical insistence upon the primacy of "belonging" in place of "alienating distanciation".[15] Gadamer criticizes Dilthey's definition of method for its adaptation of the criteria of the adversary, namely positivism, but Gadamer never recognizes the possibility of redefining method positively on the terrain of the human sciences. He thus continues Dilthey's dichtomy between understanding and explanation, as the aporia between ontology and epistemology.

Ricoeur turning to the other side of the debate, states:

> We shall approach Habermas's critique by asking whether 'the dialogue which we are' is indeed the universal element that allows hermeneutics to be deregionalized, or if instead it constitutes a rather peculiar experience, enveloping both a blindness with respect to the real conditions of human communication, as well as a hope for a communication without restriction and constraint.[16]

Habermas's critique of ideology is raised from the perspective of critical reflection and in opposition to the naivete of Romanticism and Heideggerian hermeneutics. Ricoeur shares in common with Habermas the tradition of critical reflection radicalized by the critique of subjectivity by the masters of suspicion and their concern for the relation between speech, action and emancipation.[17] Habermas challenges Gadamer's ontologizing of hermeneutics and benign interpretation of prejudice, authority and tradition. To Gadamer's rehabilitation of prejudice, Habermas opposes his notion of "interest"[18] which, Ricoeur notes, bears a family resemblance to the former.

> The concept of interest is opposed to all pretensions of the theoretical subject to situate itself outside the sphere of desire, pretensions that Habermas sees in the work of Plato, Kant, Hegel and Husserl; the task of a critical philosophy is precisely to unmask the interests which underlie the enterprise of knowledge. It is evident that however different the concept of interest may be from Gadamer's notions of prejudice and tradition, there is a certain family resemblance....[19]

Thus they both recognize that subjectivity is supported by a context and a set of presuppositions, but Habermas analyzes pre-understanding from the perspective of cloaked desire and force, which distorts the dictates of institutions. He defines ideology as a set of beliefs that function to conceal hidden interests under the mask of a rationalization that upholds the oppression of *status quo* institutions.[20] In the case of Habermas's theory of communicative action the critical social sciences parallel the place of the human sciences in Gadamer's hermeneutics. The critical sciences serve the emancipation of the individual, in that through explanatory methods, they uncover the hidden censorship and violence concealed by ideology, similar to the method of Freudian psychoanalysis. Their function is to critique the cultural foundations of institutions rather than to reappropriate and retrieve tradition as in the case of the hermeneutics of the human sciences.

While Gadamer presupposes that the authentic basis of existence resides in a prior understanding and belonging to tradition, Habermas's philosophy of communicative action, on the other hand, presupposes that prior understanding is a source of broken communication.[21] Instead he projects, through a regulative ideal of unrestricted communication the claim that authenticity is realizable only in the future.[22] Thus there is a teleological thrust to Habermas's theory of communicative action. Utopian vision[23] is the counterpart of ideology, in that it anticipates a situation of freedom that does not yet exist and thus is oriented to a future. As Ricoeur states:

A critique of ideology must think in terms of anticipation where the hermeneutics of tradition thinks in terms of assumed tradition. In other words, the critique of ideology must posit as a regulative idea, in front of us, what the hermeneutics of tradition conceives as existing at the origin of understanding. It is at this point that...the interest in emancipation, comes into play. This interest...animates the critical social sciences, providing a frame of reference for all the meanings constituted in psychoanalysis and the critique of ideology. Self-reflection is the correlative concept of the interest in emancipation. Hence self-reflection cannot be founded on a prior *consensus*, for what is prior is precisely a broken communication.[24]

Habermas's concept of ideology thus opposes Gadamer's notion of a prior consensus. For Gadamer misunderstanding is preceded and supported by the dialogue which we are; and a deeper consensus is held to be retrievable through a hermeneutics of recollection beyond the misunderstanding. In contrast, Habermas's critique of ideology by the critical social sciences attends to the interconnection between language, power and labour. These elements are involved in a hermeneutics of suspicion in order to reveal the role that privilege and power play in distorting communication, ruling out prior consensus or understanding. Explanation by way of psychoanalytic or sociological critique, is necessary to excavate the hidden violence at work in language. The recourse to a hermeneutics of suspicion is necessary since censorship and violence of this type are not open to restoration through dialogue, particularly a dialogue that is not based upon a balance of power or equality.

The critique of ideology must be placed, therefore, under the sign of a regulative idea, that of unlimited and unconstrained communication. The Kantian emphasis is evident here; the regulative idea is more what ought to be than what is, more anticipation than recollection. It is this idea which gives meaning to every psychoanalytic and sociological critique. For there is desymbolisation only with the project of resymbolisation, and there is such a project only with the revolutionary perspective of an end of violence. Where the hermeneutics of tradition sought to extract the essence of authority and to connect it to the recognition of superiority...................
....
An eschatology of non-violence thus forms the ultimate philosophical horizon of a critique of ideology. This eschatology, close to that of Ernst Bloch, takes the place of the ontology of lingual understanding in a hermeneutics of tradition.[25]

From Habermas's perspective Gadamer has hypostasized a rare experience and canonized the exceptional case of authentic authority and prejudice as pre-understanding. As Ricoeur summarizes Habermas's position:

> One cannot speak with Gadamer of the common accord which carries understanding without assuming a convergence of traditions that does not exist, without hypostatising a past which is also the place of false consciousness, without ontologising a language which has always only been a distorted 'communicative competence'.[26]

Thus, Ricoeur notes, Habermas places the critical instance above a hermeneutics of historicity, while Gadamer places the recovery of "belonging" through his concept of historical efficacy, above the critical instance.

Ricoeur's mediation of this debate clarifies his agenda to develop a critical hermeneutics that can answer to the lack of critique in Gadamer's hermeneutics of tradition, and to recognize Habermas's dependence upon hermeneutical presuppositions. Ricoeur seeks to join Gadamer's emphasis upon the recollection of the past to Habermas's eschatological thrust to the future. Ricoeur returns to Heideggerian ontology by way of the philosophy of language to bridge the gap between these conflicting philosophical positions. He notes Heidegger's admission of the need for critique,[27] (although Heidegger does not take up this problem) and observes that Heidegger's anticipatory structure of understanding,[28] insofar as it projects new ways of being in the world, parallels Habermas's eschatological thrust to the future. Ricoeur shares with Gadamer the project of working out the consequences of Heidegger's ontological redefinition of the imagination as understanding in relation to historicity. But Ricoeur takes up the problem of the imagination in relation to literary works of language as expressive of action. Since he adheres more closely to Kant's admonition that the imagination cannot be observed directly, Ricoeur's analysis of the imagination and time is carried out in terms of the creative imagination's objectification in literary works, which convey a mimesis of action. He seeks to recover the place of critique within the hermeneutic circle through making the mimetic and poetic text[29] the axis of his hermeneutics, rather than historical consciousness.

Ricoeur's turn to the philosophy of language is made at the exegetical level of hermeneutics in the tradition of Schleiermacher and Dilthey and their concern for the problems of written language.

> The idea of such a shift in the initial locus of the hermeneutical question is suggested by the history of hermeneutics itself. Throughout this history, the emphasis has always come back to exegesis or philology, that is, to the sort of relation with tradition which is based on the *mediation* of texts, or documents and monuments which have a status comparable to texts. Schleiermacher was exegete of the New Testament and translator of Plato. Dilthey located the specificity of interpretation (*Auslegung*), as contrasted with the direct understanding of the other (*Verstehen*), in the phenomenon of fixation by writing and, more generally, of inscription.[30]

Metaphoric and fictional discourse are the particular focus of his analysis, in continuity with his earlier attention to symbol and myth.[31] Ricoeur notes that it is on the return route from the fundamental level of hermeneutics to the derivative level of hermeneutics:

> that the link between pre-understanding and prejudice becomes problematic and the question of critique is raised afresh, in the very heart of understanding. Thus Gadamer, speaking of the texts of our culture, repeatedly insists that these texts signify by themselves, that there is a 'matter of the text' which addresses us. But how can the 'matter of the text' be left to speak without confronting the critical question of the way in which pre-understanding and prejudice are mixed?[32]

In comparing the absence of critique in Heidegger's project with the same in Gadamer's, Ricoeur points out that while Heidegger's radicalism prevents him from returning to the question of critique at the level of derivative hermeneutics, Heidegger admits the danger of mistaking the distortions of ideology for authentic pre-understanding.

> In the circle of understanding...is hidden a positive possibility of the most primordial kind of knowing. We genuinely take hold of this possibility only when, in our explication(*Auslegung*), we have understood that our first, last and constant task is never to allow our fore-having, fore-sight, and fore-conception to be presented to us by fancies (*Einfalle*) and popular conceptions (*Volksbegriffe*), but rather to make the

scientific theme secure by working out these anticipations in terms of the things themselves.[33]

Heidegger's critique within *Being and Time* is directed against classical metaphysics, which he assesses as concealing the question of Being. He never makes the return route to the epistemological questions of method and historicity on the level of derivative hermeneutics because of his obsessive pursuit of the question of Being. Gadamer, on the other hand, is prevented from recognizing the critical instance because the *primary* experience of hermeneutics that he seeks to recover is "belonging" and his project is directed against the alienation of distanciation and thus against a critique of critique.[34] Gadamer's development of Heidegger's ontological redefinition of the transcendental imagination is conveyed by his notion of historical efficacy, as the schematization of time, in which the past (due to his emphasis upon "belonging") dominates the dialectic of past, present and future.

As we noted above Heidegger admits the need of critique, although he does not return from his exploration of this ontology of Being to the question of epistemology, since his critique is aimed against metaphysics. The Heideggerian recognition of the need for critique implies the realization of a depth hermeneutics as the remedy to the distortions of meaning, but he does not offer any concrete instruction at the level of derivative hermeneutics for the realization of a depth hermeneutics. However Ricoeur notes the kinship between Heidegger's definition of the anticipatory structure of understanding as the projection of new ways of being in the world turned toward the future and Habermas's regulatory ideal of unconstricted communication as the eschatological horizon of emancipation.[35] For Ricoeur the Heideggerian notion of "world" as the projection of new ways of being pertains to creativity and critique. The Heideggerian definition of the hermeneutic circle of understanding, includes Gadamer's emphasis upon the past through the forestructures of pre-understanding and also Habermas's emphasis upon the future through Heidegger's notion of the anticipatory structure of understanding as the power-to-be.[36] Heidegger's advance beyond Romanticism replaces Romanticism's focus upon subjectivity and the mind of the author with the projection of a world. Ricoeur seeks to forge a kinship between Gadamer and Habermas within his own development of hermeneutics, restoring a dialectic that is in keeping with Heideggerian ontology between past and future (through his turn to the text and particularly poetic works of language, such as metaphor and fiction). Heidegger is thus the bridge back from Habermas to Gadamer.

Ricoeur's own development, while deeply indebted to Gadamer, is thrust toward innovation, the future, and the subversive power of the imagination, themes which are akin to Habermas. The emphasis upon innovation and praxis are longstanding concerns of Ricoeur in which he identifies with Habermas's political philosophy and vision of a just society.

The correlation between metaphor and the creative imagination, I will argue, is key to Ricoeur's explication of a dialectic between belonging and distanciation. This he demonstrates through showing the relation of the anticipatory structure of understanding to the intentionality of equivocal language. Ricoeur takes the long indirect route through language to resolve the aporia between ontology and epistemology, which he claims Gadamer's hermeneutics fails to overcome. As asserted in the earlier chapter, the limitations of Schleiermacher's and Dilthey's reliance upon the empathetic imagination to define the task of hermeneutics is overturned by Heidegger's radical redefinition of the hermeneutic circle, through his ontological reinterpretation of Kant's definition of the transcendental imagination. The contribution of Ricoeur's regrafting of hermeneutics to phenomenology is to incorporate a hermeneutics of suspicion by retrieving and developing the relation between language and the philosophy of the creative imagination at the exegetical level of texts.

Although both Heidegger and Gadamer make the turn to language, they do so at the level of the ontology of language[37] as such, rather than at the derivative level of written language and texts. Ricoeur sets out to overcome the dichotomy between understanding and explanation, which Gadamer adopts from Dilthey by uncovering a non-alienating distanciation that is appropriate to the functioning of language and the human sciences. Through his turn to the philosophy of language and the advances of semantics and literary criticism, he argues for a definition of explanation that is not borrowed from the natural sciences[38] but is native to the functioning of language and its strategies, in keeping with the theory of intentionality of Husserlian phenomenology (that is, as differentiated from its idealist interpretation). Thus Ricoeur's agenda is set to rectify the shortcomings of Gadamer's hermeneutics by seeking to unfold a dialectic between understanding and explanation/distanciation and appropriation that is founded upon the correlation between the creativity of language as metaphoric strategy and the philosophy of the creative imagination.

> My own interrogation proceeds from this observation. Would it not be appropriate to shift the initial locus of the hermeneutical question, to reformulate the question in such a way that a certain dialectic between the experience of belonging and alienating distanciation becomes the mainspring, the key to the inner life, of hermeneutics?
> ...[I]t seems to me that the properly hermeneutical moment arises when the interrogation, transgressing the closure of the text, is carried toward what Gadamer himself calls 'the matter of the text'—namely the sort of *world* opened up by it..........
> ....
> It may be noted in passing that the most decisive break with Romantic hermeneutics is here; what is sought is no longer an intention hidden behind the text, but a world unfolded in front of it. The power of the text to open a dimension of reality implies in principle a recourse against any given reality and thereby the possibility of a critique of the real. It is in poetic discourse that this subversive power is most alive............
> ....
> In the case of poetry, fiction is the path of redescription; or to speak as Aristotle does in the *Poetics*, the creation of a *mythos*, of a 'fable', is the path of *mimesis*, of creative imitation.[39]

With the development of four themes Ricoeur sets out to supplant Gadamer's hermeneutics of tradition through a hermeneutics of communication that incorporates critique. First Ricoeur's theory of the text as a work of language adopts Habermas's emphasis upon praxis/language and power. It is as he states the emancipation of the text that allows for the critical instance to be recognized and explicated within the hermeneutic circle.[40] Second discourse is placed under the category of a work rather than of writing. As Ricoeur notes:

> Discourse is characterized by the fact that it can be produced as a work displaying structure and form. Even more than writing, the production of discourse as a work involves an objectification that enables it to be read in existential conditions which are always new.[41]

Third the task of hermeneutics is to realize the world of the text, through following the mediation of the text from sense to reference.[42] This represents Ricoeur's attempt to circumvent Gadamer's opposition to distanciation by introducing a notion of objectification and distanciation in keeping with the nature of language, rather than one borrowed from the natural sciences. The intentionality of the text is to be actualized toward its projection of a world in front of the text, not behind it. In showing how this unfolds, Ricoeur's focus is upon metaphor and fiction and the subversive function of the imagination at work in this type of language.

Fourth subjectivity is the last reference of the hermeneutic process. The text offers to the self a critique of subjectivity and the task of actualizing new possibilities and reforming the *status quo*. In contrast with the position of Schleiermacher and Dilthey, subjectivity is the last reference not the first.[43] This type of language, as expressive of the subversive power of the creative imagination, responds to Habermas's call for a critique of ideology. Ricoeur argues that Habermas's position is dependent upon hermeneutical presuppositions by claiming that eschatology is nothing without the recitation of acts of deliverance from the past.[44] We turn now to Ricoeur's theory of metaphor as key to Ricoeur's development of a critical hermeneutics through attention to the creativity of language.

II

Metaphor is considered by Ricoeur as a poem in miniature, in which the rules of producing metaphor, in turn throw light upon the rules for interpreting larger literary works, such as fiction, defined as a mimesis of action. He begins the *Rule of Metaphor*[45] with a retrieval of Aristotle's definition of metaphor and mimesis, followed by a description of the reduction of metaphor by the subsequent history of rhetoric. He then turns to modern theorists and utilizes the work of the philosophy of language developed by Beneviniste, Searle and Austin as well as such literary theorists as Black, Beardsley, Richards, Goodman, Hester and Henle, to arrive at a theory of metaphor that can more adequately account for the dynamic, cognitive characteristics of metaphor and mimesis. The reduction of rhetoric to a taxonomy of tropes is exemplified by the nineteenth century treatise of Pierre Fontanier, *Les Figures du discours*.[46] Metaphor according to this tradition is simply decorative language, with no cognitive content. As we have discussed in previous chapters, Romanticism challenged this view of metaphor and poetic texts and developed a definition of the philosophy of the imagination, in which a much more creative role is given to poetic language, viewed as the product of the creative imagination of the genius, and thus celebrates its power to express deeper truth. But the philosophy of the imagination at this stage was defined in terms of the psychology of the creativity of the author. Schleiermacher and Dilthey were influenced by this tradition in their development of hermeneutics and, given their epistemology, they separated language from the imagination. Ricoeur's breakthrough, based on the Heideggerian reinterpretation of the imagination is to turn to the philosophy of the creative imagination and explicate it in relation to the functioning of language (as the anticipatory structure of understanding). By utilizing twentieth century advances[47] in the analysis of language he is able to define the creativity of metaphor and the philosophy of the creative imagination in terms of the rule-governed intentionality of language, rather than by attending to the psychology of the author's creativity.

Ricoeur's retrieval of Aristotle's definition of metaphor in relation to his *Rhetoric*[48] and *Poetics*[49] parallels Heidegger's return to early Greek philosophy,[50] prior to the dominance of classical metaphysics. Ricoeur's concern is the relation between speech, action and force. In this way he mirrors more closely the pragmatic concerns of Habermas. Ricoeur's interpretation of Aristotle seeks to recover a basis for a more active and dynamic definition of metaphor prior to its reduction by neo-classic rhetoric to decorative speech.[51] As Ricoeur notes Aristotle's definition of metaphor has its foot in the domains both of rhetoric and poetics. According to Aristotle:

> Metaphor consists in giving the thing a name that belongs to something else: the transference being either from genus to species, or from species to genus, or from species to species, or on grounds of analogy.[52]

Aristotle adds elsewhere:

> It is a great thing, indeed, to make a proper use of the poetical forms, as also of compounds and strange words. But the greatest thing by far is to be a master of metaphor (literally to be metaphorical). It is the one thing that cannot be learnt from others; and it is also a sign of genius, since a good metaphor (literally: to metaphorize well) implies an intuitive perception of the similarity in dissimilars.[53]

Ricoeur's analysis of Aristotle's definition leads him to note three points. First, metaphor is something that happens to the noun. Second, metaphor is defined in terms of movement, from...to, which is designated by the greek *epiphora.*[54] Third, metaphor is the transposition of an alien name and a deviant use of words.[55] But beyond this more straightforward analysis, Ricoeur draws forth three hypotheses about metaphor from Aristotle's definition, viewing them as grounds for a discursive definition of metaphor, taking into account the functioning of metaphor in the sentence, rather than simply as a substitution of words. His first hypothesis is that metaphor is a discursive statement, since the transposition of Aristotle's definition operates between pairs. It always takes two ideas to make a metaphor as a calculated error, going beyond the word, calling into play a whole network of meaning; and such categorial transgression does not remain simply on the level of the lexical but involves classification itself. As he states:

> First, in all metaphor one might consider not only *the* word alone or *the* name alone, whose meaning is displaced, but *the pair* of terms or relationships between which the transposition operates—*from* genus *to* species, *from* species *to* genus, *from* species *to* species, *from* the second *to* the fourth term (and vice versa) of a proportional relationship.... If metaphor always involves a kind of mistake, if it involves taking one thing for another by a sort of calculated error, then metaphor is essentially a discursive phemomenon.[56]

The second hypothesis is that metaphor creates new meaning through a categorial transgression.

> What is being suggested then, is this: should we not say that metaphor destroys an old order to invent a new one; and that the category-mistake is nothing but the

complement of a logic of discovery...? Pushing this thought to the limit, one must say
that metaphor bears information because it 'redescribes' reality. Thus, the category
mistake is the de-constructive intermediary phase between description and redescription.[57]

His third hypothesis follows from this:

A third, more venturesome hypothesis arises on the fringe of the second. If metaphor
belongs to an heuristic of thought, could we not imagine that the process that disturbs
and displaces a certain logical order, a certain conceptual hierarchy, a certain
classification scheme, is the same as that from which all classification proceeds?[58]

These hypotheses reveal an ambitious agenda for the theory of metaphor that
dignifies it beyond an accessorial role and implies that it is foundational to
thought.

Rhetoric and poetics, according to Aristotle, express and address the action.[59]
Rhetoric as defined by Aristotle is concerned with the modes of persuasion
through the use of probable arguments.[60] Liveliness of speech is conveyed
through metaphor through its ability to surprise the hearer into an insight. On the
other hand, poetics through drama and especially tragedy conveys a mimesis of
action that facilitates insight through the plot and its production of catharsis.[61]
Both are attentive to action and convey insight through invention and discovery,
and metaphor is identified as a key strategy to both types of speech.

Let us first consider Ricoeur's discussion of Aristotle's *Rhetoric*. Aristotle's
Rhetoric is a brilliant attempt to strike an equilibrium between the extremes of
violence and reason.

The question that sets this project in motion is the following: what does it mean to
persuade? What distinguishes persuasion from flattery, from seduction, from
threat—that is to say, from the subtlest forms of violence? What does it mean, 'to
influence through discourse'?[62]

Aristotle's *Rhetoric* differs from Plato's condemnation of it as sophistry and
flattery. Instead Aristotle binds rhetoric to philosophy and the use of probable
argument. Aristotle delimits the field of rhetoric as covering three areas: the
theory of argumentation, that is, the invention of arguments and proofs, the

theory of style, and last, the theory of composition.[63] The principal axis of his rhetoric is the theory of argumentation. Thus this definition of rhetoric is kept under the sway of logic and philosophy as a whole. Although Aristotle recognized rhetoric as arising from the public arena and the wisdom of common opinion, he did not condemn it for its contingency and particularity and its use of equivocal speech as did Plato. Aristotle characterized rhetoric more positively as following the logic of the probable, rather than the logic of necessary and immutable truths. Rhetoric is thus connected to the concrete and particular world, rather than to the essential and universal realm of *episteme*. As Ricoeur states:

> The kind of proof appropriate to oratory is not the necessary but the probable, because the human affairs over which tribunals and assemblies deliberate and decide are not subject to the sort of necessity, of intellectual constraint, that geometry and first philosophy demand. So, rather, than denounce *doxa* ('opinion') as inferior to *episteme* ('science'), philosophy can consider elaborating a theory of the probable.... The great merit of Aristotle was in developing this link between the rhetorical concept of persuasion and the logical concept of the probable, and in constructing the whole edifice of a philosophy of rhetoric on this relationship.[64]

The art of rhetoric practices the invention of proofs as a creative activity, which works to meet the particular situation of its address. It is a dialogical process, in that it is attuned to the specific character of audience and forum. Aristotle defines what he means by *art* as *techne* in his classic work *The Nicomachean Ethics*.[65] *Techne* involves a capacity to make, to create, which has its origin in its human creator, rather than by necessity as an object of nature. It is a type of expression that is inventive, rather than imitative. The rules of *techne* are formed in relation to their practical application, and they cannot be abstracted as a set of immutable directions. As Ricoeur states:

> A *techne* is something more refined than a routine or an empirical practice and in spite of its focus on production, it contains a speculative element, namely a theoretical enquiry into the means applied to production. It is a method; and this feature brings it closer to theoretical knowledge than to routine.[66]

Techne is exercised as an engagement of the human subject with reality and the conditions of her/his world. Aristotle defines *techne* as follows in *The Nicomachean Ethics:*

> *art* is identical with a state or capacity to make, involving a true course of reasoning. All art is concerned with coming into being, i.e., with contriving and considering how something may come into being which is capable of either being or not being, and whose origin is in the maker and not in the thing made; for art is concerned neither with things that are, or come into being, by necessity, nor with things that do in accordance with nature (since these have their origin in themselves).[67]

The art of persuasion, correlated with the concept of the probable, makes particular judgments as to the type of argument most suitable to the occasion. This testifies that it is an intersubjective phenomenon, affected by the concrete limits of its audience and its speaker's capacities, as reflected in Aristotle's definition of rhetoric: "the faculty of observing in any given case the available means of persuasion".[68] As a dialogical phenomenon it arises in the give and take of the common world of the everyday. As Ricoeur notes:

> set between two limits exterior to it—logic and violence—rhetoric oscillates between its two constitutive poles—proof and persuasion. When persuasion frees itself from the concern for proof, it is carried away by the desire to seduce and to please; and style itself ceases to be the 'face (figure),' that expresses and reveals the body, and becomes an ornament in the 'cosmetic' sense of the word. But this possibility was written into the origins of the rhetorical project, and moved within the very heart of Aristotle's treatise.[70]

Metaphor as described in Aristotle's *Rhetoric* is linked to its capacity to both delight and surprise the hearer. It is not defined as decorative or mere stylistic trimming. Its aim is to convey liveliness and awaken the hearer to a new avenue of understanding. As Aristotle states:

> Liveliness is especially conveyed by metaphor, and by the further power of surprising the hearer; because the hearer expected something different, his acquisition of the new idea impresses him all the more.... Well constructed riddles are attractive for the same reason; a new idea is conveyed, and there is metaphorical expression.[71]

Aristotle's *Poetics* is a domain distinct from the *Rhetoric*, but Ricoeur notes that metaphor is common to these distinct domains of discourse. "With respect to structure, it can really consist in just one unique operation, the transfer of the meanings of words; but with respect to function, it follows the divergent destinies of oratory and tragedy."[72] Its aim is not persuasion, but to purge the feelings of pity and fear and to illumine the deeper meanings of the human condition in which such fiction expresses truth. Its realm is the world of tragedy rather than politics. Its art is mimetic, attempting to capture through drama and narrative, a reading that strikes at the essential meaning of existence.[73]

Ricoeur's interpretation of Aristotle's notion of *mimesis* in relation to metaphor quarrels with traditional translations of Aristotle's term *mimesis*[74] as imitation of nature. According to Ricoeur's reading of Aristotle, *mimesis* captures an essential representation of human actions. Its method is to speak the truth by means of the tragic plot through fiction and fable. Its triad is *poiesis—-mimesis—-catharsis* in contrast to *rhetoric—proof—persuasion*. The mimesis of the *Poetics*, Ricoeur argues is not an "imitation of nature" as a copy of nature. It is a making, an art of capturing and comprehending human actions in terms of their essential meaning, which relies upon the creative configuration of a narrative, rather than the replication of events as historical chronicle. It is a portrayal of human actions, through a constructive rendition of events that mediates the meaning, value, and truth of existence through the plot. As Ricoeur states: "It is this function of ordering that allows us to say that poetry 'is more philosophic...than history' (*Poetics* 1451 b 5-6). History recounts what has happened, poetry what could have happened. History is based on the particular, poetry rises towards the universal." [75]

Ricoeur's interest in Aristotle's definition of *mimesis* lies in its capacity, on the one hand, to submit to reality and, on the other hand, to demand invention as it strives to manifest the deeper truths of human existence.

He stresses that it is active reality, that is human actions, which are grasped and given expression through the art of *mimesis*. Again the Aristotle of the *Poetics* as in the *Rhetoric* and *Nichomachean Ethics* is addressing concrete, temporal existence, rather than an absolute realm of unchanging and immutable Being as in the *Metaphysics*.

Ricoeur's interpretation of Aristotle challenges the translation of *phusis*[76] as nature, as well as the translation of *mimesis phuseos* as imitation of nature, particularly since it has tended to support a representational view of reality. But *phusis* for the Greeks, according to Ricoeur's interpretation of Aristotle's text, was not some inert given, rather it referred to living reality and lacked the subject/object dualism that informs the traditional translation of this phrase.

> But is not the word *nature* as far off the mark with respect to *phusis* as is the word *imitation* concerning *mimesis*? Certainly Greek man was far less quick than we are to identify *phusis* with some inert 'given'. Perhaps it is because, for him, nature is itself living that *mimesis* can be not enslaving and that compositional and creative imitation of nature can be possible. Is this not what the most enigmatic passage of the *Rhetoric* suggests? Metaphor, it relates, makes one *see things* because it 'represents things as in a state of activity' (1411 b 24-5). The *Poetics* echoes that one may 'speak in narrative' or present 'personages as acting and doing' (1448 a 22, 28). Might there not be an underlying relationship between 'signifying active reality' and speaking out *phusis*?[77]

Ricoeur connects the Aristotelian horizon to the contemporary hermeneutical problematic and the Heideggerian contribution of the "anticipatory structure of understanding" and "new ways of being in the world" projected by the hermeneutic circle. He notes that *mimesis* as a *poiesis* of reality has the capacity to capture a portrayal of existence that acts to surprise and to awaken its readers to an awareness of new modes of being-in-the-world that can stretch and overturn the limits of established opinion. Equivocal language as defined by the *Poetics* can function as a source of liberation that can work in partnership with the *Rhetoric* to achieve a renewal of speech, transcending and counteracting the limits of established opinion.

> But *mimesis* does not signify only that all discourse *is* of the world; it does not embody just the *referential* function of poetic discourse. Being *mimesis phuseos*, it connects this referential function to the revelation of the Real as Act. This is the function of the concept of *phusis* in the expression *mimesis phuseos*, to serve as an *index* for that dimension of reality that does not receive due account in the simple description of that-thing-over-there. To present humans *'as acting'* and all things 'as in act'—such could well be the *ontological* function of metaphorical discourse, in

which every dormant potentiality of existence appears *as* blossoming forth, every latent capacity for action *as* actualized. *Lively* expression is that which expresses existence as *alive*.[78]

Ricoeur's reading of Aristotle's *Rhetoric* and *Poetics* retrieves elements of Aristotle's philosophy which are attentive to the political world of opinion and the narrative world of tragedy and of epic, relevant to a concrete ontology, in which the rhetorical and poetic dimensions of language function to reflect and express existence as active and alive. Both rhetoric and poetics reflect the meaning and value of human actions. They represent related, practical forms of knowing that respond as productive arts to the experiential and probable conditions of human existence. But as practical in contrast to pure reason and the realm of theory, there is an active interchange between this type of reflection and the concrete, contingent world of the everyday.

The strategy of metaphor has a foot in both these domains. The poetic use of language constitutes a method for considering new possibilities in tension with the accepted order, and thus it can act to facilitate a renewal and transformation of reality through the power of the tragic narrative to describe the depth and fragility of the human condition and envision the fullest potential of the human condition. It represents an alternative to Parmenides's dictum that one cannot bend being to non-being.[79] Ricoeur's interpretation of Aristotle's notion of *mimesis* reveals the latter as a dynamic and compositional rendition of reality through emplotment, contrasting with the traditional interpretation of *mimesis* as an imitation of nature which has lent itself to a representational view of reality. But this interpretation by Ricoeur is novel. The traditional interpretation of Aristotle's *Poetics,* particularly through neo-classicism, tended on the whole to translate *mimesis* as imitation, in the sense of a reproduction of nature in an idealized form. It is to the limitations of this notion that Romanticism reacted through its celebration of the lyrical and creative capacities of language and the imagination.

Aristotle's definition of metaphor is limited by its focus upon the word, but the cognitive and creative aspects of metaphor that Aristotle's treatises recognize, within the context of the *Rhetoric and the Poetics*, lend themselves to Ricoeur's retrieval of the power of equivocal language to speak truth and facilitate his project to develop a critical hermeneutics through the philosophy of language. Like Heidegger he seeks to retrieve a concrete ontology beyond the dominant metaphysical tradition. But Ricoeur's focus is upon the functioning of language and its power to express and change human existence. The dominant tradition Ricoeur seeks to overturn is neo-classical rhetoric and the correlative influence of Hume's philosophy of the imagination, that supports a representational view of reality and truth as adequation.[80]

In summary Ricoeur recovers Aristotle's definition of rhetoric and poetics in relation to practical philosophy. Rhetoric, according to Aristotle, is tied to philosophy through the theory of argumentation and the dialectical use of probable logic, thus shaping the criteria for a valid use of persuasive speech. It is attentive to truth in the concrete. The poetic use of language is furthermore defined in the *Poetics* as a mimetic art which expresses the essential meaning and value of human actions through plot. It is a mode of reflection upon human action that can manifest important truths. Metaphor has a foot in both domains and is praised for its ability to evoke surprise and discovery in its hearer. It is lively expression that demands the ability to see similarity in dissimilarity and captures the blossoming forth of the "real" as "act". As Ricoeur states:

> The truth of imagination, poetry's power to make contact with being as such—this is what I personally see in Aristotle's *mimesis. Lexis* is rooted in *mimesis*, and through *mimesis* metaphor's deviations from normal *lexis* belong to the great enterprise of 'saying what is.'[81]

Ricoeur turns from his retrieval of the theory of metaphor in Aristotle to the contemporary context and the tools of the philosophy of language and literary criticism to develop the hypotheses he has formulated. The three studies in *The Rule of Metaphor* that are pivotal to his development of the theory of metaphor are "Studies Three, Six" and "Seven". "Study Three" sets the grounds for a contextual theory of metaphor that defines metaphor in terms of the sentence rather than the word by attending to the advances of contemporary semantic theory. In "Studies Six" and "Seven", Ricoeur develops his argument for semantic innovation in relation to the philosophy of the creative imagination, that in turn will prove key to his development of a critical hermeneutics. I will describe his definition of the theory of metaphor viewed in relation to the philosophy of the imagination, by reference to the above as well as pertinent articles.

The classic definition of metaphor by Aristotle is denominational and focussed upon the word, which Ricoeur argues is not wrong, but it fails to account for Aristotle's recognition of metaphor's power to invent, discover and form new categorizations. Ricoeur's development of the theory of metaphor seeks to explicate the grounds for the cognitive status of metaphor acknowledged by Aristotle and to break beyond the limitations of the neo-classic reduction of metaphor to decorative, figurative speech with no cognitive content, and on the other hand to overcome the limitations of Romanticism's efforts to reclaim the power of metaphoric and poetic language. The neo-classic definition is affected by the Enlightenment structures upholding a representational view of reality, while Romanticism's recognition of the creativity of metaphor is limited by its reliance upon a psychological definition of the creative imagination that is inadequate to make the case for creativity against the representative illusion.

In "Study 3" he argues for a definition of metaphor as predication that goes beyond the word to the frame and context of the sentence as a whole and a generative notion of language. Among the various theories of language he utilizes semantics rather than semiotics and structuralism,[82] since in his view the latter theory analyzes language cut off from its relation to reality, due to its implicit adherence to positivist assumptions.The theory of semantics[83] begins with the sentence, in keeping with the theory of intentionality of language that Husserl's and Frege's theory of sense and reference articulates, particularly the aim "to say something about something"; that is, to express meaning and truth. Thus it presupposes that language refers to reality. The theory of semiotics develops at another extreme and analyzes the internal structure and syntax of language, and brackets altogether the relation of language to reality.

Ricoeur defines metaphor in terms of the semantic theory of discourse which addresses language in relation to the sentence rather than the word.

Does this mean that the definition of metaphor as transposition of the name is wrong? I prefer to say that it is nominal only and not real, using these terms as Leibniz does. The nominal definition allows us to identify something; the real definition shows how

> it is brought about...as soon as rhetoric looks into generative causes, it is already
> considering discourse and not just the word. Thus a theory of the metaphorical
> statement will be a theory of the production of metaphorical meaning.... This is why
> Aristotle's definition is not abolished by a theory that no longer deals with the place
> of metaphor in discourse but with the metaphorical process itself.[84]

The phenomenological theory of intentionality as defined by Frege and Husserl was limited to univocal language, but Ricoeur applies this theory to equivocal language and thus breaks with the limits of their more narrow application to literal uses of language.

The semantic theory of discourse has a dialectical cast as Ricoeur defines it. On the whole he is following the work of Emile Benveniste. First discourse always occurs as an event, but endures as meaning. Its existential character is caught by the notion of event, while its capacity to remain in memory is defined by the concept of meaning. Second it has an "identifying function and a predicative function" that is the equation of the sentence that unites a particular subject to a predicate. The "identifying function" points out the individualizing function of the subject versus the universal function of the predicate, and that the sentence must be taken as a whole. Third it has a locutionary and illocutionary force (here Ricoeur is following the work of the philosopher John L. Austin), which describes the power of the speech act to do something; that is the locutionary force is the act of speaking, its illocutionary force is the "force" of the proposition, as for example, a promise, order or statement. Fourth discourse is characterized by sense and reference; sense is the immanent structure of meaning and reference, its capacity to transcend language and refer to reality. As Ricoeur adds:

> the transcendence-function of the intended captures perfectly the meaning of the
> Fregean concept of reference. At the same time, Husserl's phenomenological analysis
> based on the concept of intentionality is completely justified; language is intentional
> par excellence; it aims beyond itself.[85]

The fifth pair differentiates reference to reality from reference to the speaker. Reference itself is defined as dialectical in that, insofar as it refers to a situation, world, experience, reality, it also refers back to its speaker. The theory of discourse clarifies a type of distanciation that is integral to speech, particularly through the polarity between event/meaning and sense/ reference. Meaning and sense indicate a moment of objectification and structure through which the speech act endures. This offers a notion of distanciation that is based upon the functioning of language and not imported from the natural sciences.

Ricoeur develops an argument for a predicative theory of metaphor versus the traditional denominational theory of metaphor through reference to the work on metaphor by the rhetorician I. A. Richards[86], the philosopher Max Black[87] and the literary critic Monroe Beardsley.[88] All three reject the denominational definition of metaphor.

I. A. Richards establishes that words do not have a "proper meaning", rather all words have a polysemic character and the determination of their meaning is orchestrated by the context of their use which determines and limits polysemy for the sake of meaning. The interpenetration of words creates meaning from the extreme of technical, literal denotation to poetic, multiple meaning. In the former case meaning is limited to a direct and singular definition, while at the other extreme the strategy of the literary uses of language is to heighten the interplay and multiplicity of meaning. As Ricoeur states: "as opposed to the usage that fixes their meanings, the literary use of words consists precisely in restoring 'the interplay of the interpretative possibilities of the whole utterance'." [89]

Richards defines metaphor as the interaction of "tenor" and "vehicle" in a sentence that brings together two disparate semantic fields of meaning; but unlike Aristotle he does not limit the practice of metaphor to the genius, rather according to Richards, language is vitally metaphorical.

If to 'metaphorize well' is to possess mastery of resemblances, then without this power we would be unable to grasp any hitherto unknown relations between things. Therefore, far from being a divergence from the ordinary operation of language, it is 'the ominipresent principle of all its free action' (90). It does not represent some additional power, but the constitutive form of language. By restricting itself to the description of the ornaments of language, rhetoric condemned itself to treating nothing but superficial problems—whereas metaphor penetrates to the very depths of verbal interaction.[90]

Richards's definition of metaphor as the interaction of "tenor" and "vehicle", describes this bringing togther of disparate semantic fields as focussed upon the word, through which two ideas are presented.

> The two thoughts in metaphor are somehow disrupted, in this sense, that we describe one through the features of the other.... Richards suggests that we call the underlying idea the 'tenor' and that 'vehicle' be the name of the idea under whose sign the first idea is apprehended. It is very important to note, however, that the metaphor is not the vehicle alone, but the whole made up of the two halves.[91]

The limitation of Richards theory, according to Ricoeur, is its lack of precision. It remains abstract in that it describes two disparate thoughts coming together in metaphor. "The problem with these words is that they bear on 'ideas' or 'thoughts,' which are said to be 'active together,' and above all that the meaning of each of them is too ambiguous."[92] Richards's definition of metaphor is very close to his definition of the polysemy of ordinary language use, and it does not account for semantic innovation or the reference of metaphor to reality.

The American philosopher Max Black contributes greater precision to the discussion through his terms "focus" and "frame" to describe the metaphoric process of the sentence. He seeks to construct a logical grammar of metaphor in his classic book *Models and Metaphors*. Ricoeur enumerates three contributions of Black's theory. First Black distinguishes words used metaphorically in a sentence from those used non-metaphorically. He seeks to clarify the interaction of semantic fields within the sentence, which Richards's theory of "tenor" and "vehicle" had failed to specify.

> The word *focus*, then, will designate this word, and *frame* will designate the rest of the sentence. The advantage of this terminology is that it directly expresses the phenomenon of focusing on a word, yet without returning to the illusion that words have meanings in themselves. Indeed, the metaphorical use of *focus* results from the relationship between *focus* and *frame*. Now Richards saw this perfectly well; metaphor, he said, arises from the joint action of the tenor and the vehicle. Black's more precise vocabulary allows us to get closer to the interaction that takes place

between the undivided meaning of the statement and the focused meaning of the word.[93]

Second Black objects to the definition of metaphor as a substitution of words by rejecting Aristotle's definition of metaphor as a type of comparison or analogy.[94] This has the benefit of eliminating the taxonomy of figures of speech in classical rhetoric.

The third contribution of Black addresses the functioning of interaction and attempts to describe the emergence of metaphorical meaning. For example in the metaphor "man is a wolf" the interaction functions like a filter or screen that organizes and gives insight.

> The focus, 'wolf,' operates not on the basis of its current lexical meaning, but by virtue of the 'system of associated commonplaces'..... 'The wolf-metaphor suppresses some details, emphasizes others—in short, *organizes* our view of man'. In this way metaphor confers an 'insight.'[95]

But for Ricoeur the problem with this exposition is that it tends to best explain trivial metaphors through its emphasis upon "associated commonplaces", that is lexical meanings that are current; consequently the enigma of novel meaning beyond the borders of the established rules is left an enigma.

Finally Ricoeur turns to the work of the literary critic, Monroe Beardsley, and his book *Aesthetics*. He finds in Beardsley an answer to the problem of semantic innovation that Black's theory does not offer, and Beardsley also uses a semantic theory close to the semantic theory of discourse Ricoeur has sketched at the beginning of this study. Beardsley looks upon the metaphor as a poem in miniature that offers a test-case for the method of explication of larger literary works. The transition from semantics to hermeneutics also begins at this stage, in that the consideration of literary works beyond the unit of the sentence, raises the fuller question of interpretation and the implications of the theory of metaphor for the task of hermeneutics.

The focus of literary criticism as opposed to Black's logical grammar is on larger works of language (poems, essays and prose fictions), rather than the sentence. It rejoins Aristotle's comments on the relation between *muthos* and the *mimesis* of human actions. At the level of literary works, Beardsley's literary theory gives the notion of meaning a greater extension and precision, insofar as he defines meaning as referring to an inhabitable world that is projected through the configuation of the literary work, and revealed only at the level of the work as a whole. Literary criticism tends to bracket the referentiality of the work and concentrate on the analysis of its immanent sense, for example the narrative structuralist theory of Greimas.[96] However Beardsley, in keeping with Ricoeur's adaptation to literary works of language Frege's distinction between sense and reference, is interested in the power of metaphor to project and reveal a world. The Heideggerian notion of *world* is applied here to the *project* of the literary work.

Beardsley's theory focusses upon *living metaphors* rather than trivial metaphors and he describes the semantic innovation of metaphor as a type of *logical absurdity*. The production of the meaning of the text is dependent upon the reader's ability to actualize the structure of primary and secondary connotations that the metaphor constructs. As Ricoeur states:

> Beardsley's contribution differs appreciably from that of Max Black, as regards the positive role assigned to logical absurdity at the level of the primary meaning, functioning as a means of liberating the secondary meaning. Metaphor is just one tactic within a general strategy, which is to suggest something other than what is stated. Another such tactic is irony.... In all the tactics within this strategy, the trick consists in giving indicators that point towards the second level of meaning; and 'in poetry the chief tactic for obtaining this result is that of *logical absurdity*.[97]

Like Richards and Black, Beardsley defines metaphor as an interaction and his terms are "principal subject" and "modifier". What is new is the stress put on the logically empty attributions and particularly on incompatibility.[98]

> In the case of incompatibility, the modifier, by means of its primary meanings, points to characteristics incompatible with the corresponding characteristics designated by the subject at the level of its primary meanings. Accordingly, incompatibility is a conflict between designations at the primary level of meaning, which forces the reader to extract from the complete context of connotations the secondary meanings capable

of making a 'meaningful self-contradictory attribution' from a self-contradictory statement.[99]

It is the task of the reader to work out the connotations of the modifier that are meaningful in relation to the subject. Thus the act of reading[93] is like the performance of a musical score, in that it follows the rules of the metaphor-text and realizes an individual performance. Beardsley extracts two further principles from the test case of metaphor which are applicable to the level of the larger literary work, that is, a principle of congruence[100] and plenitude.[101] Beardsley's effort is aimed at answering the relativist position, that insists any reading is possible. The principle of congruence is a principle of selection. "As we read a poetic sentence, we progressively restrict the breadth of the range of connotations, until we are left with just those secondary meanings capable of surviving in the total context".[102] The second principle of plenitude counterbalances the first. All the connotations that can work in the poem must be utilized so that it means all that it can mean. The balance to be maintained is between producing as much meaning from the poem as possible without reading into it.

Beardsley's notion of logical absurdity accentuates the inventive character of metaphor and its emergent, eventful character. Thus it overcomes the shortcomings of Black's logical grammar and his reliance upon associated commonplaces that referred to already existing lexical meanings and best defined trivial metaphor. Beardsley's definition of metaphor as "figurative meaning" rather than "proper meaning" refers to contextual, emergent meaning that exists only here and now, as opposed to "proper meaning", that is established, catalogued, lexical designations of words. His characterization of metaphor as a semantic collision emphasizes the semantic innovation required by the reader to overcome the logical absurdity that arises through the clash of the semantic incompatiblility between "modifier" and "subject".

Ricoeur points out that the constructive role of the reader is crucial to this theory of metaphor and is ruled by the interaction of the network of semantic fields that the metaphor structures for the reader. This is central to getting beyond a substitution theory of metaphor. As Ricoeur states:

Only one line of defense remains open: one must adopt the point of view of the hearer or reader and treat the novelty of an emerging meaning as his work within the very act of hearing or reading. If we do not take this route, we do not really get rid of the theory of substitution. Instead of substituting (as does classical rhetoric) a literal meaning, restored by paraphrase, for the metaphorical expression, we would be substituting (with Black and Beardsley) the systems of connotations and common-places. I would rather say that metaphorical attribution is essentially the construction of the network of interactions that causes a certain context to be one that is real and unique. Accordingly, metaphor is a semantic event that takes place at the point where several semantic fields intersect. It is because of this construction that all the words, taken together, make sense. Then, and only then, the metaphorical *twist* is at once an event *and* a meaning, an event that means or signifies, an emergent meaning created by language.[103]

Ricoeur returns to his definition of discourse and defines metaphor in relation to this theory of discourse by pushing the theory of metaphor of Richards, Black and Beardsley to its limits. "Living metaphor" is both event and meaning. It is the interaction of the metaphoric statement as a whole that achieves the metaphoric twist both as an event and also as meaning that is capable of being identified and re-identified, since its construction is repeatable and endures through the objectification of the text as a work. It thus has a life beyond the moment of its first invention through the structure of language. If it becomes part of the lexical code it may be reduced to a dead metaphor. "Only authentic metaphors, that is, living metaphors, are at once meaning and event".[104]

This contextual definition calls into play a second polarity of discourse between singular identification and universal predication. All three theories utilize a predicative structure. Finally the last pair, sense and reference, is touched upon by Beardsley's extension of metaphor to larger literary works. Ricoeur develops this last polarity in "Studies Six and Seven" in relation to the philosophy of the imagination and the emergence of new meaning and its relation to reality. With the change in register from the sentence to larger literary works, Ricoeur moves from semantics to hermeneutics. Although Beardsley's theory addresses the problem of semantic innovation more successfully than Richards and Black through his notion of "logical absurdity", it still does not account for the process of assimilation that enables the reader to see similarity in difference.

"Studies Six and Seven" offer Ricoeur's pivotal contribution to the theory of metaphor in terms of the question of semantic innovation and reference, left unresolved by the theories of Richards, Black and Beardsley. Key to Ricoeur's advance on the question of innovation and reference is his correlation of the philosophy of the creative imagination to the strategy of metaphor. "Study Six" addresses the metaphoric sense, while "Study Seven" explicates the metaphoric reference.

In "Study Six" Ricoeur returns to the Aristotelian trait of resemblance as a central characteristic of metaphor. Resemblance is the key to the capacity of metaphor to forge similarity between differing semantic fields, enabling the reader to grasp a new semantic pertinence and to bridge the difference. It is poetic metaphor, rather than trivial or dead metaphor, that Ricoeur pinpoints. Poetic metaphor is at the edge not only of the emergence of new meaning but of new categorizations. The trait of resemblance resurrects the role of image and imagination in the formation of new meaning. Ricoeur draws upon the poetic theory of such authors as Le Guern, Henle and Hester, as well as the philosophy of Husserl, Pierce and Wittgenstein.

"Study Six" limits itself to the sense of metaphor as opposed to its reference. Ricoeur notes that the Husserlian strategy of bracketing reference to ordinary reality applies to the metaphoric sense. The metaphoric sense of poetic language functions as an "epoche" from the aims of ordinary and scientific language. Ricoeur describes the density of the metaphoric sense of poetic language as being like a sculpture or a lens constructed by verbal strategy to redescribe reality. The poem, and metaphor as a poem in miniature, creates new meaning and semantic innovation through the iconic power of the metaphor. He adopts the term icon[105] from Pierce, Henle and Hester and compares it to the schema of the creative imagination.

New meaning is created through the images constructed by the verbal interaction of metaphor and the images as bound images act to create for the reader the assimilation through which the reader sees similarity in difference between disparate semantic fields. He utilizes the tradition of Kant rather than Hume.[106] The synthetic and productive capacity of the imagination is defined in terms of the interplay between disparate semantic fields which the metaphoric process constructs as the synthetic and mediating function of the imagination objectified in language, the view that "Study Three" argued for through the theory of interaction. In turn the schematizing power of the imagination is governed by the tension between differing semantic fields, whereby it produces the iconic images through the verbal process. The schema is created through the metaphoric process. Images as icons are regulated by the structured clash of disparate semantic fields and the icons, as bound images create the schema for the new semantic pertinence that emerges on the ruins of literal predication. Unlike Hume's pre-cognitive theory of the imagination based on perception, and images as the residue of perception, Ricoeur's theory of the imagination builds upon Kant's synthetic and cognitive definition of the imagination, reinterpreted in relation to language as a rule-governed form of invention.[107]

Ricoeur adopts Wittgenstein's notion of "seeing as",[108] reinterpreted by Hester,[109] to explicate the semantic innovation of the metaphor. For Wittgenstein "seeing as" does not refer to poetic language or the imagination; rather Wittgenstein is considering the relation between ambiguous figures, such as an ink blot and the power of language to give it definition as a certain image. Wittgenstein makes the distinction that to say "I see this" is different from saying "I see this as". The latter involves creating the image rather than having it as a simple factual given.[110]

Hester's transfer of Wittgenstein's analysis to metaphor involves an important change. Wittgenstein's analysis of an ambiguous figure refers to a particular gestalt. Thus the Gestalt B allows figures A or C to be seen as for example either a rabbit or a duck. The problem is given the gestalt B of *seeing* it *as* a rabbit or *as* a duck. In applying this to metaphor, Hester notes A and C are given in the reading and they are what Richards describes as the tenor and the vehicle. What must be constructed is the gestalt B, in which case A and C are seen as similar. As Ricoeur says "'seeing as' orders the flux and governs the iconic deployment."[111]

The icon produced through the interaction of the predicative process of tenor and vehicle forms the matrix through which the reader sees similarity in difference. The iconic images are controlled through the verbal process and answer to how semantic innovation occurs through the interaction. The icon using Black's vocabulary acts as the lens or grid to read similarity in difference. So it is not resemblance through association of images, but a controlled production rendered through the act of predication, (which is the diaphora of the metaphor, recalling Aristotle's distinction between *diaphora* and *epiphora*) while the epiphora is the assimilation regulated through the iconic images as the bound, schema images, constructed by the metaphoric interaction. Ricoeur refers to Bachelard's notion of the reverberation of images that unite the verbal and non-verbal, sound and sense.

> Metaphorical meaning...is not the enigma itself,...but the solution of the enigma, the inauguration of the new semantic pertinence. In this connection, the interaction designates only the *diaphora*; the *epiphora* properly speaking is something else. It cannot take place without fusion, without intuitive passage. The secret of *epiphora* then appears truly to reside in the iconic nature of intuitive passage.... Bachelard has taught us that the image is not a residue of impressions but an aura surrounding speech: 'The poetic image places us at the origin of the speaking being.' The poem gives birth to the image;...'it is at once a becoming of expression, and a becoming of our being. Here expression creates being....'[112]

Metaphoric strategy in relation to the sense of metaphor exemplified by the poetic work abolishes the literal use of language and turns language in upon itself. This allows for a suspension of reality by the reader in which the negative condition of *epoche* as a bracketing of ordinary reality enables the reader to realize a metamorphosis of language through the tension and interplay of near and far, of similarity within difference, until an insight into reality emerges.

Ricoeur's development of the philosophy of the imagination in relation to language is tied to the rule-governed character of metaphor, which clarifies the synthetic and mediating function of the imagination. The synthesis of the imagination in terms of metaphor is a bringing together of disparate semantic fields and production of iconic images through the poetic work of language. Metaphoric process substantiates the schematizing, augmentative function of the imagination as defined by Kant.

Ricoeur's account of the creative imagination in terms of metaphor as productive of new meaning opposes the classic view of the imagination as representational on the one hand or on the other as seductive, drawing the reader into a world of fantasy and escapism that is not ruled by reason. Instead Ricoeur's explication of the imagination and metaphor describes a bracketing of literal reference to reality, but in order to release new meaning. He compares the development of the philosophy of the imagination and language to parallel developments in the history of painting[113] and the shift from representational art to abstract art in which the images augment and heighten our sense of reality. Iconic images spell out, condense and develop reality, as opposed to the representational image that replicates what is. The strategy of metaphoric language has the potential to rework the parameters of reality and awaken new possibilities of existence.

Thus unlike the literary theorists, who interpret metaphoric language as retreating from reality and directed in upon itself,[114] Ricoeur turns from the metaphoric sense to its reference to reality. His development of the theory of metaphor and imagination distinguishes itself from the view that poetic language is a world unto itself cut off from reference to reality. According to Ricoeur the latter view buys into the positivist assumptions that limit reality to empirical verification.

> [T]he bound image introduces into the whole process an effect of neutralization, in a word a negative moment, thanks to which the entire phenomenon of reading is placed in a dimension of unreality, the neutralized atmosphere of fiction. The ultimate role of the image is not only to diffuse meaning across diverse sensorial fields, to *hallucinate* thought in some way, but on the contrary to effect a sort of *epoche* of the real, to suspend our attention to the real, to place us in a state of non-engagement with regard to perception or action, in short, to suspend meaning in the neutralized atmosphere to which one could give the name of the dimension of fiction. In this state of non-engagement we try new ideas, new values, new ways of being-in-the-world. Imagination is this free play of possibilities. In this state, fiction can...create a *redescription* of reality. But this positive function of fiction, of which the *epoche* is the negative condition, is only understood when the fecundity of the imagination is clearly linked to that of language, as exemplified by the metaphorical process.[115]

The referentiality of metaphor is taken up in "Study Seven" of the *Rule of Metaphor*. The question of referentiality becomes a hermeneutical problem we move from the level of the sentence to the literary work and a larger network of meaning.[116] In "Study Seven" Ricoeur develops the notion of split reference[117] to fill out the development of the poetic sense of metaphoric process in relation to its referentiality. At this stage the brackets of the metaphoric process are removed to raise the question of its capacity to express truth. Ricoeur makes use of Nelson Goodman's *Languages of Art*[118] and his argument that symbolic systems make and remake the world, that is the world in terms of works and works in terms of the world.[119] The referentiality of metaphor is compared to that of models used to develop scientific understanding and exploration of new terrain.

Ricoeur develops his notion of split reference of metaphor in a parallel fashion to the split sense of metaphor. A second level reference is built upon the ruins of literal reference, just as metaphoric sense is based upon the break from literal sense. The *epoche* of the metaphoric process releases a second order referentiality and projects a world. This second level reference Ricoeur designates as primordial reference, in keeping with Heidegger. It is non-descriptive reference.

> This reference is called second-order reference only with respect to the primacy of the reference of ordinary language. For, in another respect, it constitutes the primordial reference to the extent that it suggests, reveals, unconceals—or whatever you say—the deep structures of reality to which we are related as mortals who are born into this world and who *dwell* in it for a while.[120]

This notion of split reference is dependent upon the *epoche* of the metaphoric process, sustained through a poetic work of fiction. He defines the imagination in relation to the *epoche* of metaphoric process and split reference:

> My contention now is that one of the functions of imagination is to give a concrete dimension to the suspension or *epoche* proper to split reference. Imagination does not merely *schematize* the predicative assimilation between terms by its synthetic insight into similarities nor does it merely *picture* the sense thanks to the display of images aroused and controlled by the cognitive process. Rather, it contributes concretely to the *epoche* of ordinary reference and to the projection of new possibilities of redescribing the world.

In a sense, all *epoche* is the work of the imagination. Imagination is *epoche*.... What I do want to underscore is the solidarity between the *epoche* and the capacity to project new possibilities. Image as absence is the negative side of image as fiction. It is to this aspect of the image as fiction that is attached the power of symbolic systems to "remake" reality, to return to Goodman's idiom. But this productive and projective function of fiction can only be acknowledged if one sharply distinquishes it from the reproductive role of the so-called mental image which merely provides us with a re-presentation of things already perceived. Fiction addresses itself to deeply rooted potentialities of reality to the extent that they are absent from the actualities with which we deal in everyday life under the mode of empirical control and manipulation. In that sense, fiction presents under a concrete mode the split structure of the reference pertaining to the metaphorical statement. It both reflects and completes it.[121]

Ricoeur builds his argument for the power of fiction to redescribe our world by drawing a parallel with the function of models in science. The use of models is not simply an acessory or visual aid in science but a cognitive tool that facilitates the discovery of new connections and correlations.

He draws upon the work of Max Black and Mary Hesse.[122] Black distinguishes three different types of models: scale models, analogical models and theoretical models.[123] It is the latter two that exemplify the parallel between models and the metaphoric process at work in fiction. Interpretation of analogical models and theoretical models is guided by specific rules of correlation that facilitate intepreting one domain in relation to a less well known secondary domain. This parallels the predicative definition of metaphor Ricoeur has adopted, that it is an interaction between principal subject and secondary predicate which facilitates the production of an insight. On the larger scale of fiction, the plot acts like the model in projecting a world that offers a metamorphosis of the real through redescription.[124] As Mary Hesse notes the use of models enlarges our conception of reality, enabling us to recognize that reality is continually expanding. It opens the way both to the discovery and the invention of new realities.[125]

Ricoeur returns at this point to Aristotle's definition of *mimesis*, as the portrayal of active reality through the *muthos* of the plot of tragedy. The plot conveys the metaphoric process through its configuration of events, and the time structure illuminates a poeisis of reality. Through the fiction and its negation of ordinary reference as an epoche the reader enters into the play of new possibilities and sees reality as resignified. A world is projected that offers new information and in the case of great tragedy reveals primordial being in the Heideggerian sense. The split reference of the literary work involves a definition of truth as metaphorical truth. The metaphorical *is like* must be taken in unison with the literal *is not*.[126]

> [P]oetic language is no less *about* reality than any other use of language but refers to it by means of a complex strategy which implies, as an essential component, a suspension and seemingly an abolition of the ordinary reference attached to descriptive language. This suspension, however, is only the negative condition of a second order reference, of an indirect reference built on the ruins of the direct reference.[127]

The imagination is at the heart of the act of reading, as objectified in the text and as brought to life in the act of reading. Ricoeur defines the imagination as follows:

> First, imagination can be described as a rule-governed form of invention or, in other terms, as a norm-governed productivity.... Next the imagination can be considered...as the power of redescribing reality. Fiction is my name for the imagination considered under this double point of view of rule-governed invention and a power of redescription.[128]

His definition grants a cognitive status to the imagination, building on Kant's description of the imagination as the productive, schematizing imagination of *The Critique of Judgement*.[129] Ricoeur's definition is distinguished from Kant's by his attention to language. Through his theory of metaphor as a process of creating semantic innovations of meaning, he defines the imagination as a strategy of language for the creation of new meaning.

The theory of the imagination is shifted from a basis in perceptual experience toward a power of language for enacting new meaning.[130] A second way in which Ricoeur's definition of the imagination differs from the philosophical tradition is to link the imagination to works. As Ricoeur states: "imagination is

'productive' when thought is at work. Writing a poem, telling a story, constru-
ing...a plan or a strategy: these are the kinds of contexts of work which provide
a perspective to imagination and allow it to be 'productive'."[131]

Ricoeur's definition describes the imagination through language as a rule-
governed form of invention, in which works of the imagination require a transformation and play upon existing rules of language. The ruling source of
Ricoeur's philosophy of the imagination originates in his theory of metaphoric
process, which advances his earlier theory of the double intentionality of the
symbol.[132] To summarize metaphor, according to this theory, is not simply a
name or figure of speech as an ornament of language having no cognitive
content. Neither is it simply a word or phrase that can be substituted by another
word or phrase; rather metaphor for Ricoeur is a form of predication, not simply
denomination. The shortest unit of discourse for metaphor is the sentence, while
metaphoric process can be extended to larger works of language such as
narrative.[133] But metaphor requires a context of interaction of semantic networks
and it cannot be limited to the discrete substitution of one word for another. The
classic definition fails to explain its power to create new meaning. Metaphoric
process "is essentially an 'odd' predication that transgresses the semantic and
cultural codes of a speaking community."[134] Thus creativity does not occur in a
vacuum, but it is shaped in relation to the sedimented code of meaning which it
transgresses and changes. He accepts Aristotle's classic definition of metaphor
as "the ability to see similarity in difference",[135] but Ricoeur's theory of
metaphoric process renders dynamic this classic definition, through his definition
of metaphor as interaction and production of *epiphora* through the iconic image,
an image which is shaped by the verbal construction of coalescing disparate
semantic fields. As Ricoeur states:

> Consequently, to form an image is not to have an image, in the sense of having a
> mental representation; instead it is to read, through the icon of a relation, the relation
> itself. Image is less 'associated' than evoked and displayed by the schematization.
> Language remains the bearer of the predicative relation, but in schematizing and
> illustrating itself in a pictorial manner, the predicative relation can be read through the
> image in which it is invested. The seeing created by language is therefore not a seeing
> of this or that; it is a 'seeing as'. This 'seeing-as' has little to do with the Humean

image, image as the simple residue of an impression. To see-as is to apprehend the meaning alluded to in a display of regulated images.[136]

Thus the semantic innovations of metaphoric process and redescription emerge through a disciplined breaking of rules. Two examples of metaphoric process[137] are first, Ezra Pound's poem, "The Paris Metro":

> The apparition of these faces in the crowd
> Petals on a wet, black bough

and second Carl Sandburg's poem, "The Fog":

> The fog comes
> on little cat feet

Such examples illustrate that metaphor conveys new meaning in reference to reality, but this new meaning emerges from the ruins of literal predication.

Ricoeur applies his theory of metaphor to larger literary works, particularly fictional narrative. The form of predication at work in the narrative is realized through the plot, which structures and shapes the events of the story. As we have noted above, Ricoeur draws upon Aristotle's definition of tragedy as a *poiesis* of reality, which he interprets as reality resignified. The tragic plot captures a deeper and profounder sense of reality through its creative rendition of events. The plot acts as a heuristic model to reveal new ways of being-in-the-world. To tell and follow a story is already to reflect upon events and encompass their meaning in a larger whole:

> the metaphoric process starts from those traits of the plot which make the parable either tragic or comic, namely the movement 'downward' or 'upward' from *crisis* to *denouement*. In this way, any existential transparities which can be advocated later have to be rooted in the dramatic structure itself. It is this dramatic structure which *means* that the existence may be 'lost' or 'gained.' Existence, as it were, has to be redescribed according to the basic plot movments.[138]

Fiction allows for a bracketing of the ordinary world of the everyday, manipulable world and frees the reader to consider new ideas, new ways of being-in-the-world. In this state fiction demands of the reader a rethinking of the *status quo*. Ricoeur recognizes the counter pull of two categories, that is, ideology[139] versus utopia.[140] The former is invested in preserving the established identity of a culture and community through which social identity is realized. Ideology according to this definition is not necessarily negative, rather it serves a positive function of framing, for example, a nation's identity. Myth and folktale are examples of the sedimentation of ideology in narrative, integrating the beliefs of a society and expressing its identity.[141] On the other hand utopia is a genre of fiction that strives to re-envision the world and its possibilites and acts to subvert the status quo interpretations of ideology. At its extreme utopianism can lead to escapism and visions of false grandeur. Ideology tends to act as a model *of*, conforming to what is already actual, while utopa acts as a model *for*, opening up the field of the possible, serving the function of a hermeneutics of suspicion of the status quo.[142] As Ricoeur states:

> we are not able to take hold *directly* of the creative dimension of imagination. We become aware of it thanks to the interplay between ideology and utopia. And that means that we do not even directly grasp the genuine function of ideology as the power to provide us with an *image* of what we are, nor the originary function of utopia as the power of *otherness*. We are unable to face directly these powers. We have to deal with them through their caricatures. In that sense, cultural, social and political imagination finds its expression at the surface of history as the conflict between utopia and ideology.[143]

III

It is my thesis that Ricoeur's development of the theory of metaphor in relation to the imagination is key to his development of a critical hermeneutics that overcomes the limitations of Romantic hermeneutics and incorporates critique within the arc of the hermeneutic circle, in terms of a principle of creativity. In this final section I will refer mainly to *Interpretation Theory*,[144] the article, "*Mimesis* and Representation",[145] and pertinent sections of the first and third volumes of *Time and Narrative*[146] which draw out the implications of Ricoeur's development of the theory of metaphor and *mimesis* for his own definition of a theory of interpretation. Returning to the debate between Gadamer and Habermas, we will see that Ricoeur's dialectic of *mimesis*[147] both rectifies the limits of Gadamer's notion of distanciation and answers to the challenge of Habermas for critique.

The paradigm of Ricoeur's hermeneutics is the written text[148] and the dynamic of creativity that rules the functioning of metaphor and *mimesis* through the mediating and augmentative power of the imagination at work in fiction. His concern is the relation between speech and action, and the power of literature to transform action.[149]

Ricoeur, following the suggestion of the literary critic Monroe Beardsley, compares metaphor to a poem in miniature in which the rule of metaphor is applicable to the problem of interpreting texts, particularly fiction, viewed now from the perspective of the reader enacting the schema of the text. The semantic innovation of metaphor is comparable to the creative imitation of reality through the plot of mimesis. As Ricoeur states in *Time and Narrative*, volume one:

> With metaphor, the innovation lies in the producing of a new semantic pertinence by means of an impertinent attribution.... The metaphor is alive as long as we can perceive, through the new semantic pertinence—and so to speak its denseness—the resistance of the words in their ordinary use and therefore their incompatibility at the level of literal interpretation of the sentence.... With narrative, the semantic innovation lies in the inventing of another work of synthesis—plot. By means of the plot, goals, causes, and chance are brought together within the temporal unity of a whole and complete action. It is this synthesis of the heterogeneous that brings narrative close to metaphor. In both cases, the new thing—the as yet unsaid, the unwritten—springs up in language. Here a living metaphor, that is, a new pertinence in the predication, there a feigned plot, that is, a new congruence in the organization of events. In both cases the semantic innovation can be carried back to the productive imagination and, more precisely, to the schematism that is its signifying matrix.[150]

Ricoeur explicates the process of interpretation as a series of dialectics. The primary dialectic is between the text and the reader rather than between the author and the reader. This polarity is opposed to the Romantic definition of the hermeneutics of Schleiermacher and Dilthey, which focussed upon the author and a replication of the author's creativity through the empathetic imagination.

The text, like metaphor, is consistent with his theory of discourse. The text as a larger work of language fulfills the polarity between event and meaning, sense and reference that applies to metaphor. The written text objectifies the meaning in an enduring form. It lacks the dialogical situation of the speaker and hearer. The written text is separate from its author, situation and original audience. It brings out a level of distanciation that exists in speech in a more concrete form through its passage from speech to a written work. The autonomy of the text opens it to an infinite series of readings. As Ricoeur states:

> writing renders the text autonomous with respect to the intention of the author. What the text signifies no longer coincides with what the author meant; henceforth, textual meaning and psychological meaning have different destinies.... An essential characteristic of a literary work, and a work of art in general, is that it transcends its own psycho-sociological conditions of production and thereby opens itself to an unlimited series of readings, themselves situated within different socio-cultural conditions. In short, the text must be able, from the sociological as well as the psychological point of view, to 'decontextualize' itself in such a way that it can be 'recontextualized' in new —accomplished, precisely, by the act of reading. [151]

The text as a work of language is structured and follows the rules of a particular literary genre, for example the poem, essay or novel. Its reality is not static; rather its meaning is generated through the act of reading that follows and enacts the rules that govern the work. "Interpretation is grasping the non-ostensive references of the text."[152] Ricoeur's focus is upon fiction and mimesis as a poiesis of reality that constructively mediates reality. The style of a work sets it apart from the general category of genre and defines its uniqueness, as a particular creation.[153] Unlike Romantic hermeneutics the task of interpretation is not to get behind the text to the mind of the author. Rather the task of interpretation is directed outward in front of the text and to a realization of the projected world of the text. The imagination as correlated to metaphor and mimesis rules the dialectic of the text and the reader. Ricoeur's definition of the imagination in relation to the strategy of metaphoric process and its projection of a world overcomes the Romantic emphasis upon the psychology of the imagination and the replication of the creativity of the author behind the text. It also sustains the Romantic claims for the power of poetic language to express new meaning.

Ricoeur's theory of interpretation incorporates Aristotle's emphasis upon the probable from *The Rhetoric* and his notion of *techne*[154] from the *Nicomochean Ethics*, insofar as the act of interpretation, while rule-governed is closer to *techne* than *episteme*. The act of interpretation encompasses a dialectic between understanding/explanation/understanding, in which understanding allows the reader to gain a sense of the whole of the text in relation to its parts. Explanation[155] is directed at an explication of the structure of the text, assessing its genre and the code of the literary paradigms that underlie it, particularly in relation to deciphering its plot. The reader approaches the text from the limits of a particular perspective or onesidedness[156] and through the dialectic of understanding and explanation enacts the most probable interpretation. Ricoeur distinguishes between the validity versus the verity of interpretation. The latter position he identifies with the absolutism of authoritarian systems. Instead his theory of interpretation, which concentrates on the problems of plurivocal texts, answers to a principle of validity in relation to criteria of congruence, that is an interpretation that accounts for the greatest number of factors and plenitude that allows for the fullest meaning of the text.[157] Understanding follows explanation dialectically enacting the structure of the text toward a new event of meaning and the actualization of its non-ostensive references. Understanding and explanation are complementary stages in the process of interpretation. As Ricoeur states:

> the term interpretation may be applied, not to a particular case of understanding, that of the written expressions of life, but to the whole process that encompasses explanation and understanding. Interpretation as the dialectic of explanation and understanding or comprehension may then be traced back to the initial stages of interpretative behavior already at work in conversation. And while it is true that only writing and literary composition provide a full development of this dialectic, interpretation must not be referred to as a province of understanding. It is not described by a kind of object—'inscribed' signs in the most general sense of the term—but by a kind of process; the dynamic of interpretative reading.[158]

If explanation is isolated from the two stages of understanding it is reduced to a mere abstraction. In *Interpretation Theory*, (which was published prior to *The Rule of Metaphor* and *Time and Narrative*), Ricoeur attempted to adapt structuralism to a definition of explanation that is adequate to the human sciences in terms of the rules that govern language; but in the article "*Mimesis* and Representation", he leaves structuralism behind,[159] since it is not in keeping with the dynamic of language which his theory of metaphor and *mimesis* develops, particularly the temporality of narrative. Structuralism separates language from its reference to reality and instead argues for a set of grammatical codes as revealing the paradigmatic structure of a literary work. The plot of narrative is considered a surface phenomenon, while for Ricoeur plot, building upon the dynamic theory of discourse as opposed to semiotic structuralism, is fundamental to the functioning of mimesis and its power to project a world.

The crystallization of Ricoeur's theory of interpretation is his notion of threefold *mimesis* that parallels Gadamer's notion of historical efficacy. Ricoeur develops this concept of *mimesis* in the article, "*Mimesis* and Representation", and expands upon it in volume one of *Time and Narrative*, works which follow *The Rule of Metaphor*. This dialectic of threefold *mimesis* is defined in reference to action, that is from a prefigured world of the text ($mimesis_1$) to the configured world of the text ($mimesis_2$) to a transfigured world ($mimesis_3$).[160] The notion of dialectic emphasizes continuity with the structures of understanding that preface and follow the moment of rupture and discontinuity represented by the text. Thus $mimesis_2$ is the focus of explanation in the dialectic of understanding/ explanation/understanding.

$Mimesis_2$ is the key to the process of mediation that rules the dialectic between the "text" and the "reader". Ricoeur defines $Mimesis_1$ as the pre-understanding of action that frames the possiblity of writing and reading fiction which makes possible its relation to our world and self-understanding. $Mimesis_1$ is analogous to Gadamer's notion of "belonging", while $Mimesis_3$ corresponds to Gadamer's notion of the fusion of horizons and refers to the downstream of the process of mediation in light of the fact that $Mimesis_3$ opens up new ways of understanding ourselves, our world, and our actions.

*Mimesis*₃ takes up the intersection between the world of the text and the world of the reader.

Ricoeur works to overcome the notion of the inside/outside of the text and the tendency of this conception to support a representational view of reality. The "reader" mediates the dialectic from *Mimesis*₁ to *Mimesis*₂ to *Mimesis*₃ as a concrete process that is itself an act of *mimesis* through the process of reading and remains at the level of praxis.[161] Aristotle's definition of *mimesis* is fundamental to this process, no longer as an imitation of reality in the sense of a copy, but as capturing the real as act through the plot.

*Mimesis*₁[162] describes the prefiguration of the world insofar as we are implicated already in narrative and a context of stories that we do not control, but into which we are thrown. The traits of *Mimesis*₁ are that there is a narrative quality to experience through which we experience reality and a repertoire of actions and common meaning through which we understand the narrativity of the context into which we are thrown. As Ricoeur states:

> *mimesis*₁ is this pre-understanding of what human action is, of its semantics, its symbolism, its temporality. From this pre-understanding which is common to poets and their readers arises fiction, and with fiction comes the second form of *mimesis* which is textual and literary...under the rule of fiction the pre-understanding of the world of action withdraws to the rank of being a 'repertory,' to speak as W. Iser does in his *The Act of Reading*...but it remains true that despite the break it introduces, fiction would never be understandable if it did not configurate what is already figured in human action.[163]

*Mimesis*₂[164] refers to the textual, literary work of fiction and its configuration of action through the plot of the narrative. The plot of fiction is analogous to the metaphoric process of the sentence through which the innovation of meaning emerges. The plot is the configuring act of the productive imagination, which brings the succession of events into a whole, and is analogous to the interaction of semantic fields at the level of metaphor as a poem in miniature. The plot also fulfills the second trait of metaphor as the schema that acts as an icon to augment the imitation of action. It gives a structure to temporality that reveals through the configuration of events the projection of a world. The plot makes sense of the events through integrating them in a synthetic fashion that conjoins them in other than linear time. Their integration exemplifies Kant's notion of judgment as drawing events together in a whole.

Gaps and discordances of time are made productive through the act of emplotment as a work of the productive imagination. As Ricoeur states:

> This (productive imagination) must be understood not as a psychologizing faculty but as a transcendental one. The productive imagination is not only rule-governed, it constitutes the generative matrix of rules. In Kant's first *Critique*, the categories of the understanding are first schematized by the productive imagination. The schematism has this power because the productive imagination fundamentally has a synthetic function. It connects understanding and intuition by engendering syntheses that are intellectual and intuitive at the same time. Emplotment, too, engenders a mixed intelligibility between what has been called the point, theme, or thought of a story, and the intuitive presentation of circumstances, characters, episodes, and changes of fortune that make up the denouement. In this way, we may speak of the schematism of the narrative function.[165]

Mimesis₂ breaks then with the everyday world of pre-understanding and creates a quasi-thing, an *epoche* that allows the reader to try out new ways of seeing and comprehending. This bracketing is not a route to escape from reality but a way to a fuller understanding and augmentation of the real.

The production of plot by the schematizing imagination attends to the rules of the history of narrative combinations. Ricoeur refers to the typology of Northrop Frye's *Anatomy of Criticism*,[166] which describes the range of narratives that arise from the tradition of western literature. These categories are not derived from an abstract code, in the fashion of Greimas's structural analysis of narrative. The structuralist analysis disregards the significance of plot.[167] Ricoeur prefers Frye's typology because it is based upon the organic rules of a living tradition. The schematism of the transcendental imagination and its rules are observed through their objectification in narrative genres, but it is not possible to abstract from narrative and reach the imagination directly. Thus Ricoeur follows Kant here rather than Heidegger.

> This productive imagination is not without its own rules and it lends itself to the type of typology of emplotment used by Northrop Frye in his *Anatomy of Criticism*. This

typology of emplotment cannot be derived from a logic of narrative possibilities which has to be ascribed to a second degree form of rationalization. The typology of emplotment arises rather from a schematism of the narrative function, from which derives the categorical order semioticians use in their constructions, with the help of a logic that is unaware of the transcendental genesis of this schematism of emplotment...this schematism...does not share the atemporality of the logical and syntactical laws which the semioticians appeal to. Instead, this schematism is constituted within a history, a history that has all the characteristics of a *tradition*. By this, I do not mean the inert transmission of some dead deposit but the living transmission of an innovation that is always capable of being reactivated through a return to the most creative moments of poetic making[168]

The creation of innovative works of fiction as innovative deviates from the established rules of emplotment and configures time in such a way as to heighten the gaps rather than conform to the given perspective on chronological time. Through innovation new genres and schemas of emplotment arise. But innovation is constituted nonetheless in relation to a repertoire.

Folktales, myths, and the traditional narratives in general stand close to the pole of repetition...as soon as we move beyond such traditional narrative, deviance and a gap or separation becomes the rule...This play with the constraints of paradigms is what provides emplotment with its historicity. As a background to such play, the combining of sedimentation and invention defines traditionality as such, on the basis of which we obey the models or experiment with them.[169]

Thus Ricoeur describes a dialectic between sedimentation and innovation that defines the basis of a living tradition.[170] There is no innovation without the paradigms of the history of literature and its typologies of emplotment. The paradigms are born from the history of the productive imagination and they are the product of previous innovation of established forms.

It remains, however, that the possibility of deviation is inscribed in the relation between sedimented paradigms and actual works. Short of the extreme case of schism, it is just the opposite of servile application. Rule-governed deformation constitutes the axis around which the various changes of paradigm through application are arranged. It is this variety of application that confers a history on the productive imagination and that, in counterpoint to sedimentation, makes a narrative tradition possible. This is the final enrichment by which the relationship of narrative time is augmented at the level of *mimesis* $_2$.[171]

Mimesis$_3$ denotes the intersection of the world of the text and the world of the reader, which Gadamer refers to as the fusion of horizons. It is at this stage that the subversive power of fiction to question the *status quo* and critique the established norms is most fully released. Ricoeur objects to the position that views literature as entertainment or as a self-contained aesthetic work with no reference to reality. "Fiction is precisely what makes language that supreme 'danger,' about which Walter Benjamin spoke with such awe and admiration, following Holderlin."[172]

This intersection between the configured world of the text and the transfigured world of the reader is a complex problematic. The configuration of the text may point to a confirmation of ideology and the norm or a critique of ideology. Like metaphor it depends upon whether the individual work of fiction is constructed towards innovation and a deviance from the accepted paradigms of the tradition.

The act of reading is decisive for actualizing the "sketch" of the text and is guided by the productive imagination at work in the plot. Emplotment has been defined as an act of judgment[173] and as an act of the productive imagination it is the conjoint achievement of the text and the reader. The reader accesses and enacts the interplay between sedimentation and innovation. The hermeneutics of suspicion works both ways, that is the text as innovative can give to the reader new ways of being in the world, or the reader can question the static quality of the work and its reenforcement of established ideology. As Ricoeur states:

> In the act of reading, the recipient plays with the narrative constraints, brings about the deviations, takes part in the fight between the novel and the anti-novel...it is the reader who completes the work insofar as, following Roman Ingarden and Wolfgang Iser, we say the written work is a sketch for the reader. Indeed, the written work may involve holes, lacunae, and indeterminate zones which, as in Joyce's *Ulysses*, defy the reader's capacity to configure the work which the author seemingly finds mischievous pleasure in defiguring. In this extreme case, it is the reader, whom the work almost abandons, who bears the burden of emplotment.... So I maintain that the act of

reading is that operation that conjoins *mimesis₃* to *mimesis₁* through *mimesis₂*. It is the final vector of the transfiguration of the world of action in terms of fiction.[174]

Mimesis₂ through the configuration of the plot forges a non-descriptive referential dimension, in which reality is augmented, magnified and increased. The notion of the real in keeping with this projection of new ways of being is not the given, but the invented, the real as act. The process of interpretation follows the principles of congruence and plenitude, and its validity is probable. The univocity of truth is exploded at the level of *mimesis₃* as well as the representational illusion. Ricoeur rejoins here the Heideggerian notion of truth as manifestation rather than as verification. As Ricoeur puts it:

> the univocity of truth is also exploded by *mimesis*.... Is it not the model of truth as adequation, the accomplice of the representative illusion, that blocks our way? I do admit, however, that we lack a sufficiently multivocal concept of truth, one that would fuse, at its margins, with the concept of rightness. It is not even certain that Heidegger's substitution of truth as manifestation for truth as adequation responds to what *mimesis* demands of our thinking about truth. *Mimesis*, in this sense, is ahead of our concepts of reference, the real, and truth. It thus engenders a need as yet unfulfilled to think more.[175]

Let us review now the success of Ricoeur's agenda to mediate the debate between Gadamer and Habermas that was sketched at the beginning of this chapter. As we stated above Gadamer's historical hermeneutics rejects the incorporation of critique within the hermeneutic circle, since he identifies it with positivism, and the alienation of distanciation he equates with the objectivism of the natural sciences, which hindered Dilthey's development of hermeneutics. Gadamer overturns the latter position by phenomenologically establishing the ontological priority of "belonging" as historicity over the differentiation of subject and object. Ricoeur's development of hermeneutics in relation to metaphor and *mimesis* establishes a productive notion of distanciation, that is not borrowed from the nineteenth century definition of natural science, but which emerges from within language and is supported by his theory of discourse as the polarity between event and meaning, sense and reference. In particular it is the distanciation of poetic discourse that Ricoeur's theory of metaphor and *mimesis* recovers. Ricoeur's definition of the dialectic of *mimesis₁*, *mimesis₂* and *mimesis₃* serves as a counterpart to Gadamer's notion of historical efficacy, in that *mimesis₂*, as a stage of productive distanciation, is conjoined to Gadamer's notion of "belonging" and enriches Gadamer's notion of the fusion of horizons by linking it to *mimesis₃* as mediated and transfigured by *mimesis₂*. Through the stage of *mimesis₂* this dialectic draws out the productive distanciation of the text in terms of the dynamic of emplotment and its capacity to augment reality through the configuration of the plot. The epoche of *mimesis₂* allows for a bracketing from the every-day and a transformation and critique of our ways of being. The critical moment is the fusion of the horizon of the world of the text with the world of the reader, since the stage of *mimesis₃* addresses the text's ethical and political implications for renewed actions. Ricoeur thus argues through the correlation of the productive imagination with *mimesis* for a complementarity between explanation and understanding as stages of a dialectic.

He incorporates the Heideggerian notion of temporality as the anticipatory structure of understanding, that projects a world through the play of the rule-governed creativity of the emplotment of literary works. The depth hermeneutics that Heidegger hints at is given flesh through Ricoeur's correlation between the subversive power of the imagination and works of fiction, which display new ways of being in the world. Thus Ricoeur also overcomes the limitations of Romanticism's definition of the imagination and retrieve's Romanticism's recognition of poetic texts. At the same time this notion of distanciation as exemplified by poetic texts answers to Habermas's call for a critique of ideology, but in terms of the subversive power of the imagination to project new ways of being in the world through the anticipatory structure of understanding. As Ricoeur states:

> we introduce a critical theme which the hermeneutics of tradition tends to cast beyond
> its frontiers. The critical theme was nevertheless present in the Heideggerian analysis
> of understanding. Recall how Heidegger conjoins the notion of 'the projection of my
> ownmost possibilities'; this signifies that the mode of being of the world opened up
> by the text is the mode of the possible, or better of the power-to-be: therein resides
> the subversive force of the imaginary. The paradox of poetic reference consists

precisely in the fact that reality is redescribed only insofar as discourse is raised to fiction.

A hermeneutics of the power-to-be thus turns itself towards a critique of ideology, of which it constitutes the most fundamental possibility. Distanciation, at the same time, emerges at the heart of reference: poetic discourse distances itself from everyday reality, aiming towards being as power-to-be.[176]

Ricoeur cautions against a schism between ideology and utopia for while emphasizing innovation he affirms the necessity of memory and tradition as the ground of creativity and eschatology. Utopian expectations can hinder us from action and lead us to despair through the projection of the illusion of an absolute ideal that is unrealizable. Instead Ricoeur advocates the practical power of expectations that are finite and relatively modest, which will invite responsible commitment over the distance to rectify suffering. Yet he also cautions in his dialectical fashion:

we must also resist any narrowing of the space of experience. To do this, we must struggle against the tendency to consider the past only from the angle of what is done, unchangeable and past. We have to reopen the past, to revivify its unaccomplished, cut-off—even slaughtered possibilities...these are two faces of one and the same task, for only determinate expectations can have the retroactive effect on the past of revealing it as a living tradition.[177]

In this chapter I have argued that Ricoeur's definition of a critical hermeneutics is advanced through his development of the philosophy of the productive imagination in terms of his theory of metaphor and *mimesis*. Unlike the hermeneutics of Schleirmacher and Dilthey, in which case the focus was upon the author and a replication of the creativity behind the text, with Ricoeur's development the focus is upon the text. The task of the reader is to actualize the rule-governed creativity of the text and its metamorphosis of reality through the world of the text. It is the *epoche* of fiction that allows for a distanciation from the everyday through an augmentation of reality that has the power to project new ways of being in the world. In this way Ricoeur incorporates a distanciation into the arc of the hermeneutic circle that is productive of meaning and complementary to Gadamer's definition of belonging. The imagination is the creative element that defines the axis of interpretation by actualizing the rule-governed deviations of the text that configure, magnify and augment reality to reveal the depth of temporality through the schematism of narrative. Heidegger's phenomenology of time is correlated to its indirect expression in the emplotment of narrative. My focus has been limited to explicating the role of the philosophy of the imagination in Ricoeur's development of hermeneutics, particularly its subversive and innovative function at the service of critique. The latter problem is subordinate to the larger thesis of Ricoeur's work *Time and Narrative* which proposes a dialectic between the poetics of narrativity and the aporetics of the phenomenology of time.

ENDNOTES OF CHAPTER FOUR

[1]Paul Ricoeur, "Hermeneutics and the Critique of Ideology", in *Hermeneutics and the Human Sciences*, trans. and ed. John B. Thompson (Cambridge: Cambridge University Press, 1981), pp. 63-100; also see Ricoeur, "Ethics and Culture: Habermas and Gadamer in Dialogue", trans. David Pellauer *Philosophy Today*, 17 (1973), 153-165, and "Ideology, Utopia, Faith", in *Protocol of the Colloquy of the Center for Hermeneutical Studies*, 17 (1981), pp. 21-28.

[2]Ricoeur, "My Relation to the History of Philosophy", *Iliff Review*, 35 (1978), p. 10.

[3]Ricoeur, "The Task of Hermeneutics", in *Hermeneutics and the Human Sciences*, p. 60; also see Hans-Georg Gadamer, *Truth and Method*, (London: Sheed and Ward, 1975).

[4]Ricoeur, "Phenomenology and Hermeneutics", in *Hermeneutics and the Human Sciences*, p. 106.

[5]Ricoeur, "Hermeneutics and the Critique of Ideology", p. 66.

[6]Ibid., p. 90 ff.; also see "The Hermeneutical Function of Distanciation", in *Hermeneutics and the Human Sciences*, pp. 131-132.

[7]Ibid., p. 67.

[8]Ibid., p. 68.

[9]"The Task of Hermeneutics", p. 49.

[10]"Hermeneutics and the Critique of Ideology", pp. 68-69.

[11]"The Task of Hermeneutics", p. 60.

[12]"Hermeneutics and the Critique of Ideology", p. 67.

[13]Ibid., p. 73.

[14]"The Task of Hermeneutics", p. 60.

[15]Ibid.

[16]"Hermeneutics and the Critique of Ideology", p. 78.

[17]"My Relation to the History of Philosophy", p. 12; also see "Imagination in Discourse and in Action", *Analecta Husserliana*, 7 (1978), pp. 3-22 and "Explanation and Understanding: On Some Remarkable Connections Among the Theory of the Text, Theory of Action, and Theory of History", trans. Charles E. Reagan and David Stewart in *The Philosophy of Paul Ricoeur: An Anthology of His Work* (Boston: Beacon Press, 1978), pp. 97-108

[18]"Hermeneutics and the Critique of Ideology", p. 78; also see Jurgen Habermas, *Knowledge and Human Interests*, trans. Jeremy Shapiro (London: Heineman, 1972).

[19]Ibid., p. 80.

[20]Ibid., p. 85.

[21]Ibid., pp. 86-87.

[22]Ibid., p.87.

[23]Ibid.

[24]Ibid., pp. 86-87.

[25]Ibid., p. 87.

[26]Ibid.

[27]Ibid., p. 88.

[28]Ibid., p. 93.

[29]Ibid.

[30]Ibid. pp. 94-95.

[31]Ricoeur, *The Symbolism of Evil*, trans. Emerson Buchanan (Boston: Beacon Press, 1967), pp. 10-18.

[32]"Hermeneutics and the Critique of Ideology", pp. 89-90.

[33]Ricoeur quotes from Martin Heidegger, *Being and Time*, trans. John Macquarries and Edward Robinson (Oxford: Basil Blackwell, 1962), p. 195 in "Hermeneutics and the Critique of Ideology", p. 88.

[34]Ibid., p. 90.

[35]Ibid., p. 93.

[36]Ibid.

[37]"The Task of Hermeneutics", in reference to Ricoeur's interpretation of Heidegger's position on language see p. 58, and in reference to Ricoeur's comments on Gadamer's position on language see p. 62.

[38]"Hermeneutics and the Critique of Ideology", p. 92.

[39]Ibid., pp. 90, 93.

[40]Ibid., p. 91.

[41]Ibid., p. 92.

[42]Ibid., p. 93.

[43]Ibid., p. 94.

[44]Ibid., pp. 99-100. As Ricoeur states: "This tradition is not perhaps the same as Gadamer's; it is perhaps that of the *Aufklarung,* whereas Gadamer's would be Romanticism. But it is a tradition nonetheless, the tradition of emancipation rather than of recollection. Critique is also a tradition. I would say that it plunges into the most impressive tradition, that of liberating acts, of the Exodus and the Resurrection ...nothing is more deceptive than the alleged antimony between an ontology of prior understanding and an eschatology of freedom...as if it were necessary to choose between reminiscence and hope."

[45]Ricoeur, *The Rule of Metaphor*, trans. Robert Czerny with Kathleen McLaughlin and John Costello, S.J. (Toronto: University of Toronto Press, 1977).

[46]Pierre Fontanier, *Les Figures du Cours,* (Paris: Flammarion, 1830).

[47]Ricoeur, "From Existentialism to the Philosophy of Language", *Criterion* 10 (1971), pp. 14-18.

[48]Aristotle, *The Rhetoric* (New York: Random House Modern Library, 1954).

[49]Aristotle, *The Poetics* (New York: Random House Modern Library, 1954).

[50]Heidegger, *Early Greek Thinking*, trans. David Farrell Krell and Frank A. Capuzzi (New York: Harper and Row, 1975).

[51]*The Rule of Metaphor*, p. 46.

[52]*The Poetics*, 1457 b 6-9.

[53]Ibid., 1459 a 3-8; also see *The Rhetoric* 1412 a 10.

[54] *The Rule of Metaphor*, p. 17.

[55] Ibid., p. 18.

[56] Ibid., p. 21.

[57] Ibid., p. 22.

[58] Ibid.

[59] Ibid., p. 35, pp. 42-43.

[60] Ibid., pp. 28-29.

[61] Ibid., p. 38.

[62] Ibid., p. 11.

[63] Ibid., p. 28.

[64] Ibid., pp. 11-12.

[65] Aristotle, *Nicomachean Ethics*, trans. Martin Ostwald (Indianapolis: Library of Liberal Arts, 1962).

[66] Ibid., p. 28.

[67] Ibid., p. 330, n. 30, *Nicomachean Ethics*, 1140 a 6-16.

[68] Ibid., p. 30, in *The Rhetoric*, 1355 b 25, 1356 a 19-20.

[69] Ibid., pp. 27-35.

[70] Ibid., p. 32.

[71] Ibid., p. 27, and in *The Rhetoric*, 1412 a 18-24.

[72] Ibid., p. 12.

[73]Ibid., p. 40.

[74]Ibid., p. 39.

[75]Ibid.

[76]Ibid., pp. 42-43.

[77]Ibid.

[78]Ibid., p. 43.

[79]Ricoeur, "Ontologie" in *Encyclopaedia universalis* XII (Paris, 1972), p. 95.

[80]"The Function of Fiction in Shaping Reality", *Man and the World*, 12 (1979), p. 125.

[81]*The Rule of Metaphor*, p. 43.

[82]Ibid., p. 67; also see Ricoeur, *Interpretation Theory* (FortWorth: Texas Christian University, 1976), pp. 6-8, and M. H. Abrams, *A Glossary of Literary Terms* (New York: Holt, Rinehart and Winston, 1981), pp. 187-190, for a definition of structuralism.

[83]Ibid., p. 67; also see *Interpretation Theory*, p. 8, as Ricoeur states: "Semantics the science of the sentence, is immediately concerned with the concept of sense...to the extent that semantics is fundamentally defined by the integrative procedures of language".

[84]Ibid., pp. 65-66.

[85]Ibid., p. 74.

[86]I.A. Richards, *The Philosophy of Rhetoric* (Oxford, Oxford University Press, 1971).

[87]Max Black, *Models and Metaphors* (Ithaca: Cornell University, 1962).

[88]Monroe C. Beardsley, *Aesthetics* (New York: Harcourt, Brace and World, 1958); "The Metaphorical Twist", *Philosophy and Phenomenological Research*, 22 (1967), pp. 293-307.

[89] *The Rule of Metaphor*, pp. 78-79, Ricoeur is quoting from Richards's *The Philosophy of Rhetoric*, p. 55.

[90] Ibid., p. 80.

[91] Ibid.

[92] Ibid., p. 85; also see Black, *Models and Metaphors*, p. 47, note 23.

[93] Ibid.

[94] Ibid., pp. 86-87.

[95] Ibid., p. 87; also see Black, pp. 40-41.

[96] Algirdas Julien Greimas, *Semantique structurale, Recherche de methode* (Paris: Larousse, 1966) and *Du Sens: Essais semiotiques* (Paris: Editions de Seuil, 1970).

[97] Ibid., pp. 94-95; also see Beardsley, p. 138.

[98] Ibid., p. 95.

[99] Ibid.

[100] Ibid., p. 96, as Ricoeur states, quoting Beardsley: "We now see in what sense 'the explication of a metaphor is a model of all explication' (144). An entire logic of explication is put into play in the activity of constructing meaning. Two principles regulating this logic can now be transposed from the microcosm to the macrocosm, from the metaphor to the poem. The first is a principle of 'fittingness,' of congruence: it has to do with 'deciding which of the modifier's connotations can *fit* the subject' (144)."

[101] Ibid.

[102] Ibid.

[103] Ibid., pp. 98-99.

[104] Ibid., p. 99.

[105]Ibid., p. 189; also see *Interpretation Theory*, pp. 40-43.

[106]"Imagination in Discourse and Action", p. 5.

[107]Ibid.

[108]Ibid., p. 212.

[109]Ibid.

[110]Ibid.

[111]Ibid., p. 213.

[112]Ibid., pp. 214-215. Gaston Bachelard, *The Poetics of Space*, trans. Maria Jolas (Boston: Beacon Press, 1969).

[113]*Interpretation Theory*, p. 41.

[114]*The Rule of Metaphor*, p. 6.

[115]"The Function of Fiction in Shaping Reality", *Man and the World*, 12 (1979), p. 134.

[116]*The Rule of Metaphor*, p. 6.

[117]Ibid., p. 7.

[118]Nelson Goodman, *Languages of Art: An Approach to a Theory of Symbols* (Indianapolis: Bobbs-Merrill, 1968). Also see, *The Rule of Metaphor*, pp. 231-234.

[119]*The Rule of Metaphor*, pp. 231-234.

[120]"The Metaphorical Process as Cognition, Imagination, and Feeling", *Critical Inquiry*, 1 (1978), p. 153.

[121]Ibid., pp. 154-155.

[122]Mary Hesse, "The Explanatory Function of Metaphor", appendix to *Models and Analogies in Science* (Notre Dame: Notre Dame University Press, 1966).

[123]Ibid.

[124]"The Function of Fiction in Shaping Reality", p. 141.

[125]*The Rule of Metaphor*, p. 306.

[126]Ibid., p. 255.

[127]"The Metaphorical Process", p. 153.

[128]"The Bible and the Imagination", in *The Bible as a Document of the University*, ed. Hans Dieter Betz (Chico: Scholars Press, 1979), pp. 49-50.

[129]Ibid., p. 50.

[130]"The Metaphorical Process", p. 148.

[131]"The Function of Fiction in Shaping Reality", p. 128.

[132]Interpretation Theory, pp. 53-56, 69, as Ricoeur states:"the metaphorical functioning of language...allows us to do justice to... [a] trait of symbols, which is obstinately emphasized by their defenders, yet for which they lack the key. We readily concede that a symbol cannot be exhaustively treated by conceptual language, that there is more in the symbol than in any of its equivalents; a trait which is eagerly embraced by the opponents of conceptual thinking. For them, one must choose; either the symbol or the concept. But metaphor theory leads to a different conclusion. It shows how new possibilities for articulating and conceptualizing reality can arise through an assimilation of hitherto separated semantic fields. Far from being a part of conceptual thinking, such semantic innovation marks the emergence of thought. This is why the theory of symbols is led into the neighborhood of the Kantian theory of the schematism and conceptual synthesis by the theory of metaphor. There is no need to deny the concept in order to admit that symbols give rise to an endless exegesis."(56-57) And further "there is more in the metaphor than in the symbol in the sense that it brings to language the implicit semantics of the symbol. What remains confused in the symbol—the assimilation of one thing to another, and of us to things;...is clarified in the tension of the metaphorical utterance"(69) and its explication of semantic innovation.

[133]*The Rule of Metaphor*, p. 243.

[134]"The Bible and the Imagination", p. 66.

[135]*The Rule of Metaphor*, p. 23.

[136]"The Function of Fiction in Shaping Reality", p. 133.

[137]These examples are quoted by Northrop Frye in *The Great Code: The Bible and Literature* (Toronto: Academic Press Canada, 1982), pp. 56-57.

[138]"Biblical Hermeneutics", *Semeia*, 4 (1975), p. 98.

[139]"Ideology, Utopia, and Faith", p. 23.

[140]Ibid.

[141]"Mimesis and Representation", *Annals of Scholarship: Metastudies of the Humanities and Social Sciences*, 21 (1981), p. 25.

[142]"Ideology, Utopia, and Faith", p. 25.

[143]Ibid., p. 28.

[144]See note 82.

[145]See note 141.

[146]*Time and Narrative*, Vol. 1, trans. Kathleen McLaughlin and David Pellauer (Chicago: University of Chicago Press, 1983). I will limit my attention to Chapter Three: "Time and Narrative: Threefold *Mimesis*", pp. 52-87, in which Ricoeur expands upon the article "*Mimesis* and Representation". I will bracket consideration of Ricoeur's discussion of the relation between history and fiction, since it is beyond the scope of this thesis. My thesis is limited to the question of Ricoeur's development of the philosophy of the imagination in relation to his theory of metaphor and *mimesis* and its implications for the development of a critical hermeneutics. In *Time and Narrative*, Vol. 3, trans. Kathleen McLaughlin and David Pellauer (Chicago: University of Chicago Press, 1989), I will refer only to Chapter 10: "Towards a Hermeneutics of Historical Consciousness" insofar as it is relevant to his mediation of the debate between Gadamer and Habermas. I am moreover bracketing

altogether reference to *Time and Narrative*, Vol. 2, trans. Kathleen Mclaughlin and David Pellauer (Chicago: University of Chicago Press, 1984) and Ricoeur's discussion of the configuration of time in fictional narrative, since it lends itself to the larger discussion that structures the overall theme of the three volumes, that is, the problem of the circularity and exchange between narrative and time.

[147]"*Mimesis* and Representation", p. 17.

[148]"Metaphor and the Main Problem of Hermeneutics", *New Literary History*, 6(1974-75), 95-110. "The Hermeneutical Function of Distanciation", p. 131. *Interpretation Theory*, see "Speaking and Writing", pp. 25-44.

[149]"*Mimesis* and Representation", p. 30.

[150]*Time and Narrative*, Vol. 1, pp. ix-x.

[151]"Hermeneutical Function of Distanciation", p. 138.

[152]*Interpretation Theory*, p. 94.

[153]"Hermeneutical Function of Distanciation", p. 137.

[154]Ibid., p. 136; also see *Interpretation Theory*, p. 77.

[155]"Explanation and Understanding", pp. 164-166. Ricoeur struggles to relate structuralism dialectically to the advances of his development of the theory of metaphor and *mimesis*. But his later work shows a shift away from structuralism (for example A. J. Greimas) toward the literary theorist, Northrop Frye since his work lends itself to a more organic description of the genres of western literature, which serve as a kind of grammatical code to the generation of new forms through a dialectic of sedimentation and innovation. Structuralism is a poor aid to Ricoeur because it adheres to positivist presuppositions that deny the referentiality of literature. Also see "*Mimesis* and Representation", pp. 22-25.

[156]*Interpretation Theory*, p. 75.

[157]Ibid., pp. 78-89.

[158]Ibid., p. 74.

[159]"*Mimesis* and Representation", pp. 22-23.

[160]Ibid., pp. 16-17.

[161]Ibid., pp. 17-18.

[162]Ibid., pp. 18-20.

[163]Ibid., p. 20.

[164]Ibid., pp. 20-25.

[165]*Narrative and Time*, Vol. 1, p. 68.

[166]Frye, *Anatomy of Criticism.*

[167]"*Mimesis* and Representation", p. 22.

[168]Ibid., p. 24.

[169]Ibid., p. 25

[170]Ibid.

[171]*Time and Narrative*, Vol. 1, p. 70.

[172]"*Mimesis* and Representation", p. 26.

[173]Ibid., p. 24.

[174]Ibid., p. 29.

[175]Ibid., p. 31.

[176]"Hermeneutics and the Critique of Ideology", pp. 93-94.

[177]*Time and Narrative*, Vol. 3, p. 216.

CHAPTER FIVE

RICOEUR'S BIBLICAL HERMENEUTICS: IMAGINATION AND RELIGIOUS LITERACY

In this chapter we will move from Ricoeur's consideration of general hermeneutics to biblical hermeneutics and the centrality of his theory of metaphor and imagination for the problem of interpreting biblical religious language as a form of narrative poetic discourse. I will illustrate his theory of metaphor and imagination in relation to the interpretation of a poem in Isaiah 14:4b-20b[1] and the metaphoric process at work in the poem through the intertextuality of narratives that convey the plot of the poem.

Ricoeur characterizes biblical hermeneutics[2] as regional hermeneutics in contrast to general hermeneutics. In his article "Time and Narrative in the Bible: Toward A Narrative Theology",[3] biblical hermeneutics is the necessary preparatory stage to the development of a "narrative theology"[4] instructed first by a consideration of the functioning of the primary level of religious language, particularly as poetic discourse. This starting point of a narrative theology, at the level of the primary forms of religious language, contrasts with traditional theological reflection as "speculative" theology,(in the sense of Hegel), "practical" theology (in the sense of Kant) or "existential" theology (in the sense of Bultmann).[5]

These approaches share in common the tendency too quickly to arrive at propositions without undergoing the long detour of a consideration of the functioning of the poetic forms of religious language. Ricoeur argues that this preparatory inquiry into the functioning of religious language must be undertaken before developing a narrative theology. Ricoeur's contribution to theological reflection is to focus upon texts and to recognize the distanciation of fiction and its projection of a "world in front of the text" that acts to redescribe and augment reality. The confession of faith according to his analysis is inseparable from the forms of discourse.[6] His development of biblical hermeneutics advocates following the interplay of the forms of discourse at work in the Bible considered as one great text. Narrative theology he argues to avoid the abstraction and reductionism of "speculative", "practical" and "existential" theology must make the long detour of following the significations of religious language and the intertextuality of its forms of discourse at work throughout the Bible considered as one great text.[7] As Ricoeur states:

> the biblical narratives, whether it be a question of the story of the Exodus or the story of Jesus, are always in a dialectical relation with other literary components that, even when they are entirely non-narrative, as are the wisdom writings and the psalms, include a specific temporal dimension.The crisscrossing of the narratives properly speaking with all these other forms of biblical discourse engenders a criss-crossing between temporalities of different qualities, which profoundly affects the temporality of the narratives.[8]

For Ricoeur the act of reading is identified with the productive imagination at the heart of this hermeneutical process that begins with the written text. The reader activates the rule-governed imagination that is objectified in the structure of the primary religious text as a poetic work of language.

> [T]he act of reading [is] a dynamic activity that is not confined to repeating significations fixed forever, but which takes place as a prolonging of the itineraries of meaning opened up by the work of interpretation...the act of reading accords with the idea of a norm-governed productivity to the extent that it may be said to be guided by a productive imagination at work in the text itself.[9]

His concern is not with the original *Sitz-im-Leben,* but with what he refers to as the *Sitz-im-Wort*[10] and the actualization of the "world of the text" through following the arc of *Mimesis₁* to *Mimesis₂* to *Mimesis₃* which the previous chapter described. Thus Ricoeur's biblical hermeneutics is oriented to the intentionality of the text and the "world in front of the text," rather than behind the text. The "world of the text" and the "text as a structured work of language" are central categories of Ricoeur's hermeneutics. Narrative for Ricoeur is a primary form of the imagination.[11]

> [O]n the side of the biblical text...narrative kernels occupy a central place and play an exceptional role from the election of Abraham to the anointing of David by way of the Exodus, and from the narratives of the life and teaching of Jesus to those of the Acts of the Apostles by way of the accounts of the Passion.[12]

The semantic innovation of the narrative is conveyed through the plot and the intertextuality of narratives. His synchronic characterization of the Bible encourages an actualization of the interplay of the narratives toward innovation and the disclosure of new ways of being in the world. Ricoeur adds:

> this investigation presupposes a certain methodological choice, that of a structural and synchronic reading of the biblical writings. This reading, which differs from a surface reading of the text, passes through the historical-critical method...but it does not reduce itself to the historical-critical approach.... The act of reading begins...with the *Sitz-im-Wort* of events, actions, institutions, and so on that have lost their first rootedness and only have henceforth, as a consequence, a textual existence. This textual status of the narratives, legislations, prophecies, wisdom sayings, and hymns has the effect of rendering these texts contemporary with one another in the act of reading. Read in this way, the Bible becomes a large living "intertext" that is the setting, the space of a working of the text on itself with the cooperation of the reader. The act of reading is the grasping, through the reconstructive imagination, of this working of the text on itself.[13]

The metaphoric process operates at this level through the intertextuality of the narratives in tension with one another as they are interwoven in the great tapestry that forms the Bible.[14] A further example Ricoeur gives of intertextuality is the tension between the narrative-parables in the Gospels and the encompass-ing narrative about the life of Jesus.[15] It is this interplay of narrative genres which dynamizes the meaning of the text and governs the reader's interpretation. As Ricoeur states:

> The theory of intertextuality allows us to take another step and to call not just the collision between two semantic fields in a sentence a metaphor, but also an intersection

between texts both of which carry their own semantic codes. The analysis of narrative-parables allows us to take this step and to extend the process of metaphorization to the widespread semantic conflicts instigated by the fact of intertextuality.[16]

This method of interpreting the Bible opens the way to an enrichment of our understanding of these texts that brings their imaginative productivity to life. The dialectic between the text and the reader recognizes the dynamic identity of the text and the act of reading as an active process rather than a passive one. Reading as active and critical is like the performance of a musical score. Such a performance is guided by the rule-governed structure of the text, as well as by its intersection with other texts that may transform its code toward innovations of meaning. Ricoeur parts company with structuralism[17] through his adherence to the concept of the "world of the text" and the specific type of distanciation of fiction that brackets reference to the everyday, manipulable reality to project a world that raises up the potentiality of being in the sense of Heidegger's notion of being-in-the world. As Ricoeur states:

> I would like to see in the reading of a text such as the Bible a creative operation unceasingly employed in decontextualizing its meaning and recontextualizing it in today's *Sitz-im-leben*. Through this second trait, the act of reading realizes the union of fiction and redescription that characterizes the imagination in the most pregnant sense of the term.[18]

It is the purpose of this chapter to approach the function of myth in the Hebrew Taunt Song of Isa. 14:4b-20b through the literary critical method of Paul Ricoeur's hermeneutics, specifically through his notion of intertextuality as a form of metaphoric process[19] that guides the dynamic reading of this poem. Ricoeur's method attends to the role of myth within the poem through its narrative character. He recognizes myth and metaphor as objectified works of the productive imagination that manifest truth through the subversive power of *mimesis* to project a world as the mode of the possible.

Most radically metaphor conveys new meaning through the plot of fiction which creates an *epoche* from everyday reality. It is the function of poetic fiction to weaken the first-order reference of ordinary language in order to allow this second-order reference to come forth.[20] In the case of this poem of Isaiah the metaphoric process of intertextuality is produced by the dynamic of the plot that intersects two narratives. The myth as integral to the taunt song is a key to reading the plot of the poem.

My claim is that the myth of Isa. 14:12-15, the inner taunt song of the larger passage of Isa. 14:4b-20b, is essential to shaping the narrative action of the poem's plot. Through its critical moment the myth acts by its structure in the poem to identify the oppression of a tyrant against humanity as equal to an assault against God. The plot is the dynamic structuring of the narrative events and as such the bearer of the metaphoric process. The mythical figure of Helel-ben-Sahar is at the center of this poem and serves as an iconic image[21] through which the scenes of the drama intersect and reverberate. The poem as a heuristic fiction[22] projects a vision of the victory of life over death. Through the genre of the taunt song and its plot, the poem describes a more basic comprehension of reality that redescribes tyranny as the limited and finite episode of a man, faceless in death and forgotten in life.

I

Traditionally the problem of myth in scripture has been approached through historical-critical methods[23] rather than from the direction of literary criticism, which characterizes the biblical hermeneutics of Paul Ricoeur. While Ricoeur's hermeneutics is concerned with the literary character of the text as a poem, as a work of discourse[24] in which the task of interpretation proceeds from *in front of*[25] the poem to the world of the text,[26] the traditional historical-critical method of biblical scholarship tends to move *in back of* the text in search of the original sources.[27] These methods are not in conflict, but rather are different strategies that can be brought to bear upon the text. The benefit of a literary critical approach to texts is its attention to the final state of the a text as well as the significance of literary language and genres[28] in productively reading a text. Ricoeur's hermeneutics is conceived of as a theory that regulates the dynamic transition from the structure of the work to the world of the work.

Previous studies on the problem of myth in the text of Isa. 14:12-15 have generally taken two directions: either the attempt has been make to identify the source of the myth in the surrounding culture and to reconstruct the possible route of mediation (this direction is represented by the work of such scholars as Gunkel, Grelot, McKay)[29] or the role of the myth in the text is confronted. But typically myth has been defined as in conflict with and opposed to the historical faith of the Israelite religion. This latter approach acts to reduce the significance of the mythical elements in the text. The underlying assumption is that myth is leveled through its assimilation into the text. This position is represented by Brevard Childs's work *Myth and Reality in the Old Testament*. His position in this work is "that Israel succeeded in overcoming the myth because of an understanding of reality which opposed the mythical."[30]

It is his interpretation that, although the text of Isa. 14:12-15 contains mythical elements, the historical framework of the poem has succeeded in reducing the myth. For Childs the function of myth in Isa. 14:12-15 is simply that of a vivid example, that of an extended figure of speech:

> The figure of Helel has become merely a striking illustration dramatizing the splendour of the rise to fame and the shame of the fall which is sarcastically hurled at the King of Babylon. There is no tension whatever between the myth and its Old Testament framework since the myth carries only illustrative value as an extended figure of speech.[31]

Childs's implicit understanding of metaphor is that it is simply decorative, connotative language with no denotative significance. This represents a traditional neo-classical view of metaphor. His categories of myth versus reality prevent him from acknowledging the possibility of continuity between the mythopoetic past of Israel and its more historic witness.[32] The religion of Israel is conceived of as a unique phenomenon, radically or wholly discontinuous with the "foreign mythology" of its environment. Childs defines myth as pagan cult reenacted each year to sustain harmony with the universe.[33] Myth is then reduced to a primitive explanation of reality to be gone beyond and jettisoned. Myth as "broken myth" may remain in the text as an extended figure of speech however myth as metaphor conveys no significant meaning, but functions simply as language that is cosmetic to the text and has no power to augment or innovate meaning.[34]

This understanding of myth and metaphor contrasts with Ricoeur's theory of hermeneutics, which emanates from a literary critical perspective. Ricoeur's contribution lies in his development of the theory of metaphor correlated to the philosophy of the imagination as a dynamic process, which conveys new meaning. For Ricoeur both myth and metaphor tell about reality through the narrative genres of language, and both are observed for their power to resignify reality beyond the literal use of language, particularly for their ability to transcribe a deeper sense of reality.[35] Ricoeur's understanding of metaphor is developed as a later stage to his work on myth as symbol. It represents Ricoeur's more explicit turn to the philosophy of language.[36]

Through his analysis of metaphoric process, Ricoeur has come to define metaphor as a strategy of language for semantic innovation and redescription in contrast to the ordinary and scientific uses of language. This constitutes a more precise analysis of the double intentionality of myth through attention to the narrative configuration of the plot of myth and its relation to a repertoire of narrative genres that develop through the process of the sedimentation and innovation of a narrative tradition. The theory of intertextuality parallels the tension between differing semantic fields at the level of the sentence which creates semantic innovation. Intertextuality at the level of fiction is defined as the interplay between narratives, which creates new meaning. The act of reading actualizes the individual text through an awareness of the background of its repertoire of narratives. Ricoeur's theory of the imagination and metaphor, extended to narrative, views this repertoire as the product of the dialectic of the sedimentation and innovation of narrative genres.

Myth and history share in common a narrative structure. The recognition of this common narrative structure enables one to admit the possibility of myth in history and history in myth. As narratives both myth and history tell a story and share a common origin in primitive drama. The categories of myth and history have too often been cast in conflict and alienation rather than recognized as sharing a common bond as complimentary expressions that answer to the human desire and effort to articulate the meaning of reality. It is through narratives, through stories, that we gain access to an understanding of our world and its deepest meanings.[37]

The history that confronts us in scripture is more adequately described through the literary category of epic narrative, a genre cast between the figurative and the literal. It is possible through this genre to recognize the interpenetration of myth and history. Epic narrative is a blend of myth, legend and folk tale interwoven with the common historic realm of the everyday.[38] As the biblical scholar Frank Moore Cross states:

> Epic narrative best designates the constitutive genre of Israel's religious expression. Epic in interpreting historical events combines mythic and historical features in various ways and proportions. Usually, Israel's epic forms have been labeled "historical." At the same time confusion often enters at this point. The epic form, designed to recreate and give meaning to the historical experiences of a people or a nation is not merely historical. In epic narrative a god or gods interact in the temporal course of events. In historical narrative only human actors have parts. Appeal to divine agency is illegitimate.[39]

Recognition of epic narrative as a more adequate category to describe the literary texture of scripture enables us to break beyond a conflictual view of myth and history, particularly as represented in Childs's work *Myth and Reality in the Old Testament*.[40] The categorization of epic narrative brought out by a literary critical perspective invites us to pay greater attention to the literary genres of scripture and their possible blending of mytho-poetic and realistic dimensions in the text. It is possible then to recognize the interpretive power of this use of the mytho-poetic narratives as a strategy of language to convey meaning at the service of historical witness.

For Ricoeur genre[41] is not a static category, but governs the dynamic process of reading the text as a structured work of discourse that configures time through plot and the rules of the genre. The work is ordered according to the norms of codification that constitute the structure of a particular genre, for instance as an essay, novel, or poem. The genre of the text is more like a musical score, which to be interpreted must be activated, played; and the world projected by the work is the outcome of the performance.[42]

The literary genre of Isaiah 14:4b-20b is a taunt song, a mocking comparison in the limping meter of a funeral dirge. It is a kind of prophetic spell or invocation of fate, in which, from the perpective of the future, a vision of the death of the tyrant is satirically announced.[43] It combines a striking dissonance of thought and form by a reversal of the usual themes of a lament for the dead through the satirical intention of the poem; for example, sorrow at the death of the individual has been changed to an expression of joy. The petition for the peace of the dead one is reversed to a proclamation of his state of unrest. It is a proclamation of celebration through its very reversal of the form of the lament. The genre of the taunt song in this poem of Isa.14:4b-20b produces an imaginative construction, a heuristic fiction through which the truth about tyranny can be disclosed. The poem combines both mythical and realistic scenes in its drama of the death of the tyrant. The power of the poem to transmit its message is generated by its use of myth as basic to the plot of the poem. The intertextuality of narratives is the interplay between the myth at the center of the poem with its reference to a repertoire of pre-Israelite mythology and on the other hand the encompassing narrative of the taunt song that describes the death of a tyrant.

> The effect of this embedding is twofold: on the one hand, the embedded narrative borrows from the encompassing narrative the structure of interpretation that allows the metaphorization of its meaning; in return [the encompassing narrative] is also reinterpreted due to the feedback from the metaphorized narrative. Metaphorization, therefore, is a process at work between the encompassing narrative and the embedded narrative.[44]

II

I would like to turn to an analysis of the function of myth as metaphorical process through attention to the plot of this song of Isa.14:4b-20b, as a narrative structure which is related—told through several unfolding dramatic scenes. It is the thesis of this interpretation that the myth of Isa. 14:12-15, the inner taunt song, is essential to shaping the narrative action of the poem's plot. Structurally it forms the critical moment[45] of the poem. It acts to identify the oppression of a tyrant against humanity as equal to an assault against God.

I shall attempt to demonstrate that the myth is not confined to the inner song of the poem, but is integral to the entire poem. The power of the presence of the myth in the poem is created in part by its tension with prior versions of the myth from "foreign mythology" and the myth's later transformation through the Israelite religion into Yahweh as the Divine Warrior.

First I shall describe the dramatic structure of the poem as unfolded through its several dramatic scenes. Second I shall briefly indicate the temporality conveyed by the structure of the plot in its relation to the metaphoric process of the poem. Next I shall describe the general mythical type represented in this text, according to Ricoeur's typology from *The Symbolism of Evil* as well as Cross's study of *Canaanite Myth and Hebrew Epic*. This will aid in reading the intertextuality of the poem, particularly to recognize the relation of the poem to a mythical type in the first two scenes of the poem, as well as the inner taunt song. However it is not my intention to give the exact origin of the myth. The description of the typology of the myth probably integrated into this poem is given to aid a forward reading of the text as a metaphoric process; it is not given in the interest of an attempt to lead back to some original mythic source. Finally I shall draw out the reference of this metaphoric process to reality as a heuristic fiction which redescribes the present through the genre of the taunt song which seeks to shatter the illusion that oppression is beyond relief.

The metaphoric process is borne by the whole poem as a heuristic fiction.[46] As Ricoeur states:

> Fictional narratives seem to constitute a distinctive class of metaphorical processes. The bearers of the metaphor are not the individual sentences of the narratives, but the narratives as a whole, what Aristotle has called the *mythos* in the poem.[47]

The world disclosed by the poem is in tension with everyday life and reality, which the prism of the poem acts to reconfigure. The tension evoked by the poem is conveyed by the interplay of narratives which produce the insight displayed by the poem as a fiction and the world it projects.

The Hebrew Taunt Song of Isa. 14:4b-20b is a remarkable piece of poetry, wherein the language gains a momentum and expresses a drama at several levels, from the cosmic to the everyday. Verses 12-15 form the inner taunt song that mirrors the structure of the overall song of 4b-20b. The poem as a whole tells of the death of a tyrant through four dramatic scenes: the first (4b-8) announces the proclamation, as if from a cosmic perspective, of the death of the tyrant and depicts the jubilant celebration that arises through the personified realms of earth and nature; the second scene (9-11) presents the tyrant's reception in Sheol, the realm of death, where he is mocked by the dead kings; the third scene (12-15) shifts to a cosmic level, in which the fall of the demigod Helel-ben-Sahar (Luminous Son of Dawn) is depicted, and this scene as the inner taunt song (and embedded narrative) forms the center of the poem; the closing scene (16-20b) is the most realistic as it portrays the human plane of the battlefield, on which the maimed corpse of a dead king is observed by the living. The first three scenes of the poem are described in more mythical language, while the last is the most realistic and concrete. The third scene (12-15), which forms the inner song, is the most mythical because of its recollection of the boast and subsequent fall of the demigod Helel-ben-Sahar is set in a cosmic realm. Here unlike the surrounding scenes of the encompassing narrative, the hero's active boasting is directed upward toward ascent, while the outer scenes of the encompassing narrative all portray the downward direction of the tyrant's deadly fall.

The two opening scenes portray the downfall, proclaiming the death of the tyrant and the fact that his power is broken. All of the scenes surrounding the inner song convey the downward direction of the anti-hero of the poem, from the heavens in the first scene to the very stones of a pit in the last scene. The demigod Helel's boast to reach highest heaven, from within the inner song, contrasts with the second scene's portrayal of the mockery of the dead kings, which greets the tyrant's entrance to the realm of death and reflects his mythic fall from the heights of the cosmos to the depths of Sheol.

A structure of reversal is constituted throughout the poem by the genre of the taunt song with its dissonant intention of satirizing within the form of a funeral lament. The downward direction of the outer scenes is reflective of the tragic mode, but the anti-hero of the taunt song is less than fully tragic in character.

The tone of the poem's first two scenes is musical in their evocation of a renewal of life in contrast to the former suffering inflicted by the central character. These two scenes are equally full of a rich range of feelings from anger to intense joy. The opening scene (4b-8) succeeds in conveying deep anger at the tyrant's former oppression of peoples and the corresponding joy of celebration that arises at the release from bondage. The images of that power are the rod and staff now smashed, which reflect vertical symbols of power that are now broken, just as the rise of the tyrant has been reversed toward downfall. Images of uprightness are expressed through the trees that stand tall in contrast to the felled tyrant.

In the second scene, which presents the realm of death, kings who once commanded are now commanded by Sheol, the spectre of death. The dead kings, who mockingly greet the dead tyrant, are all equal in death, for all power is reduced in the face of death. The previous glory of the tyrant is contrasted with the trappings of his present state of corruption (11), and the music of his homage is reduced to the mockery sung by powerless kings. The shock and amazement evidenced by the shades of the dead kings at his arrival add to the overall impression of his past power. The reaction of the dead kings indicates that the taskmaster was considered to be beyond the grasp of death.

The closing scene of the dramatic structure of the poem is the most realistic and human in its point of view. From this human perspective it restates the reputation of the tyrant, which had been portrayed more mythically in the first two scenes. The final scene depicts the shock of the living as they view the body of the dead king and reflect upon his true identity.

Thus the encompassing narrative (the two opening scenes and the closing scene) of this drama present the downfall of an oppressor that is greeted by universal rejoicing throughout all realms of the world, in which the level of celebration seems to match the suffering of a universal order inflicted by the tyrant. There is as well the register of surprise that even the tyrant is vulnerable to death. This satirical song is addressed to the oppressor as well as the oppressed. Throughout this prophetic vision produced by the genre of the taunt song, the true power of tyranny is disclosed by the taskmaster's fall into death.

But it is the inner taunt song (the embedded narrative) that is the key to the dynamic structure of the plot. It tells of the downfall of the mythical demigod Helel-ben-Sahar. It is here that the critical moment of the poem is placed, and the true character of the tyrant revealed through the boast of Helel (13-14) at the center of the poem. This is the catastrophe that propels the downfall of the anti-hero. It is in this scene that the depth of the tyrant's offense is disclosed as ultimately a rebellion against God. The figure and actions of Helel-ben-Sahar are the central icon[48] of the poem through which the actions of the opening and closing scenes receive their interpretation, that is, that the tyrant of the first scene and the corpse of the closing scene are *seen as* Helel, the demigod who has sought to match 'Elyon (14), to sit above El's stars (13); and Helel is *seen as* both tyrant (5) and merely human(16), oppressor of nations (6) and murderer of peoples (20). It is an example of what Ricoeur means by metaphoric process as assimilation through predication, but in this case predication as explicated by the plot of a narrative rather than by a single sentence structure.[49] As Ricoeur states:

> One could speak here of *predicative assimilation,* in order to understand by the word 'assimilation,' on the one hand, that it is not a question of a passively recorded similitude, but of an active operation, coextensive with the *'rapprochement'* performed by the metaphorical statement, and, on the other hand, by the word 'predicative' that the entire weight of the operation rests on the copula of the metaphorical statement: X *is*-like Y. This predicative assimilation enables the imagination to work as 'to see'.... 'to see similarity.'[50]

In the case of this poem of Isa.14:4b-20b, the metaphoric process is conveyed by the the intertextuality of the narratives which dynamizes the plot, and the denouement of the plot is the *mythos* of the poem.[51] The scenes of this drama are drawn together through the reverberation of the critical moment of this embedded narrative. This is the central icon of the poem.

I would like to refer briefly to the time of the narratives and its significance to the narrative action.[52] The first two scenes of the poem as well as the final scene (the encompassing narrative) are "now,"[53] while the central scene (the embedded narrative, the inner taunt song) is the "past" of deep temporality.[54] It is the "past" of the inner taunt song which propels the downward direction of the poem displayed in the outer scenes. It is from this "past" that the depth of the tyrant's offense is revealed in the upward boast of the demigod Helel-ben-Sahar at the center of the poem. The time of the poem is more complex than simple episodic time, that is a chronology of events. The time of the poem through its space/time arrangement of "mythic-now," "cosmic past" and "human-now," reflects a configurational[55] narrative construction, that is a non-chronological arrangement of events according to the configuration of the plot. This structure of time gives the poem its ontological depth as schematized by the productive imagination at work in the poem, through which the dimensions of the metaphoric process of the plot are conveyed. This adds support to my thesis that the myth of the inner taunt song, Isa. 14: 12-15 is key to the narrative structure of the poem as its critical moment. The inner song is not a superficial addition to the poem which could be stripped away with no loss of meaning to the whole. It augments and intensifies the *mimesis* of this poem as *poeisis,* conveying the cosmic depth of evil and suffering enacted by the tyrant as well as his fragility and hubris.

III

I would like now to turn to the problem of the mythical narrative that is possibly recessive to this poem of Isa. 14:4b-20b, in order to suggest that the use of the myth is not confined simply to the inner taunt song and in order to aid a further understanding of the network of symbolism that is appropriated within the context of this Israelite poem. It seems that the mythopoetic background of the Israelite religion served as a repertoire of fictive narratives that were rewoven toward the new vision of reality expressed by the Hebrew epic, which witnessed to a more concrete and specific relation between the human and the divine. As narratives both myth and epic share a kind of history, but what is unique to the history of the Hebrew epic is its concreteness and realism. This concreteness and realism is expressed through a variety of literary genres, which cannot be reduced to sheer literalism.

According to Ricoeur's hermeneutics the poem as a whole can be viewed as a heuristic fiction, in which the suspension of reality is the condition for the emergence of new dimensions of experience and reality. The integration of myth in this poem can be understood as an example of Ricoeur's theory of the metaphorization of narrative through the intertextuality of narrative, and as the product of the dialectic of the sedimentation and innovation of a tradition of narrative. In this section I shall refer to Ricoeur's earlier work *The Symbolism of Evil* as well as to Cross's study of Canaanite Myth and Hebrew Epic. Ricoeur describes myth as follows in *The Symbolism of Evil.*

> The first function of the myths of evil is to embrace mankind as a whole in one ideal history. By means of a time that represents all times, 'man' is manifested as a concrete universal; Adam signifies man. 'In' Adam, says Paul, we have all sinned. Thus experience escapes its singularity; it is transmuted in its own 'archetype.' Through the figure of the hero, the ancestor, the Titan, the first man, the demigod, experience is put on the track of existential structures: one can now *say*....existence, human being, because in the myth the human type is recapitulated, summed up...
> ....
> because its paradigm is dramatic, the myth itself is a tissue of events and is found nowhere except in the plastic form of narration.[56]

The myth that seems recessive[57] to this poem of Isaiah is the myth of the Divine Warrior as king.[58] But the myth as found in this poem is a reversal of the Divine Warrior myth. It is about the Enemy, represented in the figure of the evil king become tyrant that the Divine Warrior goes out to battle. The Divine Warrior myth belongs to the earliest mythical type, referred to by Ricoeur as the "Drama of Creation,"[59] in which order is wrested out of chaos. Order is secured through violence by the older god (in Canaanite mythology, the god El) at what is referred to as the theogonic stage of this cycle of strife among the gods. But to maintain this order the younger gods (in Canaanite mythology, the god Ba'l) of the cosmogonic stage must constantly do battle against the reemergence of chaos and order that propels the plot cycle of this mythic drama of creation itself insofar as creation is established through violence.

The myth of the Divine Warrior is a focus for mediating the relation between the cosmic and human realms, in which case cosmic harmony signifies human harmony. It is in the festival of ritual reenactment that a people played out this drama.

> A whole people, in the presence of the gods assembled in effigy, reenacts the original battle in which the world of order was won and relives the fundamental emotions of the poem—cosmic anguish, the exaltation of battle and jubilation in triumph. By the celebration of the festival the people place their whole existence under the sign of the drama of creation.[60]

In this festival of ritual re-enactment, the king plays the role of the god who battles chaos and re-establishes order. The figure of the oriental king represents the link between the cosmic drama and human harmony. "The king is both the grand penitent, in whom the service of the gods is epitomized, and the personification of the bound and delivered god".[61]

The plot of the myth, through its very instability, lends itself to a cycle of combat, and it becomes a structure for interpreting human history through a theology of the Holy War. The king represents the god who overcomes chaos, while the forces of evil in history are represented by the Enemy in the figure of the opponent as tyrant. This "mythological type of the drama of creation is marked by the *King-Enemy* relation, which becomes the political relation par excellence."[62]

> The 'cultural-ritual' vision of human existence develops a specific sort of history attached to the cult—hence to the re-enactment of the drama of creation—by means of the King. Because royalty stands between gods and humanity, it provides the figure that ties history to the cult, as the cult is itself tied to the theogonic drama.[63]

As the Enemy the figure of the king becomes "a figure of false greatness, as the caricature and no longer the image of god,"[64] no longer representative of a god of order and life. Instead the tyrant becomes associated with Yamm and Mot, the gods of disruption and death. Nor is the figure of the tyrant as the Enemy able to represent the Human-King as the mediator of the people, for the king as the tyrant corrupts this service of mediation toward an individualism which seeks to dominate and oppress peoples. The elements of the theology reflected in this reversal of the Divine Warrior myth of the Drama of Creation are: "The Enemy is a Wicked One, war is his punishment, and there are wicked ones because first there is evil and then order".[65]

But the myth as found in this poem of Isaiah is recessive to the dominance of the myth of the Hebrew epic, in which creation is good and evil contingent. As Yahweh the Divine Warrior brings a stability to this cycle of chaos and order that has constantly been in need of re-enactment through the cyle of the Creation Drama. Cross shows in his work, *Canaanite Myth and Hebrew Epic*, that there is a conflation between the old god El and Ba'l in representations of Yahweh as the Divine Warrior.[66] It would seem that Yahweh, as the Divine Warrior corresponding to El in the myth, transforms this whole cycle of chaos and order at the most fundamental level of the theogony. This exemplifies what Ricoeur means by the innovation of a sedimented tradition of narratives toward the creation of new genres.

Cross's example from Canaanite myth gives the elements of this Drama of Creation narrative, which seems to be the narrative-type recessive to this poem of Isaiah. It is as follows:

Yamm, deified Sea, claimed kinship among the gods. The council of gods assembled and told of Yamm's intention to seize the kingship and take Ba'l captive, made no protest. They were cowed and despairing, sitting with heads bowed to their knees. Ba'l rises, rebukes the divine assembly, and goes forth to war. In the cosmogonic battle he is victorious and returns to take up kingship. Presumably he returned to the assembled gods and appeared in glory, and the divine assembly rejoiced.[67]

The mythic pattern reflected by this drama is found in Canaanite and early Hebrew poetry. That pattern is:

(a) The Divine Warrior goes to battle against chaos (Yamm, Leviathon, Mot).

(b) Nature convulses and languishes when the Warrior manifests his wrath.

(c) The warrior-god returns to take up kingship among the gods, and is enthroned on his mountain.

(d) The Divine Warrior utters his voice from the temple, and Nature again responds. The heavens fertilize the earth, animals writhe in giving birth, and men and mountains whirl in dancing and festive glee.[68]

The second half of this mythic narrative pattern (c and d) form the background to the opening scenes of this poem of Isaiah. The proclamation announced from on high in the opening scene of the taunt song is like the proclamation given from the assembly of the gods by the victorious Divine Warrior.

> Ba'l's characteristic mode of self-revelation is in the storm theophany. El on the other hand makes his will known in the word or decree of the council of the gods. El's word is, in effect, the judgment or decision of the divine council, and it may be announced by the messenger of the council or more directly to mankind in dream or visitation.[69]

This taunt song of Isaiah as a prophetic oracle could be viewed in keeping with the recessive narrative as a message delivered from the council of Yahweh.

> The language of revelation in prophecy does not stem from the Ba'l epiphany and its figures and images. Rather, it originates ultimately in the judgments of El. Behind the revelation of the word of Yahweh (that is, the divine decision or judgment) lies a basic picture of the Council of Yahweh, the Israelite counterpart of the council of El.[70]

The death of the tyrant announced from on high in the opening lines of the poem parallels the proclamation of the Divine Warrior in d of Cross's mythic pattern, and this announcement is greeted by celebration from earth and nature (7-8).

IV

The myth as found in Isa. 14:4b-20b is a reversal of the Divine Warrior myth, in which the figure of the tyrant is representative of the Enemy whom the Divine Warrior has defeated. It is Yahweh who is portrayed as the Divine Warrior, but as a figure offstage to the drama of the poem. The battle and defeat of the Enemy have already occurred, and the poem depicts the downfall of the Enemy as both tyrant and demigod.

The encompassing narrative of the taunt song presents the tyrant as the man representative of the Enemy in the realm of human history, while the embedded narrative of the inner taunt song depicts the fall of the Enemy in the cosmic realm as the demigod Helel-ben-Sahar. The tyrant as the king mediates the corruption of order that transpires between the cosmic and human realms. In the encompassing narrative of the outer taunt song it is the "nations" that represent the Divine Warrior and not the tyrant. The "nations" replace the role of the "king" as the link between the human and the divine. What is perpetrated against the "nations" is perpetrated against the Divine Warrior as Yahweh. This metaphoric process discloses that the "nations" in the human realm correspond to the Divine Warrior as Yahweh in the cosmic realm. This is the radical transformation of this myth of the Divine Warrior through the new intentionality and innovation of the myth of the Hebrew epic.

There is no longer the need of the king as intermediary between the "nations" and Yahweh as Divine Warrior, because that relation as disclosed by the plot of the poem is much more direct and immediate. As Yahweh is victorious, so the nations are lifted up, are resurrected in contrast with the fall into death of the tyrant as the defeated Enemy. The Enemy's assault against El (as represented by the boast, 13-14, of Helel-ben-Sahar) in the inner taunt song is paralleled by the recollection of the tyrant's oppression of "nations" (6) in the outer taunt song.

A pattern of reversal is constituted through the interplay of the narratives adapted by the taunt song. For example the direction of the action of the encompassing narrative of the outer taunt song is "downward" revealing through the death of the tyrant, the resurrection of life and order, while in contrast Helel's boast at the center of the embedded narrative, i.e. the inner taunt song, is "upward," disclosing the catastrophic action that propels the downfall of the tyrant in the outer song. Helel,[71] the figure of light, is reversed toward a symbolism of darkness and death. Instead of functioning to give light, the demigod is destroyed by it. The boast of Helel parallels the claim of Yamm to kingship in the Canaanite myth. The claim of Yamm to kingship is the *crisis* which initiates the conflict between Ba'l and Yamm. But in the inner taunt song of Isaiah the boast of Helel is not the crisis but the *denouement* of the action of the poem. It is professed from the point of view of Yahweh as the victorious Divine Warrior. The demigod Helel-ben-Sahar is as well a lesser deity, not an equal power pitted against Yahweh as El nor as Ba'l, the son of El. In Canaanite mythology both Yamm and Ba'l are sons of El, while Helel is of more distant descent from El.[72]

The myth of the inner taunt song is the story of the foolish hubris of a lesser god, who moves beyond the bounds of his proper role in cosmic space and must be stricken down for the preservation of order and life. Helel as the Enemy is a lesser deity not equal to Yamm, thus Helel is not fully representative of a power toward chaos equal to the power of El as Yahweh toward order and life. Both Helel and the tyrant reflect a violation of limits which threatens the balance of the whole for the sake of an individual's lust for power. The reversal of the myth of the Divine Warrior as Enemy, integrated into the plot of this taunt song of Isaiah, discloses the significance of the larger community before the absolutism of the individual, corrupted king.

If we reread the poem, the final scene, which is the most realistic, is recollectively read back through the prior episodes, through the critical moment of the central scene, to the beginning. A multi-dimensional view of the death of the anti-hero is achieved through the dramatic scenes of the poem. The death of the final scene is interpreted retrospectively by those that precede it.

The poem is addressed to all who suffer under oppression and to the oppressor as well. It presents an enduring theme of universal significance that allows the poem to speak forcefully across the distance of its origin.

The poem as a heuristic fiction acts to re-describe reality, and it demands a re-reading of reality through the world that the poem discloses. It conveys a vision of hope and freedom that reveals the true power of tyranny, as opposed to the acceptance of tyranny as part of the everyday, an acceptance that blinds humanity to the presence of oppression and the oppressor. It projects to those it addresses new ways of being-in-the-world; particularly to those suffering oppression it offers hope by its disclosure of the fragility of the tyrant.

The myth is key to the dynamic intertextuality that conveys the action of the poem as told through its unfolding dramatic scenes. The myth of Isa.14:12-15 reveals the catastrophic action of the anti-hero that has brought about his downfall—retrospectively announced from the beginning. The Enemy is reduced in the final scene to a mortal man left to decay and death without honor or memory.

The poem fits the general description of epic narrative, since it contains both mythic and realistic scenes. It creatively interprets reality through its use of myth as well as the prophetic genre of the taunt song. This creative *mimesis* discloses a more fundamental truth: fiction leads to an augmentation of reality.

The myth is essential to the poem's narrative plot, and it acts to reveal the true significance of the tyrant and oppression. This is what Ricoeur means by metaphoric process as a strategy of language to create new meaning. Metaphor for Ricoeur is not denomination but predication, and in this poem of Isaiah the metaphoric process is conveyed by the plot and through the intertextuality of the narratives that intersect and fused in the denouement. The myth is key to the retelling of the identity of the oppressor and his fate.

The interpretation of myth in this study is in contrast to the position of Brevard Childs's work, *Myth and Reality in the Old Testament,* in which myth as metaphor is decorative but is not essential to cognitive content. Through the method of a literary critical interpretation, I have demonstrated the function of myth and metaphor through the biblical hermeneutics of Paul Ricoeur. This interpretation exemplifies the creative imagination at work in the text that governs the act of reading by following the intertextuality of narratives at work in the text. In Ricoeur's biblical hermeneutics the fictive and metaphoric dimensions of language convey new ways of being in the world through the epoche of fiction which releases a second order intentionality, reconfiguring and augmenting reality toward an evocation of deeper temporality. As Ricoeur states:

> My deepest conviction is that poetic language alone restores to us that participation or belonging-to an order of things which precedes our capacity to oppose ourselves to things taken as objects opposed to a subject. Hence the function of poetic discourse is to bring about this emergence of a depth-structure of belonging-to amid the ruins of descriptive discourse.[73]

Our foregoing exercise in consideration of poetic discourse has been limited to a poem in Isaiah and the intertextuality at work in the poem. Ricoeur's biblical hermeneutics continues to develop a philosophy of the imagination correlated to the functioning of metaphor and fiction. The philosophy of the imagination is central to the process of interpretation in relation to narrative as a primary form of the imagination. The dialectic between the text and the reader enacts the ruled-governed strategy of the imagination at work in narrative through the configuration of the plot and the intertextuality of the narratives. The subversive power of the imagination at work in poetic religious language gives rise to both critique and innovation within the tradition.

ISA. 14:4b-20b

How is the taskmaster vanished,
How is opression ended!
The Lord has broken the staff of the wicked,
The rod of the tyrants
That smote peoples in wrath
With stroke unceasing,
That belabored nations in fury
In relentless pursuit.

All the earth is calm, untroubled;
Loudly it cheers.
Even pines rejoice at your fate,
And cedars of Lebanon:
"Now that you have lain down,
None shall come up to fell us."

Sheol below was astir
To greet your coming—
Rousing for you the shades
Of all earth's chieftains,
Raising from their thrones
All the kings of nations.
All speak up and say to you,
"So you have been stricken as we were,
You have become like us!
Your pomp is brought down to Sheol,
And the strains of your lutes!
Worms are to be your bed,
Maggots your blanket!"

How are you fallen from heaven
Helel-ben-Sahar (O Shining One, son of Dawn!)
How are you felled to earth,
O vanquisher of nations!

Once you thought in your heart
"I will climb to the sky;
Higher than the stars of God (El)
I will set my throne.

I will sit in the mount of assembly,
On the summit of Zaphron:
I will mount the back of a cloud—
I will match the most High."
Instead you are brought down to Sheol,
To the bottom of the Pit.

They who behold you stare;
They peer at you closely:
"Is this the man
Who shook the earth,
Who made realms tremble,
Who made the world like waste
And wrecked its towns,
Who never released his prisoners to their homes?"
All the kings of nations
Were laid, every one, in honor
Each in his tomb;
While you were left lying unburied,
Like loathsome carrion,
Like a trampled corpse
(In) the clothing of slain gashed by the sword
Who sink to the very stones of the Pit.
You shall not have a burial like them;
Because you destroyed your country,
Murdered your people.*

*The Prophets: A New Translation of the Holy Scriptures (The Jewish Publication Society of America: Philadelphia, 1978).

NOTES OF CHAPTER FIVE

[1]Paul Ricoeur read and enthusiatically approved of a draft of this interpretation of Isaiah 14:4b-20b in the Spring of 1980 and with revisions it was published as "Paul Ricoeur's Biblical Hermeneutics: An Application to the Text of Isa. 14:4b-20b" in *Foundations of Religious Literacy*, ed. John V. Apczynski (Chico: Scholars Press, 1983), pp. 59-78. I have revised it here in light of Ricoeur's subsequent development of the notion of "intertextuality". The text of the poem is given on pp. 198-199 above.

[2]Ricoeur,"Toward a Hermeneutic of the Idea of Revelation", *Harvard Theological Review*,70 (1977), p. 26.

[3]Ricoeur, "Time and Narrative in the Bible: Toward A Narrative Theology" (unpublished typescript, October, 1983), pp. 1-25.

[4]John Baptist Metz, *Faith in History and Society: Toward a Practical Fundamental Theology*, trans. David Smith (New York: Crossroad, 1980) see "Narrative", pp. 205-228.

[5]"Time and Narrative in the Bible", p. 1-2.

[6]"Toward a Hermeneutic of the Idea of Revelation", p. 16.

[7]Ibid.

[8]"Time and Narrative in the Bible", p. 2.

[9]Ricoeur, "Bible and the Imagination", in *The Bible as a Document of the University*, ed. Hans Dieter Betz (Chico: Scholars Press, 1981), p. 50.

[10]"Time and Narrative in the Bible", p. 3.

[11]"Bible and the Imagination", p. 51.

[12]Ibid.

[13]"Time and Narrative in the Bible", pp. 2-3.

[14]"Bible and the Imagination", p. 53.

[15]Ibid., pp. 52-53.

[16]Ibid., p. 66.

[17]Ibid., p. 53.

[18]Ibid., p. 50.

[19]Ricoeur, "Biblical Hermeneutics", *Semeia*, 4p (1975), pp. 75-106; "Metaphor and the Main Problem of Hermenetics", *New Literary History*, 6 (1974), pp. 95-110; "Metaphorical Process as Cognition, Imagination, and Feeling", *Critical Inquiry*, 5 (1978), pp. 143-159; *The Rule of Metaphor* (Toronto: University of Toronto Press, 1977). Also see the very fine analysis and overview of Ricoeur's theory of metaphor by Mary Schaldenbrand, "Metaphoric Imagination: Kinship through Conflict" in *Studies in the Philosophy of Paul Ricoeur*, ed. Charles Reagan (Athens: Ohio University Press, 1979), pp. 57-81.

[20]"Biblical Hermeneutics," pp. 80, 84, 87. As Ricoeur states: "Here I rejoin the great idea of Aristotle in his *Poetics*. There poetry is depicted as a *mimesis* of human action (Aristotle has tragedy in mind). But this *mimesis* passes through the creation, through the *poiesis* of a fable or a myth which is the very work of the poet. In the language which I have adopted here, I would say that poetry imitates reality only by recreating it at a mythical level of discourse. Here fiction and redescription go hand in hand. It is the heuristic fiction which bears the function of discovery in poetic language" (87).

[21]*The Rule of Metaphor*, pp. 209-215; Ricoeur, *Interpretation Theory: Discourse and the Surplus of Meaning* (Fort Worth: Texas Christian University, 1976), pp. 40-43.

[22]*Interpretation Theory*, pp. 66-69.

[23]H. Gunkel was one of the first to formulate a critcal method for studying the process by which myth was assimilated into the *Hebrew Scriptures*. In his famous work of 1895, *Schöpfung und Chaos* (Göttengen, 1921), he demonstrated the process of demythologization through his examination of Israel's transformation of the creation myth. His concern lay chiefly in reconstructing the earliest stage of the myth. He assumed that the process of assimilation necessitated the demythologization of myth to be incorporated into the historical emphasis of Israel's monotheistic religion. Cf. Frank Cross, *Canaanite Myth and Hebrew Epic* (Cambridge: Harvard University Press, 1973), see especially his discussion of the imitation of the "Myth and Ritual Position" and "History of Redemption Position"; also see Lynn Clapham, "Mythopoetic Antecedents of the Biblical World View and Their

Transformation in Early Israelite Thought" in *Magnalia Dei: The Mighty Acts of God*, ed. Frank Cross, et al. (New York: Doubleday & Co., Inc., 1976).

[24]"Biblical Hermeneutics", pp. 66-68; *Interpretation Theory*, pp. 8-22.

[25]The phrase *in front of* the text refers to the world of the text, realized when a work of discourse is critically read and its meaning is actualized from the immanent sense of the text to its reference. The references of the text discloses the world of meaning it gives rise to in the event of a depth interpretation of the text. See Ricoeur, *Interpretation Theory*, p. 87.

[26]"Biblical Hermeneutics", p. 82; *Interpretation Theory*, pp. 25-44. "The Model of the Text: Meaningful Action Considered as a Text", *Social Research*, 38 (1971), pp. 529-562.

[27]Ricoeur, "Du conflit à la convergence des methodes en exégèse biblique" and "Equisse de Conclusion" in *Exégèse et herméneutique (Parole de Dieu)* (Paris: Seuil, 1971), pp. 35-53, 292-294.

[28]"Biblical Hermeneutics", pp. 68-71.

[29]P. Grelot, "Isaie XIV 12-15 et son arriere-plan mythologique", *Revue de l'Histoire des Religions*, 149 (1956), pp. 18-48; J.W. McKay, "Helel and the Dawn Goddess: A Re-examination of the Myth of Isaiah XIV 12-15", *Vetus Testamentum*, 20 (1970), 451-463; P. C. Craigie, "Helel, Athtar and Phaeton (Jes 14, 12-15)", *Zeitschrift f. alttestamentl Wiss.*, 85 (1973), 223-225. See also note 1, Raymond C. Van Leewen, "Isa. 14:12, HOLES AL GWYM and Gilgamesh XI, 6", *Journal of Biblical Literature*, 99(1980), p. 173. Van Leewen's argument is that the myth derives from the Gilgamesh myth, and he uses structural principles of Levi-Strauss to support this. The weakness of Van Leewen's argument is its focus on line 14:12. It does not take into account verses 13-15 as well as the surrounding poem and its possible relation to the Gilgamesh epic, which I think would be necessary to support his conclusion.

[30]Brevard Childs, *Myth and Reality in the Old Testament* (London: SCM Press, 1960), pp. 95-96. Childs states the purpose of the study is to show that Israel overcame myth through its understanding of reality. He recognizes a positive use of myth in the biblical text as "broken myth" for communicating the biblical understanding of reality (95). But this "broken myth" functions as language that is simply decorative to the text. Childs' definition of myth in this work strongly emphasizes the role of the cult (30, n.1) as a way of maintaining world order, but he overlooks the narrative character of myth with its origin in the dramatic

structure of the cult. In Ricoeur's defining of myth, its dramatic and narrative character is essential. This enables him to recognize a structure of continuity between the myth of the surrounding culture and the myth of the Judeo-Christian tradition and to develop a typology of myths which dynamically evolve, the "new," retaining some relation to the old. See Paul Ricoeur, *The Symbolism of Evil* (Boston: Beacon Press, 1967). Ricoeur's understanding of metaphorical process is in keeping with the notion of narrative, central to his definition of myth. In both cases myth and metaphor are defined as a strategy of language that intends reality, but through a poetic use of language. For Childs' more recent position as a "canonical approach" to the Old Testament, which attends to the final form of the text as normative and is critical of the historical critical method, see his *Introduction to the Old Testament* (London: SCM Press, 1979), pp. 71-79. Cf. John F. Priest, "Canon and Criticism: A Review Article", *Journal of the American Academy of Religion*, XLVIII, pp. 259-271). Childs's criticism of the philosophical hermeneutics of Paul Ricoeur is as follows: "the Bible is seen as a deposit of metaphors which contain inherent powers by which to interpret and order the present world of experiene, *regardless of the source* of the imagery. The concern is to illuminate what lies 'ahead'(devant) of the text, not behind. This approach shows little or no interest in the historical development of the biblical text or even in the historical context of the canonical text. The crucial intepretative context in which the metaphors function is provided by the faith-community itself (cf. David Kelsey). Such an approach fails to take seriously the essential function of the canon in grounding the biblical metaphors within the context of the historical Israel" (77). Cf. Ricoeur, "Biblical Hermeneutics", pp. 134-135. As Ricoeur states: "I am ready to admit that the *initial* application and interpretation....has a kind of priority and, in that measure, is controlling with respect to reinterpretation. But we must add, at the same time, that no interpretation can exhaust their meaning, not even the 'historical' interpretation" (134).

[31]Childs, *Myth and Reality*, p. 72.

[32]Ibid., pp. 96-97.

[33]Ibid., pp. 19ff.

[34]Ibid., p. 72.

[35]Ricoeur, "Biblical Hermeneutics", p. 87.

[36]Ricoeur, "From Existentialism to Philosophy of Language", *Criterion*, 10 (1971), pp. 14-18.

[37] *The Symbolism of Evil,* p. 170; "Narrative Function", *Semeia,* 13 (1978), pp. 177-202.

[38] Robert Scholes and Robert Kellogg, *The Nature of Narrative* (London: Oxford University Press, 1966), p. 12.

[39] Cross, *Canaanite Myth and Hebrew Epic,* p. viii.

[40] See note 29 above.

[41] See note 28 above.

[42] An analogy helpful to grasp Ricoeur's productive notion of genre is the example of film. A film on one level consists of a series of pictures that capture various phases of action. When the film is run we are given a sense of fluid action, while on another level, film is structured through the editing process which juxtaposes various scenes to tell a story. When the film is played we are given a sense of dramatic process, which conveys a story as a world of meaning.

[43] R.B.Y. Scott, *Introduction and Exegesis to Isaiah 1-39: Interpreter's Bible,* V (New York: Abington Press, 1956), p. 259.

[44] "Bible and the Imagination", p. 55.

[45] "Biblical Hermeneutics", 32; also see M. H. Abrams, *A Glossary of Literary Terms* (3rd ed.; New York: Holt, Rinehart, and Winston, Inc., 1971), p. 130.

[46] "Metaphor and the Main Problem of Hermeneutics", p. 96; "Biblical Hermeneutics", pp. 77-80.

[47] "Biblical Hermeneutics", p. 94.

[48] "Metaphorical Process", p. 146.

[49] "Biblical Hermeneutics", pp. 31, 93-94, 97-98.

[50] "The Function of Fiction", p. 131.

[51] "Biblical Hermeneutics", p. 94.

[52]"Narrative and Time", p, 169-190.

[53]Ibid., pp. 172-177.

[54]Ibid., pp. 181-184.

[55]Ibid., pp. 179-180.

[56]*The Symbolism of Evil*, p. 162, 169.

[57]Ibid., p. 198.

[58]Cross, *Canaanite Myth and Hebrew Epic*, pp. 71-111.

[59]*The Symbolism of Evil*, pp. 175-206.

[60]Ibid., p. 192.

[61]Ibid., p. 193.

[62]Ibid., pp. 197-198.

[63]Ibid., p. 191.

[64]Ibid., p. 205, note 44.

[65]Ibid., p. 198.

[66]Cross, *Canaanite Myth and Hebrew Epic*, p. 163.

[67]Ibid., p. 93.

[68]Ibid., pp. 162-163.

[69]Ibid., p. 177.

[70]Ibid., p. 186.

[71]Helel means the "shining one," and refers to the brightest star in the morning sky. According to P. Grelot's article, cited above in note 15, the Greek myth resembles the myth of Helel in this poem of Isaiah. According to the Greek myth, Phaeton demands to drive his father's sun-chariot, but as he drives the chariot he discovers he is too weak to control the solar horses, and he endangers the heavens and the earth by setting fire to them as the chariot goes out of control. Finally to save the earth and the heavens, Zeus strikes Phaeton down with a thunderbolt and Phaeton falls to the earth, consumed by fire. The symbolism of fire in the figure of Helel and Phaeton seems to offer potential to represent good and evil. Cf. Gaston Bachelard, *The Psychoanalysis of Fire* (Boston: Beacon Press, 1964).

[72]See Cross's reference to El's son Sahar, Dusk, in *Canaanite Myth and Hebrew Epic,* p. 22.

[73]"Toward a Hermeneutic of the Idea of Revelation", p. 24.

CONCLUSION

This thesis has followed Ricoeur's long route to the development of a critical hermeneutics, modelled upon the creativity of language. Ricoeur's correlation of the theory of metaphor with the philosophy of the creative imagination is key to his explication of a creative interpretation of poetic discourse as well as contributing to his development of a critical hermeneutics. Ricoeur's focus is on poetic discourse and its conceptual potentialities and its capacity to innovate and stretch the expressive power of language and to project the depth dimensions of human existence in terms of the heuristic power of fiction to augment and resignify reality. Ricoeur's hermeneutics brings to the forefront an awareness of the sedimentation and innovation of literary genres, which sustain the dynamic process of the interpretation of a tradition as "living" tradition. His contribution to theological hermeneutics is through an analysis of the of the primary expressions of religious language as poetic discourse. As I discussed in the first chapter, the theological tradition of Christianity has tended to ignore the cognitive significance of metaphorical/poetic/narrative forms of discourse. But developments in scholarship since the nineteenth century have encouraged a rethinking of the model of theological reflection, particularly in view of contemporary hermeneutics.

Before constructing a "narrative theology" or "correlative theology", Ricoeur counsels it is necessary to engage in the work of a preparatory analysis of the intertextuality of discourse within the Bible, considered as one great text. His model for the dialectic of the past with the present oriented to a future is through the arc of $Mimesis_1$ to $Mimesis_2$ to $Mimesis_3$. Poetic and philosophic/ theological discourse remain separate repertoires of discourse that intersect and the process of interpretation is balanced by the pull of their opposite demands. Poetic discourse gives rise to thought to which philosophic/theological discourse replies in terms of a limit concept. It is a dialectic weighted in the direction of poetic discourse, which provokes conceptual innovation. Ricoeur's enduring philosophical method is that of the dialectic, which seeks kinship in conflict.

Chapter two established the philosophical influences, which shaped Ricoeur's allegiance to a type of philosophical reflection responsive to the human condition and the praxis of justice. The significance of Ricoeur's prisoner-of-war experience, as a time of enforced leisure, served as a kind of *epoche* in his life, influencing his post-war development of a philosophy of freedom. Heidegger is an enduring reference for Ricoeur's development of hermeneutics and the philosophy of the imagination, but the war experience throws light upon a level of antipathy which Ricoeur's work registers toward Heidegger. Unlike Heidegger Ricoeur's fidelity in the post-war situation is to the humanist tradition and the effort to reconcile phenomenology to a concrete ontology.

Chapter three described the context of Ricoeur's turn to hermeneutics and his early correlation of the philosophy of the creative imagination with language and symbolic discourse. He brings together the strengths of the Enlightenment and Romantic traditions, which influenced the nineteenth century founders of contemporary hermeneutics, that is, Schleiermacher and Dilthey. But Ricoeur recognizes the necessity of overcoming the gap between language and the psychology of the imagination, which hindered Schleiermacher's and Dilthey's development of hermeneutics. This is the first *aporia* of hermeneutics Ricoeur sets out to overcome. He accepts the validity of Heidegger's ontological hermeneutics and its success in depsychologizing the imagination. But Ricoeur maintains that the shortcomings of this ontological hermeneutics lie in its failure to make the return route from ontology to epistemology and to address the problems of derivative hermeneutics on the level of history and texts.

He takes the longer route through the study of language and an adaptation of Husserl's theory of intentionality to equivocal language. In *Fallible Man* he joins the philosophy of the imagination to language by adapting Husserl's theory of intentionality to Kant's philosophy of the transcendental imagination. While Ricoeur agrees with Kant's comment that the imagination can be defined only indirectly, Ricoeur identifies language as the indirect objectification of the mediating function of the imagination. Thus he grafts hermeneutics to phenomenology by returning to the theory of intentionality of the early Husserl, but separated from Husserl's idealist position. Through the axis of the symbol he dialectically interrelates and finds the limits of the hermeneutics of suspicion of

Freudian psychoanalysis versus the teleological thrust of Hegelian phenomenology. At this stage he critiques the absolute idealism of the *cogito* as well as the finality of the Hegelian concept of absolute knowledge. The symbol testifies to the priority of the hermeneutic circle, which precedes the *cogito* and limits the Hegelian assumption of the possibility of absolute knowledge. Symbol and interpretation are defined correlatively.

Chapter four argues that Ricoeur's development of the theory of metaphor, in relation to the philosophy of the creative imagination at the level of general hermeneutics, advances his analysis of the functioning of symbolic language and facilitates his realization of a critical hermeneutics. Ricoeur defines the theory of metaphor in *The Rule of Metaphor* as a dynamic discursive process of language, which creates semantic innovation through the interaction of semantic fields. The assimilation of the metaphoric process occurs through its verbal construction, which creates iconic images that enable the reader "to see similarity in difference".

Ricoeur develops Kant's philosophy of the creative imagination in relation to metaphoric strategy. The imagination both mediates the interaction between semantic fields and creates the assimilation through the iconic images produced by the verbal construction. Thus Ricoeur goes beyond Hume's non-cognitive definition of the imagination. Ricoeur makes a case for the capacity of poetic discourse to create new meaning through his notion of split reference which builds upon the *epoche* of the imagination. Split reference is a second level reference that projects a world on the ruins of literal reference. Split reference refers to reality by an augmentation and resignification of it. At the level of fiction, the metaphoric process is conveyed by the plot and through the "intertextuality" of the work in relation to a repertoire of narratives. The semantic tension is between the trajectory of episodic and configurational dimensions of the plot. Thus fiction is a form of distanciation that is both productive of meaning and refers to reality.

Ricoeur builds upon Aristotle's comments on metaphor and *mimesis* as creative of new meaning and new categorization, while parting company from his denominational characterization of metaphor. Ricoeur's development of the theory of metaphor and *mimesis* enables him to respond to the lack of critique in Gadamer's definition of hermeneutics, particularly his negative definition of distanciation. He argues for a complementarity between understanding and explanation through the model of the text as a work of discourse. The poetic text of metaphor and fiction uncovers a productive form of distanciation at work in language through the rule-governed invention of the imagination.

The task of the reader is to activate the non-ostensive references of the text and to realize the world of the text through the dynamic of the structure of the text and the world it projects. Fiction allows for *epoche*, a moment of bracketing through which the reader enters the world of the text and is affected by its metamorphosis of reality. The imagination is at the heart of reading through the dialectic of the ruled-governed structure of the text and the reader's actualization of the rules of the text.

Ricoeur also responds, through this development of the theory of interpretation, to Habermas's call for a critique of ideology, in view of his distrust of tradition and authority. Ricoeur sketches a dialectic of ideology and utopia as works of the social imagination. The subversive power of the imagination functions through the innovative moments of poetic making and the projection through the world of such texts of new ways of being, which critique the *status quo*.

The arc of Ricoeur's hermeneutics is through *Mimesis*$_1$ to *Mimesis*$_2$ to *Mimesis*$_3$ by which action is prefigured, configured and transfigured. The move from *Mimesis*$_2$ to *Mimesis*$_3$ raises questions of praxis in terms of the challenge for justice that the reading provokes through its course of meaning.

Chapter five moves from the level of general hermeneutics to regional hermeneutics as biblical hermeneutics. Before developing a narrative theology, Ricoeur argues it is necessary to pursue the preparatory stage of biblical hermeneutics and an analysis of the Bible and its forms of poetic discourse. The theory of the imagination correlated to the theory of metaphor and *mimesis* is central to Ricoeur's development of biblical hermeneutics. Here I applied his theory of metaphor and imagination to a poem in Isaiah 14:4b-20b in order to recover the myth at the center of this narrative as a form of metaphoric process, demonstrating that it is key to the plot of the poem. The imagination is the creative element of religious literacy, which governs the dialectic between the text and the act of reading. This poem is an example of an heuristic fiction through its redescription of the power of tyranny and an end of oppression.

Ricoeur's theory of metaphor and *mimesis* correlated to the philosophy of the creative imagination resurrect the power of poetic discourse and make a case for poetic discourse's capacity to invent and project new ways of being in the world. On the one hand, it enables Ricoeur to overcome the *aporia* between language and the imagination, which is the legacy of Schleiermacher's and Dilthey's hermeneutics, due to their reliance upon the psychology of the imagination and a limited epistemology. On the other hand it facilitates Ricoeur's development of a positive definition of distanciation as productive and critical. This enables him to overcome the second *aporia* between ontology and epistemology, the legacy of Heidegger and Gadamer, and to establish a complementarity between understanding and explanation.

Ricoeur's development of hermeneutics points theology in the direction of rhetoric, poetics, literary criticism and the philosophy of language. Moreover his philosophy of the creative imagination and its singular importance to the renewal and innovation of the interpretation of the Judeo-Christian tradition, particularly through a recovery of the potentiality of poetic and narrative discourse to project new ways of being in the world.

BIBLIOGRAPHY

I must gratefully acknowledge the bibliographical compilation of D. Vansina, "Bibliographie de Paul Ricoeur," in *Rev. Phil. de Louvain* 60(1962), pp. 394-414; 66(1968), 85-101; 72(1974), 156-181; and J.W. Van Den Hengel, *The Home of Meaning*, (Washington, DC: 1982) pp. 261-329.

A. Paul Ricoeur[1]

I. Books

Ricoeur, Paul. *Démythologisation et herméneutique*. Nancy: Centre Europeen universitarire, 1967.

———. *Entretiens Paul Ricoeur-Gabriel Marcel*. Paris: Aubier, 1968.

———. *Être, essence et substance chez Platon et Aristote*. Paris: Centre de Documentation Universitaire, 1957.

———. *Idées directives pour une phénoménologie*. Paris: Gallimard, 1950. (Translation of E. Husserl, *Ideen zu einer reinen Phanomenologischen Philosophie*, with commentary by Ricoeur.)

———. *De l'interprétation. Essai sur Freud*. Paris: Seuil, 1965. (English translation by Denis Savage. *Freud and Philosophy: An Essay on Interpretation*. New Haven: Yale University Press, 1970).

———. *Interpretation Theory: Discourse and the Surplus of Meaning*. Fort Worth, Texas: The Christian University Press, 1976.

———. *La métaphor vive*. Éditions du Seuil, 1975. (English translation by Robert Czerny with Kathleen McLaughlin and John Costello, S. J. *The Rule of Metaphor*. Toronto: University of Toronto Press, 1977.)

———. *Philosophie de la volonté. I: Le volontaire et involontaire.* Paris: Aubier,1950. (English translation by Erazim V. Kohak. *Freedom and Nature: The Voluntary and the Involuntary*. Evanston: Northwestern University Press, 1966.)

———. *Philosophie de la volonté. Finitude et Culpabilité. I. L'homme fallible*. Paris: Aubier, 1960. (revised English translation by Charles Kebley. *Fallible Man*. New York: Fordham, 1986.)

————. *Philosophie de la volonté. Finitude et Culpabilité.II. La symbolique du mal.* Paris: Aubier, 1960. (English translation by Emerson Buchanan. *The Symbolism of Evil.* New York: Harper & Row, 1967).

————. *Temps et Récit.* Éditions du Seuil, 1983. (English translation by Kathleen McLaughlin and David Pellauer.*Time and Narrative* I. Chicago: University of Chicago Press, 1984).

————.*Temps et Récit.* II. Éditions du Seuil, 1984. (English translation by Kathleen McLaughlin and David Pellauer. *Time and Narrative.* II. Chicago: University of Chicago Press, 1985.

————. *Temps et Récit.* III. Éditions du Seuil, 1985. (English translation by Kathleen McLaughlin and David Pellauer. *Time and Narrative.* III. Chicago: University of Chicago Press, 1988.

II. Articles

Ricoeur, Paul. "L'acte et le signe selon Jean Nabert", *Les études philosophiques,* 17 (1962), pp. 339-349. (Repris dans *Le conflit des interprétations,* pp. 2ll-221. English translation by Peter McCormick. "Nabert on Act and Sign", in The Conflict of Interpretations, pp. 211-222.)*

————."Analyses et problèmes dans Ideen II de Husserl", *Revue de métaphysique et de morale.* 56 (1951), pp. 357-394. (English translation by E. G. Ballard and L. E. Embree. "Husserl's Ideas II: Analyses and Problems", in *Husserl,* pp. 39-81.)*

————."L'antinomie de la réalité humaine et le problème de l'anthropologie philosophique". *Il Pensiero.* 5 (1960), pp. 273-290. (English translation by Daniel O'Connor. "The Antimony of Human Reality and the Problem of Philosophical Anthropology", in *The Philosophy of Paul Ricoeur,* pp. 20-35.)*

————. "Belief or *Anamnesis*: Is a Rapprochment Between History of Religions and Theology Possible?", *Journal of Religion,* 52 (1972), pp. 150-169.

————. "The Bible and the Imagination" in *The Bible as a Document of the University.* Edited by Hans Dieter Betz. Chico: Scholars Press, 1981, pp. 49-75.

————. "Biblical Hermeneutics", *Semeia,* (1975), No. 4, pp. 29-148.

————. "R. Bultmann", *Foi-Education,* 37 (1967), No. 78, pp. 17-35.

————. "Bultmann: Une theologie sans Mythologie", *Cahiers d'Orgemont* (*Importance de la théologie de Rudolf Bultmann*), (1969), No. 72, pp. 21-37, 38-40.

————. "Can Fictional Narratives be True (Inaugural Essay)" in *The Phenomenology of Man and of the Human Condition. Individualization of Nature and of the Human Being. Vol. I.: Plotting the Territory for Interdisciplinary Communication.* (Analecta Husserliana, The Yearbook of Phenomenological Research, XIV). Edited by A. T. Tijmieniecka. Dordrecht: D. Reidel, 1983, pp. 3-19.

————. "Le christianisme et le sens de l'histoire. Progrès, ambiguité, espérance", *Christianisme social,* 59 (1951), pp. 261-274. (English translation. "Christianity and the Meaning of History, Progress, Ambiguity, Hope", in *History and Truth,* pp. 81-97.)*

————. "Du conflit à la convergence des méthodes en exégèse biblique", dans *Exégèse et herméneutiques: (Parole de Dieu).* Paris: Seuil, 1971, pp. 35-53.

————."Le conflit des hermémeutiques: épistémologie des interprétations", *Cahiers internationaux de Symbolisme,* 1 (1963), No. 1, pp. 152-184.

————."Le conscient et l'inconscient", dans *L'Inconscient (IV Colloque de Bonneval) (Bibliothèque Neuro-Psychiatrique de Langue Francaise,* sous la direction de H. Ey. Paris: Descle de Brouwer, 1966, pp. 409-422. (Repris dans *Le conflit des interprétations.* English translation by Willis Domingo."Consciousness and the Unconscious", *The Conflict of Interpretations,* pp. 99-120.)*

————. "Contribution d'une réflexion sur le langage à une théologie de la parole", *Revue de th'eologie et de philosophie,* 18 (1968), pp. 333-348.

————. "Creativity in Language, Word, Polysemy, Metaphor", *Philosophy Today,* 17 (1973), pp. 97-111. (Reprinted in *The Philosophy of Paul Ricoeur,* pp. 120-133.)*

————. "Critical Discussion: Ways of Worldmaking by Nelson Goodman", *Philosophy and Literature,* 4 (1980), pp. 107-120.

————. "Critique of Religion and the Language of Faith", *Union Seminary Quarterly Review,* 28 (1973), pp. 203-224.

————. "The Critique of Subjectivity and the Cogito in the Philosophy of Heidegger", in *Heidegger and the Quest for Truth.* Ed. M. S. Frings. Chicago: Quandrangle Books, 1968. (Publié en francais."Heidegger et la question du sujet", dans *Le conflit des interprétations.* English reprinted as "Heidegger and the Question of the Subject", in *The Conflict of Interpretations,* pp. 223-235.)*

————. "Démythiser l'accusation", *Archivio di Filosofia (Demitizazione e morale),* 35 (1965), Nos. 1-2, pp. 49-65, 67-75. (Repris dans *Le conflit des interprétations.* English translation by Peter McCormick."The Demythization of Accusation", in *The Conflict of Interpretations,* pp. 335-353.)*

————. "Les Directions de la Recherche Philosophique sur l'Imagination", pp. 1-8, "Imagination productive et Imagination reproductive selon Kant", pp. 9-13, "Husserl et le probléme de l'image (I-II), pp. 24-30. "Métaphore et Image", pp. 66-73. Recherches

Phenomenologiques Sur L'Imaginaire (Seminaire 1973-1974). Centre de Recherches Phenomenologiques. Typescript 81 pages.

————. "Ebeling", *Foi-Education,* 37 (1967), No. 78, pp. 36-53, 53-57.

————. "Ethics and Culture: Habermas and Gadamer in Dialogue", *Philosophy* Today, 17 (1973), pp. 153-165.

————. "L'enseignant protestant en face du catholicisme d'aujourd'hui", *Foi-Education,* 28 (1958), pp. 7-13.

————. "Etude sur les *Méditations Cartésiennes* de Husserl", *Revue philosophique de Louvain,* 52 (1954), pp. 75-109. (English translation by E. G. Ballard and L. E. Embree. "A Study of Husserl's Cartesian Meditations I-IV", in *Husserl,* pp. 82-114.)*

————. "Evènement et sens dans le discours", dans *Ricoeur ou la liberté selon l'espérance par M. Philibert.* Paris: Seghers, 1971, pp. 177-187.

————. "Excursus: Ideology, Utopia, and Faith". *Center for Hermeneutical Studies in Hellinistic Studies,* No. 17. Berkeley, 1976, pp. 21-28.

————. "Existence et herméneutique", dans *Interpretation der Welt, Festshrift für Romano Guardini zum archtzigsten Geburtstag.* Ed. H. Kuhn, H. Kahlefeld et K. Forster. Wurzburg: Im Echter-Verlag, 1964, pp. 32-31. (Repris dans *Le conflit des interprétations,* pp. 7-28. English translation by Kathleen McLaughlin. "Existence and Hermeneutics", in *The Conflict of Interpretations,* pp. 3-24.)*

————. "Expliquer et Comprendre", *Revue Philosophique de Louvain,* (1977), pp. 126-147. (English translation by Charles Reagan and David Stewart in *The Philosophy of Paul Ricoeur,* pp. 149-166.)*

————. "Faith and Action: A Christian Point of View. A Christian Must Rely on His Jewish Memory", *Criterion,* 2 (1963), pp. 10-15.

————. "The Father Image: From Phantasy to Symbol", *Criterion,* 8 (1968-69), pp. 1-7.

————. "Foi et langage: Bultman-Ebeling", *Foi-Education,* 37 (1967), octobre-décembre.

————. "Foi et philosophie aujourd'hui", *Foi-Education,* 42 (1972), No. 100, pp. 1-12, 12-13.

————. "La fonction narrative", *Etudes théologiques et religieuses*, 54 (1979), pp. 209-230. (English translation by John B. Thompson in *Hermeneutics and the Human Sciences*, pp. 274-296.)*

————. "Foreword", in *Hermeneutic Phenomenology: The Philosophy of Paul Ricoeur* by Don Ihde. Evanston: Northwestern University Press, 1971.

————. "From Existentialism to the Philosophy of Language", *Criterion*, 10 (1971), pp. 14-18.

————. "From Proclamation to Narrative", *Journal of Religion* 64 (1984) pp. 501-512.

————. "The Function of Fiction in Shaping Reality", *Man and the World*, 12 (1979), pp. 123-141.

————. Gadamer, H-G. *Vérité et méthode. Les grandes lignes d'une hermenéutique que philosophie*. Translation E. Sacre et P. Ricoeur. Paris: Seuil, 1976.

————. "Geschichte der Philosophie als Kontinuierliche Schopfung der Menschheit auf dem Wege der Kommunikation", dans *Offener Horizont: Festschrit fur Karl Jaspers zum 70. Geburtstag.* Ed. Kl. Piper, Munich: R. Piper, 1953. (Traduction francaise, "L'histoire de la philosophie et l'unité du vrai", *Revue internationale de philosophie*, 8(1954), pp. 266-282. English translation by Charles Kebley. "The History of Philosophy and the Unity of Truth", in *History and Truth*, pp. 47-56.)*

————. "Heidegger et la question du sujet" dans *Le conflit des interprétations*, pp. 222-232. (English translation in *The Conflict of Interpretations*, pp. 223-235.)*

————. "Hégel aujourd'hui", Études théologiques et religieuses, 49 (1974), No. 3, pp. 335-355.

————. "The Hermeneutical Function of Distanciation", *Philosophy Today,*17 (1973), pp. 129-141. (English translation by John B. Thompson in *Hermeneutics and the Human Sciences, pp. 131-144.)* *

————. "Herméneutique et critique des idéologies", *Démythisation et idéologie*. Ed. E. Castelli. Paris: Aubier, 1973. (English translation by John B. Thompson in *Hermeneutics and the Human Sciences*, pp. 131-144.)*

————. "Herméneutique et réflexion", *Archivio di Filosofia: Demitiszasione e immagine.Atti del Colloquio interazionale, Roma,11-16 gennaio* 1962, 32(1962), Nos. 1-2, pp. 19-34, 35-41. (Repris dans *Le conflit des interprétations*. English translation by Charles Freilich. "The Hermeneutics of Symbols and Philosophical Reflection II", in *The Conflict of Interpretations*, pp.315-334)*

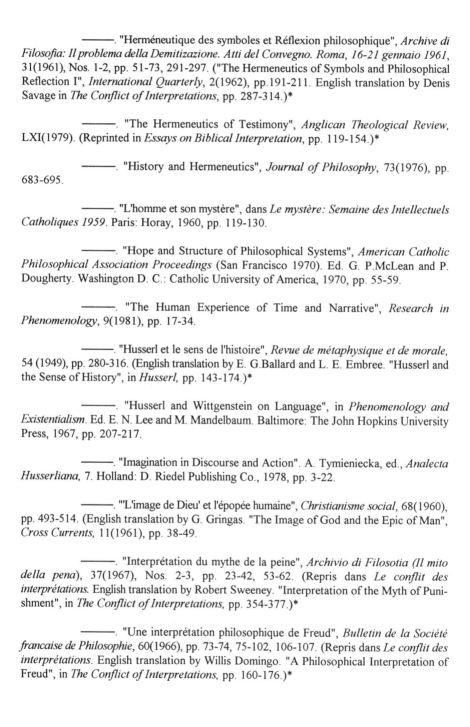

————. "Herméneutique des symboles et Réflexion philosophique", *Archive di Filosofia: Il problema della Demitizazione. Atti del Convegno. Roma, 16-21 gennaio 1961*, 31(1961), Nos. 1-2, pp. 51-73, 291-297. ("The Hermeneutics of Symbols and Philosophical Reflection I", *International Quarterly*, 2(1962), pp.191-211. English translation by Denis Savage in *The Conflict of Interpretations*, pp. 287-314.)*

————. "The Hermeneutics of Testimony", *Anglican Theological Review*, LXI(1979). (Reprinted in *Essays on Biblical Interpretation*, pp. 119-154.)*

————. "History and Hermeneutics", *Journal of Philosophy*, 73(1976), pp. 683-695.

————. "L'homme et son mystère", dans *Le mystère: Semaine des Intellectuels Catholiques 1959*. Paris: Horay, 1960, pp. 119-130.

————. "Hope and Structure of Philosophical Systems", *American Catholic Philosophical Association Proceedings* (San Francisco 1970). Ed. G. P.McLean and P. Dougherty. Washington D. C.: Catholic University of America, 1970, pp. 55-59.

————. "The Human Experience of Time and Narrative", *Research in Phenomenology*, 9(1981), pp. 17-34.

————. "Husserl et le sens de l'histoire", *Revue de métaphysique et de morale*, 54 (1949), pp. 280-316. (English translation by E. G.Ballard and L. E. Embree. "Husserl and the Sense of History", in *Husserl*, pp. 143-174.)*

————. "Husserl and Wittgenstein on Language", in *Phenomenology and Existentialism*. Ed. E. N. Lee and M. Mandelbaum. Baltimore: The John Hopkins University Press, 1967, pp. 207-217.

————. "Imagination in Discourse and Action". A. Tymieniecka, ed., *Analecta Husserliana*, 7. Holland: D. Riedel Publishing Co., 1978, pp. 3-22.

————. "'L'image de Dieu' et l'épopée humaine", *Christianisme social*, 68(1960), pp. 493-514. (English translation by G. Gringas. "The Image of God and the Epic of Man", *Cross Currents*, 11(1961), pp. 38-49.

————. "Interprétation du mythe de la peine", *Archivio di Filosofia (Il mito della pena)*, 37(1967), Nos. 2-3, pp. 23-42, 53-62. (Repris dans *Le conflit des interprétations*. English translation by Robert Sweeney. "Interpretation of the Myth of Punishment", in *The Conflict of Interpretations*, pp. 354-377.)*

————. "Une interprétation philosophique de Freud", *Bulletin de la Société francaise de Philosophie*, 60(1966), pp. 73-74, 75-102, 106-107. (Repris dans *Le conflit des interprétations*. English translation by Willis Domingo. "A Philosophical Interpretation of Freud", in *The Conflict of Interpretations*, pp. 160-176.)*

————. "Interrogation philosophique et engagement", dans *Pourquoi la philosophie?* Ed. G. Leroux. Montreal: Les Éditions de Sainte-Marie, 1968.

————. "Introduction et un appendice consacré à quelques figures contemporaines", dans *Histoire de la philosophie allemande* par E.Brehier. 3rd ed. Paris: Vrin, 1954, pp. 185-258. (English translation by E. G. Ballard and L. E. Embree. "Introduction: Husserl (1859-1938)", in *Husserl*, pp. 3-12.)*

————. "Introduction", *Idées directives pour une phénoménologie* par E. Husserl. Paris: Gallimard, 1950. (English translation by E.G. Ballard and L. E. Embree. "Introduction to Husserl's Ideas I", in *Husserl*, pp. 13-34.)*

————. "Introduction au problème des signes et du langage", *Cahiers de philosophie. Publiés par le groupe d'etudes de philosophie*, 1(1962-1963), No. 8, pp. 1-76.

————. "Le jugement (suite et fin)", *Bulletin du groupe d'études de philosophie (de l'Université de Paris)*, (1958-1959), No.8, pp. 27-70.

————. "Le jugement", *Cahiers de philosophie. Publiés par le Groupe de Philosophie de l'Universite de Paris*, 2(1963-1964), No. 5, pp. 1-87.

————. "Kant et Husserl", *Kant-Studies*, 46(1954-1955), pp. 44-67. ("Kant and Husserl", *Philosophy Today*, 10(1966), pp. 147-168. (English translation by E. G. Ballard and L. E. Embree in *Husserl*, pp. 175-212.)*

————. "Langage religieux. Mythe et symbole", dans *Le Langage. II. Langages. Actes du XIII Congrès des Sociétée de philosophie de langue francaise.* Neuchatel: La Baconniere, 1967, pp. 129-137, 138-145.

————. "La liberté selon l'espérance", dans *Le conflit des interprétations*, pp. 393-415. (English translation by Robert Sweeney in *The Conflict of Interpretations*, pp. 402-425.)*

————. "Life: A Story in Search of a Narrator" in *Facts and Values: philosophical Reflections from Western and non-Western Perspectives.* Edited by M. C. Doeser and J. N. Kraay. Dordrecht: Martinus Nijhoff, 1986, pp. 121-132.

————. "Listening to the Parables of Jesus: Matthew 13: pp. 31-32 and 45-46", *Criterion*, 13(1974), pp. 18-22. (Reprinted in *The Philosophy of Paul Ricoeur*, pp. 239-244.)*

————. "The Logic of Jesus, the Logic of God", *Anglican Theological Review*, LXII(1980), pp. 37-41.

————. "Manifestation et proclamation", *Archivio di Filosofia*, (1974), 57-76. (English translation by David Pellauer, "Manifestation and Proclamation", *The Journal of the Blasdell Institute*, XII(1978), pp. 13-35.)

————. "The Metaphorical Process as Cognition, Imagination, and Feeling", *Critical Inquiry,* 5(1978), pp. 143-159.

————. "La métaphore et le problème central de l'herméneutique", *Revue philosophique de Louvain,* 70(1972), pp. 93-112. (English translation. "Metaphor and the Main Problem of Hermeneutics", *New Literary History,* 6 (1974), pp. 95-110. (Reprinted in *The Philosophy of Paul Ricoeur,* pp. 134-148. English translation by John B. Thompson in *Hermeneutics and the Human Sciences,* pp. 165-181.)*

————. "Méthodes et tâches d'une phénoménologie de la volonté", dans *Problémes actuels de la phénoménologie.* Ed. H. L. Van Breda. Bruges-Paris: Desclée de Bouwer, 1952, pp. 110-140. (English translation by E. G. Ballard and L. E. Embree. "Methods and Tasks of a Phenomenology of the Will", in *Husserl,* pp. 213-233.)*

————. "*Mimesis* et répresentation" in *Actes du XVIIIe Congres des Sociétés de philosophie de langue francaise* (Strassbourg, 1980). Strassbourg: Université des Sciences humaines de Stassbourg, Faculté de philosophie, 1982, pp. 53-63. (English translation by David Pellauer. "*Mimesis* and Representation", *Annals of Scholarship: Metastudies of the Humanities and Social Sciences,* 2(1981), pp. 15-32.)

————. "The Model of the Text: Meaningful Action Considered as a Text", *Social Research,* 38(1971), No. 3, pp. 529-562. (Reprinted in *Hermeneutics and the Human Sciences,* pp. 197-121.

————. "'Morale sans péché' ou péché sans morale?", *Esprit,* 22 (1954), pp. 294-312. (English translation. "'Morality without Sin' or Sin without Moralism", *Cross Currents,* 5(1955), pp. 339-352.

————. "My Relation to the History of Philosophy", *Iliff Review* 35 (1978), pp. 5-12.

————. "Mythe 3. "L'interpétation philosophique", dans *Encyclopaedia universalis.* XI Paris: Encyclopaedia Universalis.

————. "Mythe et proclamation chez R. Bultmann", *Le cahiers du Centre Protestant de l'Ouest,* (1967), pp. 21-33.

————. "Naming God", *Union Seminary Quarterly Review,* 34 (1979), pp. 215-227.

————. "The Narrative Function", *Semeia,* 13(1978), pp. 177-202.

————. "Narrative Time". University of Chicago, 1978-1979. Unpublished typescript, 39 pages.

————. "New Developments in Phenomenology in France: the Phenomenology of language", *Social Research,* 34(1967), pp. 1-30.

————. "Objectivité et subjectivité en histoire", *Revue de l'enseignement philosophique. Bulletin de l'Association des Professeurs de Philosophie de l'Enseignement public*, 3(1953), pp. 28-40, 41-43. (Repris dans Histoire et Verite. English translation by Charles A. Kebley. "Objectivity and Subjectivity in History", in *History and Truth*, pp. 21-40.)*

————. "On Parables", three unpublished lectures: I. "The Structural Approach", II. "The Poetic Approach", III. "Parables and Religious Discourse". Given at the Divinity School at the University of Chicago, May, 1973.

————. "La parole est mon royaume", *Esprit*, 23(1955), pp. 192-205.

————. "Parole et symbole", *Revue des Sciences Religieuses*, 49 (1975), pp. 142-161.

————. "Le 'Péché Originel': etude de signification", *Eglise et Théologie. Bulletin trimestrial de la Falculté de Théologie Protestante de Paris*, 23(1960), pp. 11-30. (English translation by Peter McCormick. "'Original Sin': A Study in Meaning", in *The Conflict of Interpretations*, pp. 269-286.)*

————. "Phénoménologie existentielle", dans *Encyclopédie francaise* XIX, *Philosophie et religion*. Paris: Larousse, 1957, 19. 10-12a.10-12. (English translation by E. G. Ballard and L. E. Embree."Existential Phenomenology" in *Husserl*, pp. 202-212.)*

————."Phénoménologie et herméneutique", in *Phanomenologische et Forschungen*, 1. Edited by Ernst Wolfgang Orth. Freiburg: Karl Alber, 1975, pp. 31-77. "Phenomenology and Hermeneutics", *Nous*, 9(1975), 85-102. (English translation by John B. Thompson in *Hermeneutics and the Human Sciences*, pp. 101-128.)*

————. "Philosophical Hermeneutics and Theological Hermeneutics", *Studies in Religion/Sciences Religieuses*, 5(1975-1976), No. 1, pp. 14-33.

————. "Philosophie et Ontologie. Retour à Hégel", *Esprit*, 23 (1955), pp. 1378-1391.

————. "Philosophie et Religion chez Karl Jaspers", *Revue d'histoire et de philosophie religieuses*, 37(1957), pp. 207-235.(English translation."The Relation of Jaspers' Philosophy to Religion", in *The Philosophy of Karl Jaspers: A Critical Analysis and Evaluation*. Ed. P. A. Schilpp. New York: Tudor, 1957, pp. 611-642.)

————. "Philosophie, sentiment et poésie. La notion d'a priori selon Mikel Dufrenne", *Esprit*, 29(1961), pp. 504-512. (English translation by E. Casey as "Preface" to *The Notion of A Priori* by M. Dufrenne. Evanston: Northwestern University Press, 1966.)

————. "La philosophie et la spécificité du langage religieux", *Revue de l'histoire des religions*, 55(1975), No. 1, pp. 13-26.

————. "Philosophy and Religious Language", *The Journal of Religion,* 54(1974), pp. 71-85.

————. "Philosophy of Will and Action", in *The Philosophy of Paul Ricoeur,* pp. 61-74.*

————. "Philosophy of Will and Action", in *Phenomenology of Will and Action.* Ed. E. W. Straus and R. M. Griffith. Pittsburgh: Duquesne University Press, 1967, pp. 7-33, 34-60.

————. "Préface", *L'être et la vérité chez Heidegger et Saint Thomas* par B. Rioux. Mont'eal-Presses universitaires de France.

————. "Préface à Bultmann", dans *Le conflit des interprétations,* pp. 373-392. (English translation by Peter McCormick in *The Conflict of Interpretations,* pp. 381-401.

————. "The Problem of the Foundation of Moral Philosophy", *Philosophy Today,* 22(1978), pp. 175-192.

————. "Le problème du doublé-sens comme problème herméneutique et comme problème sémantique", *Cahiers internationaux de Symbolisme,* (1966), No. 12, pp. 59-71. (English translation by Kathleen McLaughlin. "The Problem of Double-Meaning as Hermeneutic Problem and as Semantic Problem", in *The Conflict of Interpretations,* pp. 62-78.)

————. "Le Problème du fondement de la morale", *Sapienza,* 28(1975), pp. 313-337.

————. "Problèmes actuels de l'interprétation (d'après Paul Ricoeur)", Centre Protestant d'Etudes et de Documentation (Dossier Nouvelles Théologies), (1970), No. 148, 51/163-170/182.

————. "Problèmes du langage, Cours de M. Ricoeur (1965-1966, Nanterre), *Cahiers de Philosophie,* 1(1966), No. 4, pp. 65-73.

————. "Psychoanalysis and the Work of Art". J. H. Smith, ed. *Psychiatry and the Humanities.* New Haven: Yale University Press, 1976.

————. "Qu'est-ce qu'un texte? Expliquer Comprendre", dans *Hermeneutik und Dialektik. Aufsatze II. Sprache Logik. Theorie der Auslegung und Probleme der Ein elwissenschaften.* Ed. Rudiger Bubner et al. Tubingen: J. C. B. Mohr, 1970, pp. 181-200. ("What is a Text? Explanation and Interpretation", in *Mythic-Symbolic Language and Philosophical Anthropology* by D. M. Rasmussen. The Hague: M. Nijhoff, 1971, pp. 135-150. English translation by John B. Thompson in *Hermeneutics and the Human Sciences,* pp. 145-164.)*

————. "La question du sujet: le défi de la sémiologie", dans *Le conflit des interprétations*. Paris: Seuil, 1969, pp. 233-362. (English translation by Kathleen McLaughlin."The Question of the Subject: The Challenge of Semiology", in *The Conflict of Interpretations*, pp. 236-266.)*

————. "La Recherche philosophique peut-elle s'achever?", *Orientations,* (1966), pp. 31-44.

————. "Réflexions sur 'Le diable et le Bon Dieu'", *Esprit*, 19(1951), pp. 711-719.

————. "Renouveau de l'ontologie", dans *Encyclopédie francaise* XIX. *Philosophie et religion*. Paris: Larousse, 1957, 19.16 a 19.18-3.

————. "A Response", *Biblical Research*, XXIV-XXV(1979-80), pp. 70-80.

————. "Responses"(to Lévi-Strauss, etc.), *Esprit*, 31(1963), pp. 628-653.

————. "Retourner à Kant au passer par Kant", *Esprit*, No. 89, (1986), pp. 155-6.

————. "Rhetorique-poetique-hermeneutique", in *De la Metaphysique à la rhetorique: Essais à la mémoire de Chaim Perelman*. Ed. Michel Meyer. Bruxelles: Éditions de l'Université de Bruxelles, 1986, pp. 143-155.

————. "Religion, athéisme, foi", dans *Le conflit des interpétations*, pp. 431-457. (English translation by Charles Freilich in *The Conflict of Interpretations*, pp. 440-467.)

————. "Royaume dans les parables de Jesus", *Études theologiques et religieuses,* 51(1976), No. 1, pp. 15-19.

————. "Sartre and Ryle on the Imagination" in *The Philosophy of Jean-Paul Sartre*. Edited by A. Schlipp. La Salle: Open Court, 1981, pp. 168-178.

————. "Schleiermacher's Hermeneutics", *The Monist*, 60(1977), pp 181-197.

————. "Science et idéologie", *Revue philosophique de Louvain*, 72(1974), pp. 328-356.

————. "Signe et sens", dans *Encyclopaedia Universalis.* XIV Paris: Encyclopaedia Universalis, 1972, 1011-1015.

————. "Structure et herméutique", *Esprit*, 31(1963), pp. 596-627. (English translation by Kathleen McLaughlin. "Structure and Hermeneutics", in *The Conflict of Interpretations*, pp. 27-61.)*

————. "La structure, le mot, l'événement", *Esprit*, 35(1967), pp. 801-821. (English translation by Robert Sweeney. *Philosophy Today*, 12(1968), pp. 114-129. Reprinted in *The Conflict of Interpretations*, pp.79-96.)*

————. "Structure et signification dans le langage", dans *Pourquoi la philosophie?* Ed. G. Leroux. Montreal: Les Editions de Sainte-Marie.

————. "Sur l'exégèse de Genèse 1, 1-2, 4a", *Exégèse et hermenéutique (Parole de Dieu)*. Paris: Seuil, 1971, pp. 67-84, 85-96.

————. "Le symbole et le mythe", *Le Semeur: Le sacré*, 61(1963), no.2, pp. 47-53.

————. "Le symbole donne à penser", *Esprit*, 27(1959), pp. 60-76. (English translation by Francis Sullivan. "The Symbol: Food for Thought", *Philosophy Today*, 4 (1960), pp. 196-207.)

————. "Le symbolisme et l'explication structurale", *Cahiers internationaux de Symbolisme*, 2 (1964), No. 4, pp. 81-96.

————."Sympathie et respect. Phénoménologie et éthique de la seconde personne", *Revue de metaphysique et de morale*, 59(1954), pp. 380-397.

————."The Task of Hermeneutics", *Philosophy Today*, 17(1973), pp. 112- 128. "La tâche de l'herméneutique", dans *Exegesis: Problèmes de methode et exercices de lecture*, Ed. par Francois Bovon and Grégoire Rouiller. Neuchatel: Delachaux et Niestl'e, 1975, pp.179-200. (English translation by John B. Thompson in *Hermeneutics and the Human Sciences*, pp. 43-62.)*

————. "Technique et non-technique dans l'interprétation", *Archivio di Filosofia: Tecnica e casistica*, 34(1964), Nos. 1-2, pp. 23-37, 39-50.(English translation by Willis Domingo in *The Conflict of Interpretations*, pp. 177-195.)*

————."That Fiction 'Remakes' Reality", *Journal: The Blaisdell Institute*, 12(1978), pp. 44-62.

————."Time and Narrative in the Bible: Toward a Narrative Theology" University of Chicago, 1981. Unpublished typescript. 25 pages.

————."Toward a Hermeneutic of the Idea of Revelation", *Harvard Theological Review*, 70(1977), pp. 1-37. (Reprinted in *Essays on Biblical Interpretation*, pp. 73-118.)*

————."Le *Traité de Metaphysique* de Jean Wahl", *Esprit*, 25(1957), pp. 529-540.

——. "L'unité de volontaire et l'involontaire", *Bulletin de la Société francaise de Philosophie*, 45(1951), 1-2, pp. 3-22, 22-29. (English translation by N. Lawrence and D. O'Connor. "The Unity of the Voluntary and the Involuntary as a Limiting Idea", in *Readings in Existential Phenomenology*. Ed. Nathaniel Lawrence and Daniel O'Connor. New York: Prentice-Hall, 1976. Reprinted in *The Philosophy of Paul Ricoeur*, pp. 3-19.)*

——. Vérité et mensonge", *Esprit*, 19(1951), pp. 753-778. (English translation by Charles Kebley. "Truth and Falsehood", in *History and Truth*, pp. 165-191.)*

——. "Volonté, dans *Encyclopaedia universalis*. XVI. Paris: Encyclopaedia Universalis, 1973, 943-948.

——. "Writing as a Problem for Literary Criticism and Philosophical Hermeneutics", *Philosophical Exchange*, 3(1977), pp. 3-15.

The items marked with an asterisk (*) refer to collections of Ricoeur's writings, and are as follows:

III. Collections

Ricoeur, Paul. *Le conflit des interprétations: essais d'hermeneutique*.Paris: Seuil, 1969. (English translation edited by Don Ihde. *The Conflict of Interpretations: Essays in Hermeneutics*. Evanston: Northwestern University Press, 1974.)

——. *Essays on Biblical Interpretation*. Edited by Lewis S. Mudge. Philadelphia: Fortress Press, 1980.

——. *Hermeneutics and the Human Sciences*. Edited and translated by John B. Thompson. Canbridge: Cambridge University Press, 1981.

——. *Histoire et Vérité*. Paris: Seuil, 1955. (Seconde édition augmentee de quelque textes). Paris: Seuil, 1964. English translation by Charles A. Kebley. *History and Truth*. Evanston: Northwestern University Press, 1967.

——. *Husserl: An Analysis of His Phenomenology*. Translation by Edward G. Ballard and Lester E. Embree. Evanston: Northwestern University Press, 1967.

——. *The Philosophy of Paul Ricoeur: An Anthology of His Work*. Edited by Charles E. Reagan and David Stewart. Boston: Beacon Press, 1978.

——. *Du texte à l'action: Essais d'herméneutique, II*. Edited by Olivier Mongin. Collection Esprit. Paris: Seuil, 1986.

B. Secondary Material

Bès, Y. "P. Ricoeur. Le règne des hermeneutiques ou un long d'etour", *Revue Philosophique de la France et de l'Etranger*, 94(1969), pp. 425-429.

————. "Review of *De l'interprétation* and Le conflit des interprétations", *Revue Philosophique de la France et de l'Etranger*, 94(1969), pp. 425-429.

Bourgeois, P. "Hermeneutics of Symbols and Philosophical Reflection", *Philosophy Today*, 15(1971), pp. 231-241.

————. "Paul Ricoeur's Hermeneutical Phenomenology", *Philosophy Today*, 16(1972), pp. 20-27.

————. "Phenomenology and the Science of Language", *Research in Phenomenology*, 1(1971), pp. 119-136.

Couch, Beatriz Melano. "Religious Symbols and Philosophical Reflection", Charles Reagan, ed. *Studies in the Philosophy of Paul Ricoeur*. Athens: Ohio University Press, 1979, pp. 115-132.

Doran, R. "Paul Ricoeur: Toward the Restoration of Meaning", *Anglican Review*, (1973), pp. 443-458.

Dornisch, L. "An Introduction to Paul Ricoeur", *Theological Digest*, 24(1976), pp. 147-153.

————. "A Theological Interpretation of the Meaning of Symbol in the Theory of Paul Ricoeur and Possible Implications for Contemporary Education", Ph. D. dissertation, Marquette University, 1973.

Farris, W. J. S. "The Hermeneutical Arc", *Toronto Journal of Theology*, 4(1988), pp. 86-100.

Fialowski, A. "Paul Ricoeur et l'hermeneutique des mythes", *Esprit*, 35(1967), Nos. 7-8, pp. 73-89.

Gerhart, M. "Imagination and History in Ricoeur's Interpretation Theory". *Philosophy Today*, 23(1979), pp. 51-68.

————. "The 'New' Literature and Contemporary Religious Consciousness", *Anglican Theological Review*, LXII(1980), pp. 42-63.

————. "Paul Ricoeur's Notion of 'Diagnostics'": Its Function in Literary Interpretation", *Journal of Religion*, 56(1976), pp. 137-156.

————."The Question of Belief in Present Criticism: A Reformulation from the Perspective of Paul Ricoeur's Hermeneutical Theory", Ph.D. dissertation, University of Chicago, 1973.

Hackett, S. "Philosophical Objectivity and Existential Involvement in the Methodology of Paul Ricoeur", *International Philosophical Quarterly,* 9 (1969), pp. 11-39.

Hartmann, K. "Phenomenology, Ontology, and Metaphysics", *Review of Metaphysics,* 22(1968), pp. 85-112.

Ihde, D. "From Phenomenology to Hermeneutics", *Journal of Existentialism,* 8(1967-1968), pp. 111-132.

————. *Hermeneutic Phenomenology: The Philosophy of Paul Ricoeur.* Evanston: Northwestern University Press, 1971.

————. "Rationality and Myth", *The Journal of Thought,* 2(1967), pp. 10-18.

————. "Some Parallels Between Analysis and Phenomenology", *Philosophy and Phenomenological Research,* 27(1967), pp. 577-586.

Javet, P. "Imagination et réalité dans la philosophie de Paul Ricoeur", *Revue de Theologie et de Philosophie,* 17(1967), pp. 145-157.

Kohak, E. "The Philosophy of Paul Ricoeur", translator's introduction to *Freedom and Nature: the Voluntary and the Involuntary.* Evanston: Northwestern University Press, 1966.

Kossel, C. "Reflections on the Phenomenology of Sin", *International Catholic Review,* 1(1974), pp. 197-207.

Muto, S. "Reading the Symbolic Text: Some Reflections on Interpretation", *Humanities,* 8(1972) pp. 169-191.

Philibert, M. "The Philosophic Method of Paul Ricoeur" in *Studies in Paul Ricoeur,* pp. 133-140.

————. *Ricoeur.* Paris: Seghers, 1971.

Rasmussen, D. *Mythic-Symbolic Languages and Philosophical Anthro*pology. The Hague: Nijhoff, 1971.

————. "Myth, Structure and Interpretation in the *Origin of Cosmos and Man.* Edited by M. Dhavenony. Rome: Gregorian University Press, 1969.

————. "Ricoeur: The Anthropological Necessity of a Special Language", *Continuum,* 7(1969), pp. 120-130.

Reagan, C. "Ricoeur's Diagnostic Relation", *International Philosophical Quarterly*, 8(1968), pp. 586-592.

Sales, M. "Un colloque sur mythe de la peine", *Archives de Philosophie*, 32(1969), pp. 664-675.

Schaldenbrand, Mary. "Metaphoric Imagination: Kinship Through Conflict" in *Studies in the Philosophy of Paul Ricoeur*, pp. 57-82.

Spiegelberg, H. *The Phenomenological Movement: A Historical Introduction*, 2. The Hague: Nijhoff, 1960, pp. 563-578.

Stewart, D. "In Quest of Hope: Paul Ricoeur and Jurgen Moltmann", *Restoration Quarterly*, 13(1970), pp. 31-52.

———. "Paul Ricoeur and the Phenomenological Movement", *Philosophical Quarterly*, 12(1968), pp. 227-235.

———. "Paul Ricoeur's Phenomenology of Evil". Ph. D. dissertation, Rice University, 1965.

———. "Paul Ricoeur's Phenomenology of Evil", *International Philosophical Quarterly*, 9(1969), pp. 572-589.

Thie, M. "The 'Broken' World of Myth: An Analysis", *New Scholasticism*, 45(1971), pp. 38-55.

Tillette, X. "Réflexion et symbole. L'enterprise philosophique de Paul Ricoeur", *Archives de Philosophie*, 24(1961), pp. 574-588.

Van Den Hengel, J. *The Home of Meaning: The Hermeneutics of the Subject of Paul Ricoeur*. Washington, D. C.: University of America Press, 1982.

Vansina, D. "Esquisse, orientation et signification de l'entreprise philosophique de Paul Ricoeur", *Revue de metaphysique et de morale*, 59(1964), pp. 179-208; 305-320.

Waelhens, A. "Pensée mythique et philosophique du mal", *Revue philosophique de Louvain*, 59(1961), pp. 315-347.

Wells, H."Theology and Christian Philosophy: Their Relation in the Thought of Paul Ricoeur", *Studies in Religion*, 5(1975-1976), pp. 45-56.

C. Further Secondary Literature of Interest on the Topic

Abrams, M. H. *The Mirror and the Lamp*. London: Oxford University Press, 1981.

Aristotle. *The Nicomachean Ethics*. Trans., introd., and notes by Martin Ostwald. Indianapolis: Bobbs-Merrill, 1962.

———. *The Rhetoric and the Poetics*. Introd. and notes by Friedrich Solmsen. New York: Random House Modern Library, 1954.

Auerbach, E. *Mimesis: The Representation of Reality in Western Literature*. Trans. William Trask. Princeton: University Press, 1968.

Bachelard, G. *La Psychanalyse du Feu*. Paris: Gallimard, 1938. English translation by Alan C. M. Ross. *The Psychoanalysis of Fire*. Boston: Beacon Press, 1964.

———. *La Poétique de la Rêverie*. Paris: Presses Universitaires de France, 1960. English translation by Daniel Russell. *The Poetics of Reverie*. Boston: Beacon Press, 1971.

Barrett, W. *Irrational Man*. New York: Doubleday & Co., 1958.

Beardslee, W. *Literary Criticism of the New Testament*. Philadelphia: Fortress Press, 1970.

Beardsley, M. C. *Aesthetics*. New York: Harcourt, Brace & World, 1958.

———. "The Metaphorical Twist", *Philosophy and Phenomenological Research*, 22(1962), pp. 293-307.

Benveniste, E. *Problèmes de linguistique générale*. Paris: Gallimard, 1968. English translation by Mary Elizabeth Meek. *Problems in General Linguistics*. University of Miami Press, 1971.

Berlin, I. *The Age of Enlightenment*. New York: New American Library, 1956.

———. *Vico and Herder*. London: Hogarth Press, 1976.

———. *Against the Current: Essays in the History of Ideas*. Ed. Henry Hardy. London: Hogarth Press, 1974.

Black, M. *Models and Metaphors*. Ithaca: Cornell University Press, 1962.

Boelen, B. "Martin Heidegger as a Phenomenologist" in *Phenomenological Perspectives: Festschrift in Honor of H. Spiegelberg*. The Hague: Nijhoff, 1975, pp. 93-114.

Bultmann, R. "The Problem of Hermeneutics", in *Essays: Philosophical and Theological.* Trans. James C. G. Greig. New York: MacMillan & Co., 1955, pp. 234-261.

Bultmann, R. and Jaspers K. *Myth and Christianity: An Inquiry into the Possibility of Religion Without Myth.* Tran. Norbert Guteman. New York: The Noonday Press, 1958.

Burrell, D. *Analogy and Philosophical Language.* New York: Yale University Press, 1973.

Cassirer, E. *Language and Myth.* Trans. Susanne Langer. New York: Dover Publications, 1953.

Childs, B. *Myth and Reality in the Old Testament.* London: SCM Press, 1960.

Collingwood, R. G. *An Essay on Metaphysics.* Chicago: Henry & Co., 1961. (Oxford University Press, 1939).

Crites, S. "The Narrative Quality of Experience", *Journal of the American Academy of Religion,* 39 (1971), pp. 291-303.

Cross, F. M. *Canaanite Myth and Hebrew Epic.* Cambridge: Harvard University Press, 1973.

Crossan, John. *In Parables.* New York: Harper & Row, 1973.

Duggan, W. *Myth and Christian Belief.* Notre Dame: Fides Publishers, 1971.

Dulles, A. "Symbols, Myth and Biblical Revelation", *Theological Studies,* 27(1966), pp. 16-16.

———. "Symbol and Revelation", *The New Catholic Encyclopedia.* New York: McGraw-Hill, 1967, Vol. 13: 861-863.

Dupré W. "Myth and Reflective Thought", *The New Catholic Encyclopedia,* New York: Mc Graw-Hill, 1967, Vol. 10: 189-190.

Durand, G. *Les structures anthopologiques de l'imaginaire.* Paris: Presses Universalitaires de France, 1968.

Eliade, M. *Images and Symbols: Studies in Religious Symbolism.* New York: Sheed & Ward, 1961.

———. "Myth in the Nineteenth and Twentieth Centuries", in *Dictionary of the History of Ideas: A Study of Selected Ideas.* New York: Charles Scribner's Sons, 1973, Vol. 3:307-318.

————."Methodological Remarks on the Study of Religious Symbolism", in *The History of Religions: Essays on Methodology*. Edited by Mircea Eliade and Joseph Kitagawa. Chicago: University of Chicago Press, 1959.

Feldman, B. "Myth in the 18th and Early 19th Centuries" in *Dictionary of the History of Ideas: A Study of Selected Ideas*. New York: Charles Scribner's Sons, 1973, Vol. 3:300-307.

Frei, H. W. *The Eclipse of Narrative: A Study in Eighteenth and Nineteenth Century Hermeneutics*. New Haven: Yale University Press, 1974.

Frye, N. *The Anatomy of Criticism*. Princeton: Princeton University Press, 1957.

————.*The Great Code: The Bible and Literature*. Toronto: Academic Press Canada, 1982.

Furst, L. *Romanticism*. London: Methuen & Co., Ltd., 1969.

Gadamer, H.-G. "On the Scope and Function of Hermeneutical Reflection", *Continuum*, 8(1970), pp. 77-95.

————. *Truth and Method*. Trans. Garrett Barden and John Cumming. New York: Sheed & Ward, 1975.

Gilkey, L."Modern Myth-Making and the Possibilities of Twentieth Century Theology", in *Theology of Renewal*. Vol. 1. Edited by L. K. Shook. New York: Herder & Herder, 1968.

Hart, R. *Unfinished Man and the Imagination*. New York: Herder & Herder, 1968.

Heidegger, M. *Being and Time*. Trans. John Macquarrie and Edward Robinson. New York: Harper & Row, 1962.

————. *An Introduction to Metaphysics*. Trans. Ralph Mannheim. New Haven: Yale University Press, 1959.

————. *Kant and the Problem of Metaphysics*. Trans. James S. Churchill. Bloomington, Indiana, 1962.

————. *Poetry, Language, Thought*. Trans. Albert Hofstadter. New York: Harper & Row, 1971.

————. *What is Called Thinking?* Trans. J. Glenn Gray. New York: Harper & Row, 1968.

————. *What is a Thing?* Trans. W. B. Barton, Jr. and Vera Deutsch. Chicago: Henry Regnery Co., 1967.

Henle, P. "Metaphor", in *Language, Thought, and Culture.* Ed. Paul Henle. Ann Arbor: University of Michigan Press, 1958.

Hesse, M. "The Explanatory Function of Metaphor", Appendix to *Models and Analogies in Science.* University of Notre Dame Press, 1966.

Hester, M. B. *The Meaning of Poetic Metaphor.* The Hague: Mouton, 1967.

Hirsch, E. D. *The Validity of Interpretation.* New Haven: Yale University Press, 1967.

Iser, W. *The Act of Reading.* Baltimore: John Hopkins University Press, 1978.

————. *The Implied Reader.* Baltimore: John Hopkins University Press, 1974.

————. "The Reality of Fiction: A Functionalist Approach to Literature", New Literary History, 7(1975), pp. 7-38.

Jauss, H.R. *Aesthetic Experience and Literary Hermeneutics.* Minneapolis: University of Minnesota Press, 1982.

————. *Toward an Aesthetic of Reception.* Minneapolis: University of Minnesota Press, 1982.

Johnson, M. *The Body and the Mind: The Bodily Basis of Meaning, Imagination, and Reason.* Chicago: The University of Chicago Press, 1987.

Kant, I. *The Critique of Judgment.* Trans. J. H. Bernard. New York: Hafner Press, 1951.

————. *Critique of Practical Reason.* Trans. Lewis White Beck. New York: Liberal Arts Press, 1956.

————. *Critique of Pure Reason.* Trans. Norman Kemp Smith. New York: Macmillan & Co., 1929.

————. *Prolegomena to Any Future Metaphysics.* Trans. Carus and revised by Lewis Beck. Indianapolis: The Library of Liberal Arts Press, 1950.

Krell, D. F. "On the Manifold Meaning of *Aletheia*: Bretano, Aristotle, Heidegger, *Research in Phenomenology*, 5 (1975), pp. 77-95.

Küng, H. "Toward a New Consensus in Theology" in *Consensus in Theology?* Ed. Leonard Swidler. Philadelphia: Westminster Press, 1980, pp. 1-17.

Lakoff, G. and Johnson, M. *Metaphors We Live By*. Chicago: University of Chicago Press, 1980.

Lamb, M. *Solidarity With Victims*. New York: Crossroad, 1982.

Liss, J. "Kant's Transcendental Object and the Two Senses of the Noumenon: A Problem in Imagination". *Man and the World*, 13(1980), pp. 133- 153.

McFague, S. *Metaphorical Theology*. Philadelphia: Fortress Press, 1982.

————. *Models of God*. Philadelphia: Fortress Press, 1987.

————. *Speaking in Parables*. Philadelphia: Fortress Press, 1975.

Marcel, G. *The Mystery of Being*. 2 Vols. I: *Reflection and Mystery*. Trans. G. S. Fraser. Chicago: Gateway Editions, 1969. II: *Faith and Reality*. Trans. R. Hague. Chicago: Gateway Editions, 1968.

Metz, J. B. M. *Faith in History and Society*. Tran. David Smith. New York: The Seabury Press, 1980.

————."A Short of Apology of Narrative", *Concilium* 9(1973), pp. 84-96.

Ogden, S."The Task of Philosophical Theology", in *The Future of Philosophical Theology*. Ed. Robert A. Evans. Philadelphia: Westminster Press, 1971, pp. 55-84.

————. "What is Theology?", *Journal of Religion*, 52(1972), pp. 22-40.

Palmer, R. *Hermeneutics: Interpretation Theory in Schleiermacher, Dilthey, Heidegger, and Gadamer*. Evanston: Northwestern University Press, 1969.

Perrin, N. *Jesus and the Language of the Kingdom: Symbol and Metaphor in New Testament Interpretation*. Philadelphia: Fortress Press, 1976.

Reardon, B. M. G., *Religious Thought in the Nineteenth Century*. Cambridge: Cambridge University Press, 1966.

Richards, I. A. *Principles of Literary Criticism*. New York: Harcourt, Brace, 1925.

————. *The Philosophy of Rhetoric*. Oxford: Oxford University Press, 1936.

Rorty, R. *Philosophy and the Mirror of Nature*. Princeton: Princeton University Press, 1979.

Ruether, R. R. "Is a New Christian Consensus Possible?", in *Consensus in Theology?* Ed. Leonard Swidler. Philadelphia: Westminster Press, 1980, pp. 63-68.

Schillebeeckx, E. *Christ*. Trans. John Bowden. New York: Seabury Press, 1980.

Schüssler-Fiorenza, E. *Bread Not Stone*. Boston: Beacon Press, 1984.

Todorov, T. *Theories of the Symbol*. Trans. Catherine Porter. Ithaca: Cornell University Press, 1982.

Tracy, D. *The Analogical Imagination*. New York: Crossroad, 1981.

————. *Blessed Rage for Order*. New York: Seabury Press, 1975.

————."Particular Questions Within General Consensus", in *Consensus in Theology?* Ed. Leonard Swidler. Philadelphia: Westminster Press, 1980, pp. 33-39.

————. *Plurality and Ambiguity*. San Francisco: Harper & Row, 1987.

————."The Task of Fundamental Theology", *Journal of Religion,* 54(1974), pp. 13-34.

Wellek, R. and Warren, A. *Theory of Literature*. New York: Harcourt, Brace and World, 1949.

Wheelwright, P. *The Burning Fountain: The Study of Language and Symbolism*. Bloomington: Indiana University Press, 1968.

————. *Metaphor and Reality*. Bloomington: Indiana University Press, 1962.

Young-Bruehl, E. *Hannah Arendt*. New Haven: Yale University Press, 1982.

INDEX

Abrams, M. 143n.

Arendt, H. 33f, 37, 42n, 43,n.

Aristotle. 31, 52f., 79, 99-110, 122, 124f, 131, 141., 142n, 143n, 160.

Augustine. 53.

Austin, J. 99, 110.

Bachelard, G. 119, 145n, 181n.

Beardsley, M. 99, 111, 113-116, 127, 143n, 144, 144n.

Benjamin, W. 134.

Barrett, W. 28, 33, 41n, 43n, 44n.

Beneviste, E. 99, 110.

Black, M. 99, 111-116, 119, 122, 143n, 144n.

Bloch, E. 93.

Bultmann, R. 151.

Childs, B. 26n, 156, 158, 177n,178 n.

Cross, F. 158, 160, 165, 167f., 176n, 179n, 180n, 181n.

de Lubac, H. 21n.

Descartes, R. 32, 50, 64, 67f.

Dilthey, W., 6f., 32, 48f., 51-53, 56, 59f., 62, 64-66, 76, 79f., 89-91, 97, 99f., 127, 135, 137, 184, 187.

Dufrenne, M. 35.

Fontanier, P. 100. 141n.

Frege, G. 109, 114.

Frei, H. 21n, 22n.

Freud, S. 38, 40, 50, 74, 77f., 82n, 85n.

Frye, N. 1, 21n, 132f., 147n, 148, 149n.

Furst, L. 22n.

Gadamer, H.G. 2, 14f, 21n, 22n, 40, 58, 66, 81, 87-99, 127, 130, 135, 138n, 141, 147, 186f.

Greimas, A. 114, 144n, 148.

Grelot, P. 156, 177n, 181n.

Goodman, N. 99, 121, 145n.

Gunkel, H. 156, 176n.

Habermas, J. 87f., 91-94, 96, 99, 127, 135f., 147, 186.

Hart, R. 44n.

Hegel, G. 16, 38, 48, 64, 68, 74f., 77, 78, 92, 152.

Heidegger, M. 14f., 25n, 28, 31-37, 39f., 41, 42n, 43n, 47-52, 59, 61-66, 71-73, 75, 78-81, 81n, 83n, 88-90, 94-97, 100, 135f., 138, 140n, 141n, 154, 184, 187.

Henle, P. 99, 117.

Hesse, M. 19, 122, 146n.

Hester, M. 99, 117f.

Holderin, J. 134.

Hume, D. 117, 185.

Husserl, E. 27, 31f., 34-36, 38, 48, 59, 61, 63f., 92, 109f., 117, 184.

Jaspers, K. 27, 31-36, 38

Johnson, M. 82n, 84n.

Kant, I. 5, 19, 22n, 31, 33, 37, 40-41, 49, 54, 60, 64, 66-74, 79, 82n, 84n, 92, 94, 123, 132, 151, 184-185.

Kelbley, C. 45n.

Kellogg, R. 179n.

Kierkegaard, S. 29, 35.

Küng, H. 8-11, 23n, 24n.

Lamb, M. 3, 21n.

Lindbeck, G. 9.

McKay, J. 156.

Marcel, G. 27-32, 34, 38, 51.

Marx, K. 38, 40, 49.

Merleau-Ponty, M. 40.

Mounier, E. 27-31, 34, 37.

Nabert, J. 76.

Nietzsche, F. 35, 38, 40, 49.

Palmer, R. 6-8, 22n, 23n.

Pascal, E. 68.

Pierce, C.S. 117.

Plato. 68, 91, 102.

Pound, E. 125.

Rahner, K. 21n.

Reardon, B. 4, 8, 22n, 23n.

Richards, I.A. 99, 112.

Rorty, R. 25n

Rousseau, J.J. 38.

Ruether, R. 9, 23n.

Sandburg, C. 124.

Sartre, J.P. 39.

Schaldenbrand, M. 26n, 44n, 47, 74, 81n, 85n.

Schillebeeckx, E. 9-11, 13, 23n, 24n.

Schleiermacher, F. 5-8, 48, 52-56, 95, 99f., 127, 137, 184, 187.

Scholes, R. 179n.

Scott, R.B.Y. 179n.

Searle, J. 99.

Spielgelberg, H. 41n.

Steiner, G. 42n.

Todorov, P. 22n.

Tracy, D. 9-11, 13, 24n.

Wittgenstein, L. 117-118.

DATE DUE

			Printed in USA